critical zone 3

critical zone 3
A FORUM OF CHINESE AND WESTERN KNOWLEDGE

Edited by Douglas Kerr, Q. S. Tong and Wang Shouren

香港大學出版社
HONG KONG UNIVERSITY PRESS

南京大学出版社
NANJING UNIVERSITY PRESS

Hong Kong University Press
14/F Hing Wai Centre
7 Tin Wan Praya Road
Aberdeen
Hong Kong

Nanjing University Press
22 Hankou Road
Nanjing 210093
PRC

© Hong Kong University Press 2008

British Library Cataloguing-in-Publication Data
A catalogue record for this book is available from the British Library.

Printed and bound by NanJing Amityprinting Co., Ltd.

Contents

Introduction

Douglas Kerr, Q.S. Tong, and Wang Shouren

Locations

In the beginning (which was in 2004), *Critical Zone* committed itself to playing a part in the articulation of a global community of scholarship — articulation both in the sense of expression, and in something like the physiological sense of constituting a joint or connection, binding different parts to work together. We wanted the publication to be a forum enabling a dialogue across regions and boundaries, and in particular helping scholars in China and elsewhere to know about each other's work and to take part in the collective effort to create and benefit from an intellectual globalism. As we publish the third number of *Critical Zone*, the remarkable development of China and changes elsewhere are every day altering the material and psychological conditions in which we do our work, but that original aim has not lost its urgency or its value. It is reflected, as in previous numbers, in the architecture of this volume, in which a section of original English-language essays is followed, in Part II, by a sample of publications from China, in English translation, on themes chosen to show important developments and preoccupations in work being done in Chinese.

It is an important part of the ethos of *Critical Zone* that it is a collaborative venture, a collaboration partly expressed in the sharing of editorial and publication labours between Hong Kong and Nanjing. This scene of publication exemplifies a leading theme of the current volume, in being located in two places, in Hong Kong and the mainland of China, and we begin this volume with a number of essays devoted to Hong Kong topics. It seemed undesirable, though, to segregate these essays away in a section of their own, and so in Part I there is an open border, as it were, between the Hong Kong material and other matters. Its openness has always been, for good or ill, constitutive of Hong Kong — an early bastion of "free trade" and the open market, a refuge and opportunity for different generations of immigrants, a factor in the often painful "opening" of China and a conduit for the forces of modernization; in the absence of much in the way of natural resources or its own space, Hong Kong could be said to be the creation of its openness, and to depend on this quality. It has always been open to traffic and, in Rey Chow's felicitous phrase, "a particular kind of passageway";[1] so here Part I begins with four essays on aspects of Hong Kong's culture and history, but then after John Carroll's narrative of an episode in Hong Kong's involvement in a phase of twentieth-century geopolitics, takes passage elsewhere in the globe in the two essays that follow. Appropriately Part I of the essays in this volume has the shape of an opening-out, from Hong Kong to the world. But this is not simply a move from the local to the global, though these terms certainly come under scrutiny here. Hong Kong, if anywhere, is already a global location, a condition reflected in one way or another in all of the Hong Kong essays here — in literary, ethnomusicological, cultural and historical studies. Meanwhile Jonathan Arac's essay on W.D. Howells, while pursuing a particular American argument about the rhetoric of realism and the politics of demography in the United States, is also putting the same questions as motivate Kwai-Cheung Lo's essay about Hong Kong's "minorities". Who is my neighbour? How can they be rightly represented? The subject of Ronald Judy's essay, the last in Part I, is how the human future is imagined (and misimagined). The topic could hardly be more global in scope. Yet when he appraises the trope of a new Middle Ages, Judy's account of orality in pre-print cultures and the constitutive relation between storytelling and community picks up a strangely moving resonance from Bell Yung's essay on Dou Wen, the blind Cantonese "singer of tales". It is a question of the critical practice of sympathetic imagination — another of Ronald Judy's concerns — to shuttle back and forth between familiar and unfamiliar locations, to see the connections between the large scale and the small. In particular, those of us who work in the humanities need to remind ourselves — because there is never a lack of intellectual acrimony and institutional squabbling to help us forget — that the humanities constitute one thing, a body of knowledge and a project of investigation in which boundaries are there to be crossed and nothing human can be considered foreign.[2] Part I of this volume tries to acknowledge this idea of humanistic knowledge as a neighbourhood.

---

1. Rey Chow, *Ethics after Idealism* (Bloomington: Indiana University Press, 1998), 168.
2. The point is eloquently argued in Edward W. Said, *Humanism and Democratic Criticism* (New York: Columbia University Press, 2004), 1–56.

The perception of location is partly a matter of scale; we all live in a building, and a planet. You can type your home address into Google Earth — benefiting from a technology developed for less amiable forms of surveillance — and watch the onscreen image zoom in from a point in space to an aerial photograph of your street; a click, and you are again looking down at the turning globe. (Poets have always had this sort of vision. There is an example at the beginning of Louise Ho's "Migratory", discussed in the essay that follows.) The modalities of the small and the large scale seem to shift sometimes disconcertingly into each other. An example is that of the Hong Kong and Shanghai Bank, established with a single branch in the colony of Hong Kong in 1865; a century later it had become a corporation on a global scale, which went on to mask its China-coast patrimony with the uninformative acronym HSBC, yet recognizes its global customers' desires in the marketing slogan "The world's local bank". If this means anything it's an instance of the corporation's interest in identifying and even promoting local communities and their needs in order to target and service them, and a reminder that it may be sentimental to assume a natural antagonism between local particularities and capitalist globalization, even if the latter's most visible effect on everyday life is often a dismal homogenization and the levelling of local differences.

An exercise in the phenomenology of location was undertaken around 1820 by a schoolboy with poetic ambitions, who asserted his ownership of a text of Virgil by writing in the flyleaf:

A. Tennyson
Somersby
In Lincolnshire
In England
In Europe
In the world
In the air
In space

With this inscription the young Alfred Tennyson may have only been enjoying an already ancient schoolboy joke.[3] Still, most of us probably never quite shake off this childish theory of our concentric relation with place, each of us starting from the body and name we inhabit, and working outwards into circles of increasing diameter and vagueness, decreasing knowability and emotional affect. It might be possible to feel attached to Somersby but who could feel they belonged in space? And yet oddly in this instance too there was an imaginative shift from the intimate to the vast and back. In 1874 Tennyson described a kind of waking trance he was able frequently to induce, from boyhood, through repeating his

---

3. Christopher Ricks, *Tennyson*, 2nd edition (Basingstoke: Macmillan, 1989), 11.

own name to himself silently, "till all at once, as it were out of the intensity of the consciousness of individuality, the individuality itself seems to dissolve and fade away into boundless being...". In this process he shortcircuited the steps from "Tennyson" to "space", from the ground zero of location to a sense of being everywhere, and from personality to the extinction of individual difference, "the loss of personality (if so it were) seeming no extinction but the only true life".[4] The schoolboy's inscription anticipates by a couple of generations a better-known instance, which we find early in James Joyce's *A Portrait of the Artist as a Young Man.*

> Stephen Dedalus
> Class of Elements
> Clongowes Wood College
> Sallins
> County Kildare
> Ireland
> Europe
> The World
> The Universe[5]

This is, as far as the evidence of the novel goes, Stephen Dedalus' very first piece of writing, this scrupulous record of the nine degrees of separation between himself and the universe. But in the spatial form of the novel, he is heading for incarnation as the writer who aspires to a positively Google-Earth vision, from above, refined out of existence, paring his fingernails. And meanwhile of course, in the transtextual life that awaits him, as his author's ironic avatar Stephen Dedalus will have a part to play in *Ulysses*, that great cosmopolitan novel which, still, has both feet firmly planted in the realist representation of a given historical day and the location of particular neighbourhoods, navigable streets, addresses that might be visited, and colloquial palaver.

The focus on Hong Kong which gives this volume its starting point articulates a distinctive Hong Kong experience, in less familiar forms and narratives than the films which are Hong Kong's most familiar cultural exports. There is room for more knowledge of Hong Kong both in the rest of China, and further afield. That knowledge can sharpen a sense of the place's differences but also its Chinese commonalities, a decade after it ceased to be a colony and was replaced, as it

---

4. *The Letters of Alfred Lord Tennyson*, eds. Cecil Y. Lang and Edgar F. Shannon, volume III 1871–1892 (Oxford: Clarendon Press, 1990), 78–79.

5. James Joyce, *A Portrait of the Artist as a Young Man*, ed. Seamus Deane (London: Penguin, 2000), 12. The rubric is then reformulated on the opposite page as "Stephen Dedalus is my name, / Ireland is my nation. / Clongowes is my dwellingplace / And heaven my destination." To the young Stephen there is an aesthetically satisfying teleology to this. "He read the verses backwards but then they were not poetry."

were, in the geography of China. For Hong Kong has not always been easy to see, and not just for the reason that in recent decades it has been changing so fast as to create something of a blur around it. The commonplace descriptors of the place, from the "barren rock" famously despised by Queen Victoria's Foreign Secretary Lord Palmerston, to the cultural desert which it has more recently seemed to some of its neighbours and indeed inhabitants, have spoken of a kind of emptiness, while more positive characterizations — contact point between East and West, bridge, gateway, port, hub, exchange — often still tend to reduce the place down to a point, a position without extension of its own, or a function always serving something else. Even Hong Kong's spectacular material success has been read as a sign indicating an emptiness — of idealism, national identity, political agency, cultural capital.[6] In reflecting on Hong Kong, this number of *Critical Zone* tries to do something to substantiate a place which is sometimes seen (or not seen) as an empty and frictionless medium through which trajectories pass at speed, whether human or material traffic or the transaction of ideas — this seeming featurelessness perhaps now exacerbated by the flattening process of globalization with its tendency to make everywhere indistinguishable from everywhere else. The idea is to make some space, to enable the place to be seen not as a dimensionless point of contact, but as a zone.

The juvenile Tennyson and Dedalus both place their national location in the unobtrusive middle of the expanding gyre of their address — rather misleadingly, as it happens, since both were to go on to become writers who in different ways had ambitions to be a poet for their nation. In some obvious ways globalization is a problem for the nationalism which for centuries made coherent the map of the world, with now a new proliferation of transnational forces and groups and identities, a political fragmentation and decentralization especially in the developing world, and the emergence of new cosmopolitanisms. An announcement of the death of nationalism would be premature however, and especially in Asia.[7]

The reinvention and institutionalizing of the Olympic Games by the International Olympic Committee in 1894 was seen by some of its sponsors as promoting individual sportsmanship as an antidote to the combative nationalisms of the nineteenth century, but for many others it was another and spectacular medium for expressing them. The nation, its achievement and claims, has inevitably been one of the principal themes of public discourse throughout 2008, China's Olympic year. And meanwhile for both the central and the Hong Kong governments, participation and pride in China's Olympics, and the prodigious economic development symbolized by the Games, has been a focus to consolidate

---

6. See Chow, *Ethics After Idealism*, 168–178.
7. The debate between nationalism and forms of cosmopolitanism is staged in *Cosmopolitics: Thinking and Feeling beyond the Nation*, eds. Pheng Cheah and Bruce Robbins (Minneapolis: University of Minnesota Press, 1998).

Hong Kong people's sense of national belonging, a participation in the national imaginary which has always seemed incomplete or compromised as a result of Hong Kong's colonial history. Since 1997, and in fact since some time before the official resumption of Chinese sovereignty, large-scale economic, financial and infrastructural initiatives have been afoot to integrate Hong Kong more fully into national systems. To the poet Louise Ho in her 1997 poem "Island", it seemed she was living in "an international city becoming national"; yet it was not simply an international city before 1997 nor is it straightforwardly a national one today. There is no seamless fit between Hong Kong and the mainland, and there seems to be a recognition, on both sides of what is still a border, that although Hong Kong is certainly a Chinese location, it is not or not yet simply another Chinese city. The place's awkwardness, though open to misprision, may in the long run be of as much value to China as its stock market and other vaunted amenities.

As Bell Yung tells the story, in his youth the blind singer Dou Wen could slip easily across the border between Guangzhou and the colony of Hong Kong, yet later in his life he found himself stranded, because of changes in technology and musical taste, in a place where he and his talent were no longer much regarded; he had not moved but a cultural displacement around him produced an effect of alienation which threatened his livelihood. Meanwhile Kwai-cheung Lo's essay shows that a similar struggle to be visible characterizes Hong Kong's non-Chinese minorities, some of whose families have lived in the city for generations. For the poet Louise Ho, a desire to bear witness to what is unique and valuable about Hong Kong, while all the time the place was in the grip of historical forces that would change it forever, leads not simply — as it might have done — to melancholy and nostalgia but to a foregrounding of the problematic of location, as the first essay here tries to show. Exile may be elected, for any number of reasons, or it may be enforced by economic or political violence. Then again, being onsite, even being tolerated to an extent, is not the same thing as belonging or being allowed to belong. For the refugee or immigrant or indeed for long-term (even aboriginal) inhabitants of a place, belonging too may be chosen but it can equally be denied. In the relational positioning of self and other, located and estranged modalities, commonality and difference seem to pursue each other round in a circle. How can both be justly represented? In the case of the Howells novel at the centre of Jonathan Arac's essay, the orthography of every word of the immigrant's speech that acknowledges his difference also confirms his dislocation, suggesting he has no natural place in the community to which he has in fact contributed so much.

The problematics of location can be studied anywhere; in this number of *Critical Zone* we start with Hong Kong. Ronald Judy's essay begins with the idea that imagination has played a key role in the history of cartography. In the years of Cold War, Hong Kong's location made it — to its own discomfort — a strategic point on the map of the world, a geopolitical space. John Carroll's historical essay, in his words, "tries to move beyond the idea that space is a stage — a static backdrop to events — or that space is a determinant of human affairs, trying instead to understand space as a dynamic and dialectic vehicle that both shapes and is shaped by those affairs in important symbolic and material ways". A dynamic cartography needs to take account both of where we are and what we do, whether it is a matter of what we experience of the immediate and local, or how we imagine (if we can) our global future.

Translations

Like its predecessors, this volume of *Critical Zone* includes a collection of essays translated from Chinese. Although independent from the first part of the volume, these translations in Part II are concerned with China in its global contexts and they resonate with some of the essays in Part I. In different ways, they all attempt to respond to the question of China's place in the world — how it should see itself as a member of the world, rather than as the world, and especially how it should understand its historical relationships with the major world powers, which continue to function as important terms of reference for China's perception of itself in the world. Since the Opium War in the mid nineteenth century, which led to the collapse of the myth of China as self-sufficient, autonomous, and independent of the need to cultivate and develop productive relations with the rest of the world, the modern history of China has never been able to transcend the collective memories of its repeated experience of humiliation in its encounters with the West and Japan. Within the critical paradigm of the local in relation to the global, nationalism presents one of the most challenging issues that China is faced with today, not least because it often sets down the terms in which Chinese national identity is discussed and debated, though perhaps not so much as an ontological issue as an epistemological one.

Nationalism is an entrenched local feeling inscribed and preserved in a nation's collective memories. As "an inflamed condition of national consciousness," nationalism, Isaiah Berlin observes, "usually seems to be caused by wounds, some form of collective humiliation."[8] Derived from the collective experience of loss and defeat at the hands of foreign powers, nationalism is a negative feeling; it inculcates as well as profits from a sense of collectivity and solidarity among members of the nation, imagined or otherwise, especially at times of major national crisis or during a period of national ascendancy. As a collective attitude, psychology or consciousness, nationalism is developed and consolidated through the passage of time, and its historical depth constitutes the basis of the

8. Isaiah Berlin, "The Bent Twig: On the Rise of Nationalism," in *The Crooked Timber of Humanity: Chapters in the History of Ideas,* ed. Henry Hardy (London: John Murray, 1990), 245.

moral authority with which it defines and determines a citizen's position on matters related to the nation as a whole.

In Europe, nationalism was invented, we're told, at the beginning of the nineteenth century, although the term nationalism might have been coined in the late eighteenth century by Herder.[9] If the desire for the establishment of the nation-state, and for self government, was the major condition of possibility for the rise of European nationalism, in China nationalism emerged in the late nineteenth century primarily as an emotional reaction to external aggressions or coercive trade arrangements. Given the particularities of the modern history of China, Chinese nationalism is often intertwined with the imperatives of national survival and territorial integrity. Not surprisingly, therefore, it's often compounded and confused with patriotism, and as such it has received very little critical attention in China. It's then of special interest to note the emergence in recent years of more sober critical reflections on some of the major historical events in modern China which not only take to task established historical verdicts on those events but also argue for the need to rethink the past in order to understand the present and develop a clearer sense of the future.

In "Modern Chinese Nationalism and the Boxer Movement", Li Weichao offers a discussion of Chinese nationalism as a structure of historical feeling that has played a decisive role in defining China's relations with the Western powers. According to Li, nationalism expresses itself, typically, in the form of mass movements; it demands unquestioned faith and action on the part of individual members of the nation, especially at moments of national crisis, and its emotional intensity is comparable to religious zeal. For Li, the expression of such intense nationalistic feeling is nowhere more manifest than in the Boxer Rebellion at the beginning of the twentieth century. However, as Li shows in the essay, valorization of such historical events as the Boxer Rebellion is inseparable from larger political or ideological convictions in China. While political leaders such as Dr. Sun Yat-sen and Mao Zedong, who considered revolution to be the only or most effective means to their political objectives, were more inclined to draw on the Boxer Rebellion as a source of legitimation for large-scale social movements, leading progressive intellectuals such as Chen Duxiu, Li Dazhao, and Lu Xun were critical of it for its anti-modern and anti-progressive ethos. This divergence in opinion on the Boxers is significant, not only because it shows how Chinese historiography often responds to political demands, but also because it is indicative of an absence and therefore the need of a general recognition of the dangers of nationalism and organized social violence as its manifestation.

---

9. See Isaiah Berlin, *Three Critics of the Enlightenment: Vico, Harman, Herder,* ed. Henry Hardy (Princeton: Princeton University Press, 2000), 206. *Oxford English Dictionary* records the earliest appearance of "nationalism" in the English language in 1798.

In "The Cultural Origin of the Boxer Movement's Obscurantism and Its Influence on the Cultural Revolution", Wang Yi shares that suspicion of mass movements as a strategy for obtaining political objectives. What is of special interest in Wang's critical account is the link he makes between the Boxer Rebellion and the Cultural Revolution, two large-scale mass movements of extraordinary social violence that bear striking similarities in their mobilization of the masses in resisting, destabilizing and overthrowing the existing order of things or the established structure of power. Wang Yi understands the historical continuity between the two not only in terms of their shared commitment to mass violence, but more importantly, on the basis of the fact that the Boxer Rebellion was evoked and appropriated for the justification of the Cultural Revolution. For Wang, mass movements in China often have a shared belief in the myth of the totality, sanctity, and inviolability of the will of the masses.

In China, history writing has never been simply a scholarly endeavour, and a revision of historical events can become a major public issue. Controversies surrounding the history textbooks in Shanghai, as discussed in the interviews with the two historians Su Zhiliang and Zhu Xueqin, included in this volume, tell us perhaps more about the complexities and difficulties in the representation of history than the technical question of what should be included in the textbooks. History has always had a prominent presence in the contemporary life of China.

To revisit the past is to reflect on the present. The modern history of China starts with the Opium War, a war that not only exposed China's total inability to defend its coastal lines but also radically altered the course of its modern history. For more than 150 years since the Opium War, China has been obsessed with the idea of the need for superior military architecture. The perception of China's naval capabilities, for example, has been an important measure of China's military modernity and for that matter China's modernity more generally. Several essays in this volume are concerned with the modernization of China's naval capabilities and what it might mean for China in the world. Ye Zicheng and Mu Xinhai's essay "On the Development Strategy for China's Sea Power" considers the very notion of sea power and its ramifications and argues for the urgent need to understand the relationship between political structure and military structure. A nation's sea power doesn't necessarily depend on the size of its naval forces, a lesson which one would think China should have already learned from its defeat in the Sino-Japanese war in 1896. Although some of the most informed thinkers in the late Qing period such as Guo Songtao and Yan Fu argued for the need to reform China's social, cultural and legal institutions in order to maximize its military capabilities, how to plan for the development of China's military power in relation to or as part of its overall social development remains, as Ye and Mu demonstrate in their essay, an unresolved question.

Similarly, Zhang Wenmu in "On China's Sea Power" argues that the development of China's naval power should be contemplated with the nation's practical needs and ultimate interests in mind. Considering the conditions of

China's economic development, Zhang believes that it's only realistic and sensible for the country to seek the establishment of limited sea power for the protection of its territorial integrity. Like many others, Zhang is concerned that historical memories of repeated setbacks the Chinese navy has experienced since the mid nineteenth century might inspire more assertive military ambitions at present. He argues that China must forgo the paths of the global sea powers such as Britain in the nineteenth century and the US in the twentieth century, and should be always on guard against the possibility of repeating the failure of the former Soviet Union in seeking to establish unlimited hegemony at sea. However, Zhang also notes that insofar as the future of Taiwan and long-term economic development remain China's core interests, it must make all efforts to keep abreast of the newest military technologies in the world and develop in all possible ways asymmetrical military capabilities by, for example, developing submarines and underwater military technology. This line of thinking seems to have been developed out of a broad consensus among the strategists in China and may therefore be suggestive of the possible emergence of similar strategies in other areas in the near future.

In a world that's increasingly globalized, China is an inevitable part of an emergent new international order, and its development is necessarily a world development. In "On China's Foreign Policy Strategy," Yu Xilai and Wu Zichen present an overview of the mutations and shifts of China's foreign policy in accordance with or perhaps in response to political and ideological demands at different times. Worth noting in their discussion in particular is the conspicuous lack of a more formalized procedure in which a consistent foreign policy might be conceived, formulated and implemented. That China's foreign policy has been *ad hoc* shows just how it has been shaped by the local ideological demands of the Cold War, and how political needs were sometimes prioritized over national interests. Based on their historical analysis of China's foreign policy and of its inadequacies during the Mao era, Yu and Wu argue that China should adopt a pragmatic foreign policy without ideological influence, and must pursue the path of peaceful rise or peaceful development, not just as a strategy but as a long-term policy that is informed by a historical understanding of the needs as well as limits of China in relation to the rest of the world.

Over the past decade or so, the growth of China's economic power and its possible rise to a world power have been the main source of a particular structure of feeling in China — a combination of excitement and depression, hope and disappointment, pride and fear. Underlying this structure of feeling is a whole set of problems, prominent among which is the question of where to locate what could be clearly defined as Chinese, be it Chinese thought, learning or value. The double task is to locate what is Chinese in Chinese culture, and to find China's place in the twenty-first-century world. Admittedly, China's economic achievement over the past three decades has had no historical precedent, its present social and political conditions are vastly different from those under which the Boxers were mustered as a collective response to the coercive presence of the foreign powers, and China's newly-acquired confidence shouldn't be confused with nationalism. However, insofar as the forces of nationalism remain active in China, it's only pertinent to remind ourselves that the tension between the local and the global continues to be a challenge that can't be evaded. Further, unless a more sophisticated and mature understanding of such historical events as the Boxer Rebellion is reached, it will continue to be difficult to imagine China's economic ascendancy as a historical opportunity to redefine China's place in the world, and to help bring about a new world order conducive to peace, growth and international democracy.

Part I

Locality

Locating Louise Ho: The Place of English Poetry in Hong Kong

Douglas Kerr

Three locations

Louise Shew Wan Ho is a Hong Kong poet who writes in English. She was born and educated in Hong Kong, taught English at the Chinese University of Hong Kong, and now spends most of her time in Australia. Here is one of her poems which is a favourite of anthologists.

> "Home to Hong Kong"
> A Chinese
> Invited an Irishman
> To a Japanese meal
> By the Spanish Steps
> In the middle of Rome
> Having come from Boston
> On the way home.

The poem attracts attention not on account of any intellectual complexity or emotional intensity, nor for any particularly original or beautiful use of language. Its appeal consists, I think, in an image or story of a Chinese cosmopolitanism, apparently available to Hong Kong people though still, in the nineteen-eighties when the poem was written, not much more than a dream to most mainland Chinese. It exercises a kind of flourish, grounded by a cumulative structure that resembles that of a joke. The act of invitation narrated in its main verb is one that places the inviter in the position of host, at home, wherever the invitation is actually issued. It is a cosmopolitan illocution. Here is a life of international friendship, of eclectic taste, of frictionless mobility between scholarly, spiritual, and commercial centres, old world and new, West and East. The poem, like the traveller, is in circulation, beginning and ending at "home," with the only end-rhyme anticipating the bump of arrival, the return to the starting place, laden with each line's trophy of experience or traveller's tale. What could be more desirable, simpler, or more fun? "Home" underwrites the poem, as homecoming underwrites the travelling. Local belonging is the warrant for global mobility and gives it a shape.

So this is one story about the local. The poem first appeared in Louise Ho's collection *Local Habitation* (1994), a book whose title invokes by quotation, typically enough, a Shakespearean notion of poetry.[1] The theory of poetry which Theseus expounds in Shakespeare's *A Midsummer Night's Dream* (V. i. 7–22) is one that foregrounds an idea of landing, or grounding. The poet's eye may glance from heaven to earth and from earth to heaven, but the poet's pen, says Theseus, has the power to materialize thought, "and gives to airy nothing / A local habitation and a name" — embodying it in language, but also putting it somewhere on the map. Creativity in this construction is the articulation between that airy nothing and the local embodiment that gives it form, without which it would remain nothing. Theseus the Renaissance prince gives a conventional and courtly account of the poet, which nonetheless retains elements of the magical and shamanistic, with the poet transcribing messages from the supernatural realm. But though the poet traffics through the unconscious in "the forms of things unknown," it is a process that depends on a necessary groundedness and orientation in the material world. In this sense the poet is somebody who needs to know his or her place, a recognition shared after all by the Biblical poet in exile (Psalm 137) who sat down and wept by the waters of Babylon, fearing that creativity could not survive a loss of place. "If I forget thee, O Jerusalem, let my right hand forget her cunning."

So what happens when a location is lost, or given up?[2] Such is the odd history of Hong Kong that it used to be quite common to meet a disbelief that the place could be thought of as home. It was a city of exiles, populated by people who had come, for the most part, from the mainland of China in search of business opportunities or political refuge, and the wind that had blown them to the colony

---

1. Louise Ho, *Local Habitation* (Hong Kong: Twilight Books, 1994). The poem is reprinted in Louise Ho, *New Ends Old Beginnings*, intro. by Michael Hollington (Hong Kong: Asia 2000, 1997). All my quotations from Louise Ho's poetry will be taken from *New Ends Old Beginnings*. For many years, as a professor at the Chinese University of Hong Kong, Louise Ho lectured on Shakespeare and other poets.

2. In this discussion of the dynamic of location and dislocation in Louise Ho's work I am indebted to groundbreaking work in Elaine Yee Lin Ho, "'People Like Us': The Challenge of a Minor Literature," *Journal of Asian Pacific Communication* 9, no. 1&2 (1999): 27–42.

might just as easily carry them further in due course, to other cities in South-East Asia, to Australia or North America. Hong Kong was a transit camp of the Chinese diaspora, a city of sojourners, economic migrants and refugees, and not a place to develop sentimental ties. From the point of view of the Chinese mainland, it was hard to imagine people feeling at home in a modern Chinese city that, however rich, differed from other Chinese cities in being the colonial possession of a foreign power, won by force legitimated by unequal treaty. Besides, since the signing of the last of those treaties in 1897, the colony's days were exactly numbered. Hong Kong in the past had not participated in the narrative of the Chinese revolution; it had no future as itself. Anomalously insulated, for a while, from Chinese history, to observers in the mainland it often seemed culturally empty too, a place without an inner life of its own, where materialism was the only language. As for the non-Chinese population, this was essentially expatriate, consisting of people who after a contract or a career would take their money and go home. There were reasons why people might want to live in Hong Kong, but who could really belong to such a place, or wish to?

And yet there were more than sufficient conditions of difference to constitute Hong Kong as a locality, its own place, a place of affective investment, to know and belong to. The closing of the border in 1950 (hitherto there had been free traffic of people to and from mainland China) drew a line between the colony and the People's Republic and "turned the Chinese population of Hong Kong into a settled one."[3] If Hong Kong sometimes worried that it might be a "cultural desert," it suffered no Cultural Revolution. The colonial government, certainly not democratic, was subject to the rule of law. By the early 1970s a majority of the population was local-born. In recognition of this, and prompted too by its alarm at the repercussions of the upheavals over the border in the form of serious disturbances on the Hong Kong streets in the mid-1960s, the colonial government began actively to encourage an already emergent sense of a Hong Kong identity, crystallizing round indigenous popular music, film and television, and campaigns of civic responsibility, and articulated, for the most part, in Cantonese.[4] This is a well-known story and a classic case, it might seem, of the emergence of identity out of difference, in this case a difference from *both* the colonial *and* the national culture which in turn differentiates Hong Kong from other examples of local identity-formation in the twilight and the aftermath of the experience of colonization. One apocalyptic narrative of this development has it emerging, in the decade or so before 1997, only to be overtaken and swallowed up by the renationalizing of Hong Kong in China's resumption of sovereignty.[5] The mayfly

---

3.   Steve Tsang, *A Modern History of Hong Kong* (Hong Kong: Hong Kong University Press, 2004), 181.

4.   See *Hong Kong Sixties: Designing Identity*, edited by Matthew Turner and Irene Ngan (Hong Kong: Hong Kong Arts Centre Publications, 1995).

5.   Ackbar Abbas, *Hong Kong: Culture and the Politics of Disappearance* (Hong Kong: Hong Kong University Press, 1998).

existence of a Hong Kong subjectivity, in this telling of the story, appears poignantly only in the fleeting moment of its disappearance. It appears, to be lost. (Perhaps understandably, the post-1997 morphology of the phenomenon had proved difficult to descry).[6]

Something of the fragility of this position is perhaps signaled in Louise Ho's poem "Living on the Edge of Mai Po Nature Reserve." The location, in Hong Kong's northern "New Territories" near the Chinese border, is quite specific, and the scene opens in the mode of pastoral.

> This garden this stream these marshes
> A bird sanctuary among the mangroves,
> Herons perch egrets glide,
> The hills gather from afar.

The place of nature is protected from history; nothing happens here. The scene is set with no verbs at all, then traversed by the intransitive activities of herons, egrets, and hills. This first impression is deceptive, however. Within sight of this enclave are shadows of city blocks, and at night "a long row of lights like jewels" marks the electrified high fence separating the colony from mainland China. The line of lights written across the landscape is also a sentence, in the future tense, pointing to the reclamation of Hong Kong, and the "gathering" of the hills in the first stanza starts to emerge into transitivity as the landscape reveals its animate and political meanings (for to gather means to cluster, but also to scoop up). The poem ends like this:

> The horizon closes in like two long arms.
> We are surrounded,
> China holds us in an immense embrace.
> Merely the lie of the land.

This is the first we have heard in the poem of "us," the locals of this locality, now present as the passive victims, or beneficiaries, of being where they are. The edginess of this poem seems to capture a very characteristic divided state of mind in the years leading up to the transfer of sovereignty in 1997, years when the nation over the border impended increasingly over everyday life in Hong Kong. The horizon — the future — is felt as claustrophobic, but may also be sheltering. "Surrounded" is ominous, but "embrace" is reassuring — but then "an immense embrace" seems out of scale for a gesture of maternal solace, and is, besides, not something open to dissent. Who wants, or could refuse, to be held in an *immense*

---

6. See John Nguyet Erni, "Like a Postcolonial Culture: Hong Kong Re-Imagined," *Cultural Studies* 15, no. 3/4 (2001): 389–418, and Anthony Fung, "What Makes the Local? A Brief Consideration of the Rejuvenation of Hong Kong Identity," ibid., 591–601. This is a special number on Hong Kong.

embrace? The tropes applied to the inanimate topography of the scene begin to stir into a story, and a disquieting one; living on the edge of Mai Po Nature Reserve is indeed living on the edge. So the poem's last line is an apotropaic gesture; it moves in to defuse the situation, disarm the tropes of surrounding and enclosing and holding — these were after all only a manner of speaking, it seems, and the poem itself is simply a description of landscape, nothing more. "Merely the lie of the land." The last line like the first is verbless, static, and pictorial. This after all, it seems to say, is just a poem about scenery. But this classic *démenti* puts the preceding lines, we might say, under erasure, without expunging them. It contradicts what comes before, but a contradiction is not a resolution. The ending does not take the edge off the poem. There is, besides, the worrying ambiguity of "the lie of the land," which could indicate simply topography — this is just the way the contours run, no reason to read anything more into it — but also contains a hint of duplicity.[7] And if the look of the landscape is misleading, what is misleading about it: the claustrophobia, or the embrace? Denial, a classic defensive trope, often draws attention towards what it wants not to see.

There is, however, a world elsewhere, and a third poem, "Migratory," reaches for it uncertainly.

> I floated alone in my kingsize bed
> I steered between abysses
> To my left 1997
> To my right 1788
> I hugged the shorelines
> Crossed the high seas
> And drifted here
> Landing on terra firma
> Terra Australis.

This is travel of a different sort from the sociable globetrotting of "Home to Hong Kong," for this time the journey is isolating, alienating, and sounds dangerous, even in fantasy form. It is the journey of exile, and despite the new immigrant's dutifully taking note of "new shapes new sounds / And endless possibilities," the glance is drawn backwards, inevitably, to locations left behind.

> At first the heart longs
> For the absent familiar
> Cosmopolitan Hong Kong
> Its chaos, its anomalies, its power
> Or England, my other world
> Or some landmark somewhere
> A villa by Serlio on the way
> To Erbusco, outside Milan

---

7. In William Empson's taxonomy, this is an ambiguity of the third type. See William Empson, *Seven Types of Ambiguity*, third edition (Harmondsworth: Penguin, 1972), 127–59.

> Or family, relatives
> In New York, San Francisco
> Vancouver, Toronto...
>
> Then, like lightning
> The shock of the void struck.

We can listen to the way the poem in this drifting sentence tries to console its losses by a nostalgic reverie of being once more at home in the world, travelling effortlessly in memory between favourite places ("Just reeling off their names is ever so comfy," to appropriate Auden), in a sort of global freedom like that enjoyed in "Home to Hong Kong." But that cosmopolitanism was anchored and guaranteed by the local groundedness from which it departed, to which it would return; and here in "Migratory," as the title had warned, that groundedness is no longer a given. Hence the interruption — "like lightning" — that shows up that catalogue of geographical alternatives as empty air. The shock of the void "struck" — the historic tense is an ungrammaticality, incongruent with the present tense in which the sentence started, yet functioning paradoxically to drag the mind back to the present, from "the absent familiar" to the alien here and now, to having to live in history.

Meanwhile Australia in "Migratory" is not so much a place as the loss of place, a dislocation. This may seem unfair — after all "The neighbours are kind, the dogs are friendly / The land is veritable Eden" — but these amenities can only be enjoyed by someone who is really there, who has successfully negotiated the enigma of arrival and made landfall.

> Space-tost, land-lost
> I float, I drift, I hover
> Cannot settle
> Cannot come to stay

Hovering, a recurrent idea in Ho's poems, is not bad in itself, but here it indicates an incomplete exchange of places, one land lost and a new one not yet inhabited. For the cosmopolitan the globe is mapped by pathways, relationships, histories, but the would-be migrant is adrift over a landscape without known landmarks, the subject pronoun helplessly repeating itself only to state its lack of agency and purchase. The southern landscape is seen as an existential void, and the migrant needs to embark on the discursive task of knowing it — "Measure the land / Foot by foot / Step by step" — so as to acquire the weightiness to "Sink the ankles / Touch the ground / Walk normally." It does not seem an extravagant ambition. Measures, and feet, belong to the language of poetry as well as to that of surveying, for poetry too is a form of knowledge, both a cartography and a way of asserting tenancy in a place — claiming it, and settling it, hopefully without the bitterness these actions inherit from Australian history. There is, of course, an Australian precedent for the discourse of inhabitation which this poem enacts or promises: "These are my songlines":

Claiming by declaiming
Over my land
O land, walk with me
May the dust settle
Wherever I may stand.

Dislocation makes necessary relocation and this makes possible, though it does not guarantee, a new and much more difficult kind of freedom, one that is not given but made. In "Migratory" we see it establish a narrow and precarious foothold, where the home lost or abandoned is replaced by a more abstract location, a modality and subject position, wherever the subject pronoun makes a stand. But in this move, "Migratory" is paradigmatic of Louise Ho's poetry as a whole. For the Hong Kong poet of her generation, who has known a Hong Kong colonized, internationalized, globalized, decolonized, and renationalized, locality — a place to belong to — has always been something to be created, brought into being, through writing. Writing is a way of finding your feet. One thing that makes Louise Ho particularly interesting is that she finds hers in English.

The place of English

A Hong Kong poet writing in English has, it seems, some explaining to do. Why does she not write in the local language? Trade and empire spread European languages around the globe. No one thinks it odd that Borges wrote in Spanish: the former imperial language is the national language in Argentina. Nor is it mystifying to find a great Indian writer like Narayan using English, an option which was a way of reaching a large readership of his own countrymen in a multilingual nation, besides others around the world. But Hong Kong is a Chinese city, full of Chinese people, and there is a Chinese language, with, of course, an incomparable literary tradition. Why articulate a modern Hong Kong Chinese experience in a residual colonial language brought to the China coast with the traders, the missionaries, and the gunboats of empire?

It was never, to be sure, a simple choice or contention between a local language and that of a distant imperial authority. When Hong Kong was colonized there was already an imperial, Mandarin, language in China, but in the minds of many European missionaries and educators it was the medium of a sclerotic bureaucracy, a privileged class, and an irredeemable cultural conservatism, of an empire which had had its day; the cultivation and use of Chinese vernaculars might be one way of freeing China from the dead hand of tradition, a linguistic dimension of the discourses of "opening" and modernization in which so much of the European action on China in the nineteenth century (and later) narrated and justified itself. European linguists recorded regional varieties of Chinese and promoted dialect literacy, while in Hong Kong the practical attentions of missionaries, scholars and teachers fixed more on the local variety of southern Chinese which most people used.[8] Such activities only reinforced perceptions of the difference and distance of the region and particularly the colony from the Mandarin centre. English and the Cantonese regional variety of Chinese became the languages of Hong Kong, though with different functions and in very unequal proportions. Cantonese was the Hong Kong vernacular, the main form of Chinese in use, while English was the language of government and the courts, and of the more prestigious schools and colleges.

This was the history that formed the linguistic character of Hong Kong, reflecting its colonial formation, but at the same time reinforcing a sense of local identity different from the Chinese mainland and its political and linguistic regimes. This sense of difference only deepened at the time of the foundation of the People's Republic, with the population of Hong Kong swollen fourfold between 1945 and 1951 by people escaping the turmoil on the mainland. Cantonese began to play a more important role in public domains, while immigrants from the different dialect areas of Guangdong and Fujian adapted their speech "to meet the norms of urban metropolitan Cantonese," and the use of indigenous dialects like Hakka declined.[9] English was the official language of government in Hong Kong — to be joined in 1974 by a scrupulously non-specific "Chinese"[10] — while the Cantonese "mother tongue" continued to broaden its functions in the territory, in education, administration, and media; but meanwhile on the mainland of a now reunified China there was a nationalist policy of homogenization, with a vigorous promotion of Standard Written Chinese, simplified characters, and Putonghua. In this sense, it was the language of nationalism and not of colonialism that ranged itself against Hong Kong's distinctness.

> While in many people's minds, the juxtaposition of Cantonese and English is an ideological one between the local and the colonial, it is also true to say that there is a complex symbiosis between the two languages, reflecting two aspects of Hong Kong's alternative linguistic "modernity": the vernacular language as incipient prestige language (Cantonese) on the Romantic model and English as a product of colonial modernity.[11]

---

8. See Christopher Hutton, "Writing and Speech in Western Views of the Chinese Language," vol. 2 of *Critical Zone*, eds. Q.S. Tong, Wang Shouren and Douglas Kerr (Hong Kong and Nanjing: Hong Kong University Press, 2006), 83–105.

9. Kingsley Bolton, Introduction to *Hong Kong English: Autonomy and Creativity*, ed. Kingsley Bolton (Hong Kong: Hong Kong University Press, 2002), 2.

10. "As pressure increased in Hong Kong for recognition of Chinese in public life, the spoken form adopted was Cantonese by default." Hutton, Writing and Speech, 101.

11. Hutton, Writing and Speech, 102.

In Hong Kong, Cantonese, incidentally fostered and promoted by Western missionaries and ideologues as a regional identity independent of the Chinese empire, became the language of the local, the community's "mother tongue" with which the colonial power had to reckon and communicate; in the colony Cantonese was the language of "localization" and access, while English was the language of social mobility. Cantonese was the organic alternative to the colonial language, and both played a more important role in forming the territory's sense of itself than the state or national language of China. In such circumstances it cannot be adequate to claim that Chinese is the local language in Hong Kong; further, the existence of a literature in English in Hong Kong, however tenuous, at least makes it a little harder to think of the place in terms of the hoary binaries of West and East.[12] Finally, with the anticipation of renationalization in 1997 and now in its aftermath, there has been a very significant increase in Putonghua speakers, and Putonghua use, in Hong Kong.

Cantonese however remains overwhelmingly the language of common speech and popular culture, but the fate of Cantonese was, for some, one focus of an anxiety about the consequences of a homogenizing renationalization. So we have the apparent anomaly of Louise Ho, in "Flags and Flowers," using English to make a plea for Cantonese after the handover, in what looks very like a version of a trope belonging to the nativist phase of postcolonial discourse. "Change our flag as you must / But let us keep our speech," the qualities of that local speech being the expression of a locality but also — since it is believed Cantonese is phonologically closer to older forms of Chinese — an important bearer of an ethnic tradition.

> Our local voices
> Our nine tones
> Our complex homophones
> Our own configurations of meaning
> Our own polite formalities
> Our resonances from the Hans of old.

In these circumstances, what does it mean for a Chinese writer to use English? The more common postcolonial scenarios do not apply: English is not the national language in Hong Kong, it is not a linguistic hegemon threatening to engulf a relatively weak indigenous language, nor is it the only medium available whereby a local writer might hope to reach a larger readership. English is, to be sure, a "world" language in a way that Chinese at the moment is not, and the literary-historical paradigm influentially proposed by Pascale Casanova in *The World*

---

12. For recent Hong Kong literature in English, see the anthology *City Voices: Hong Kong Writing in English 1945 to the Present*, eds. Xu Xi and Mike Ingham, foreword by Louise Ho (Hong Kong: Hong Kong University Press, 2003).

Republic of Letters may help us to think about this, up to a point. Casanova argues that what she calls "world literary space" is now organized in terms of an opposition between an autonomous "literary and cosmopolitan pole" on one side, and a heteronomous "political and national pole" on the other.[13] Her contention that the latter is "composed of relatively deprived literary spaces at early stages of development" scarcely bears on either the traditions or the institutions of Chinese writing; however, there is more potential explanatory power in her view that the internal configuration of each national space is similarly bipolar in structure, and shaped by a rivalry between what she calls "'national' writers (who embody a national or popular definition of literature) and 'international' writers (who uphold an autonomous conception of literature)."[14] International writers in Casanova's sense are those who, often in exile, seek greater freedom for their work by appealing to a common "universal" measure of literary value, authorized in a "denationalized" universal capital, such as Paris, through metropolitan aesthetic models, publishing networks, and critical functions.[15] What clearer sign of this intent than to write not in a national language like Chinese but in an international language like English?[16]

   In considering how useful this is as a way of thinking about Hong Kong writing in English, it is instructive to turn to a neighbouring case, that of the body of English-language poetry written by Malaysian Straits-born Chinese, principally Ee Tiang Hong, Wong Phui Nam, and Shirley Lim. (Lim, who went into American exile as a student, and much of whose subsequent writing might be described as Asian American, is for this reason a somewhat different case from the other two.) These writers grew up in the ethnically and culturally distinct *Baba* communities of the peninsula, but fell foul of the nationalist myth of the *Bumiputra* (son of the soil) promoted in postcolonial Malaysia, assisted by a traditional resentment of the commercially successful Chinese minority and a vigorous promotion of Bahasa Malaysia, displacing English in education and public life, as the national language. Some writers, notably the poet Muhammad Haji Salleh, gave up working in English to devote themselves to nationalist cultural projects and the Malay

---

13. These modalities are understood by Casanova to stand in oppugnancy, rather than, for example, in dialogue; the model seems to be one of economic rivalry or even military hostility. If letters is a republic, it is in a state of civil war.

14. Pascale Casanova, *The World Republic of Letters*, trans. M.B. DeBevoise (Cambridge, Mass.: Harvard University Press, 2004), 108.

15. "Every work from a dispossessed national space that aspires to the status of literature exists solely in relation to the consecrating authorities of the most autonomous places." Casanova, *World Republic of Letters*, 109.

16. Also of relevance to this question of internationalization is a recent anthology of translations, *Hongkong: Poems/ Gedichte*, eds., Louise Ho and Klaus Stierstorfer (Tübingen: Stauffenburg, 2006).

language. Others, like Ee and Wong, though Malayan born and in Ee's case Straits Chinese of the seventh generation, experienced the distinctly cold shoulder of "Malaysian Malaysia." "The alienation of the *Baba* Malay, as in the case of Ee Tiang Hong," writes the Singaporean scholar Rajeev S. Patke, "shows how the political idea of autonomy was fetishized along exclusionary, nativist and fundamentalist lines."[17] And as language policies in Malaysia drained English out of the national life, the English-using poets who stayed on found themselves increasingly marginalized and beleaguered in terms of readership, publication and sponsorship. Wong Phui Nam, whose first language was Cantonese, reflects gloomily on the predicament of the writer of verse in English in Malaysia in his essay "Out of the Stony Rubbish," with its title's quotation from Eliot flagging its affiliations with a distant metropolis, where furthermore *Ways of Exile*, the book containing the essay, was published.[18] The rivalry Casanova finds between internationally oriented writers and those involved in the nation-building project could hardly be more clear-cut than in this instance.

Wong Phui Nam himself writes a grave and dark-grained poetry which is the product of a cultural experience felt as tragic, of traditional ways and minority practices — including the "scant inheritance" brought from China by Wong's impoverished migrant ancestors[19] — now disregarded or worse in the homogenizing vulgarity of a new nation, and becoming unavailable, lost to decay and exile. The cast of his own literary identity in English is itself part of the tragedy, for writing in English not only limited his readership at home and might even be construed, as Alan Durant says, as "a form of cultural dissent" in nationalist Malaysia,[20] but also seems not to have compensated him with a sense of being at home in the other language. In internal exile in the culture of his own country, his facility in English does not provide him with a passport to citizenship of the world, for the history inscribed in it keeps reminding him that it belongs to somebody else.

> To internalize a language is to allow it and the broad assumptions that the community of its native speakers hold about the universe to become a part of oneself. The non-English writer who writes in English and has no similar recourse to his own language is thus, in allowing English to take over his affective faculties, in a very deep sense a miscegenated being, very much and yet not an heir to the tradition of Shakespeare

---

17. Rajeev S. Patke, "Nationalism, Diaspora, Exile: Poetry in English from Malaysia," *Journal of Commonwealth Literature* 38, no. 3 (2003): 71–85, at 73.
18. Wong Phui Nam, *Ways of Exile: Poems from the First Decade* (London: Skoob Books, 1993).
19. Wong Phui Nam, "Out of the Stony Rubbish," in *Ways of Exile* 133–44, at 134.
20. Alan Durant, "Making One's Language as One Goes Along: Wong Phui Nam's *Ways of Exile*," in Wong, *Ways of Exile*, 145–57, at 150. The essay by Durant, a London professor of English, appended to this collection of Wong's poems is, it could be argued, a further instance of Casanova's "international" writing's bid for consecration by metropolitan authorities.

and Milton. The language he uses to name, organize and express his experience of the life around him removes him from that life and, whether he is aware of it or not, he becomes a stranger cut off and always looking in as an outsider into that life. In that sense, the more facility he has with the adopted language, the more unauthentic he becomes. Culturally and so, spiritually, he is induced to place himself in exile from England and be cast out of an imagined Eden.[21]

The intellectual integrity of Wong Phui Nam's position is due the greatest respect, and so is the creativity of his response to this dilemma, a process he describes as involving "a flooding out of English words with one's own immediate apprehension of the world to clean out their traditional English connotations whenever they intrude inappropriately into the texture and feel of the writing."[22] But having said this, it seems also important to say that Wong's dilemma is not one than can be generalized as an affliction of all English-language writers in what Casanova calls "peripheral" literary spaces. Certainly the language has to be adapted to express local experience — and the creativity of such transformations by postcolonial writers is by now a hoary truism of the literary history of English — but the distance between that experience and the habits and conventions established in the metropolitan tradition need not necessarily burden the writer with fears of inauthenticity.

There are several reasons for this. First, what Wong describes as "the native tradition" of English poetry never had a stable centre, or rather its centre was always subject to continuous shifts under the pressure of revolutions and reformations in idiom and subject matter from various points of what had been the periphery (Dryden and Wordsworth being as revolutionary, in this narrative, as Robert Burns or Gertrude Stein), a process which Malaysian or Caribbean or Hong Kong English poets honour and continue. Second, the character of local poetry in English is not just the product of the *agon* of the peripheral poet with the metropolitan, formerly colonial, language. Rather, as Bruce Clunies Ross has shown in an important essay, it is marked by the complex linguistic interactions of the local scene itself, and these may include several varieties of English as well as different forms of indigenous speech and writing. "It is these," says Ross, "and not the imperially transposed English heritage, which impel the creation of poetic language."[23] Third, Wong Phui Nam's frustration at being, as a poet in English, "a stranger cut off and always looking in as an outsider into [the life around him]" is perhaps well answered by Louise Ho herself in her observation that "[l]iterary

---

21. Wong, "Out of the Stony Rubbish," 140.

22. Ibid., 141.

23. Bruce Clunies Ross, "'Rhythmical Knots': The World of English Poetry," *Debating World Literature*, ed. Christopher Prendergast (London: Verso, 2004), 291–318, at 312.

language is an alienated language, anyway."[24] Formally and rhetorically — and institutionally too — poetic writing is already apostatic, standing aside; though it must be rooted in ordinary discourse it is also a divergence from it, and would not otherwise be poetry.

It may be the fate of the local always to confound the global, to spoil the pattern, to qualify the grand statement with a stubborn footnote. Louise Ho at least appears quite content to work with a language that might be thought a colonial residue, or a cargo of inappropriate and distorting associations, without seeking to purge it of its traditions, which on the contrary she is quite ready to make use of, or to sport with. At times she uses Cantonese words or sounds within her English poems (as in the macaronic "Jamming," with its carnivalesque Cantonese nonsense-refrain, "geeleegulu"),[25] and she describes one of her goals as the creation of "a space where the English literary language expresses as well as is incorporated into the local ethos, thus becoming almost a *tertium quid*, but which remains at the same time definitely English."[26] At the same time, while certainly oriented outward to international readers and outlets, she is from beginning to end a poet of Hong Kong experience and history. And while hers is not the kind of work readily harnessed to nation-building projects or a national moral and aesthetic agenda — far from it — nor is it shaped by a rejection of local aesthetic and linguistic practices, especially as instantiated in Cantonese. The poem "Well-Spoken Cantonese," in *Local Habitation*, describes an eloquent man, and ends like this:

> His modulated resonance
> Creates a civilized space
> Or a proper silence
> Which was not there
> Before he spoke.

The medium of written English and the subject of Cantonese speech collaborate, as it were, to make "a civilized space." Language builds the city.

English and Chinese are not bound to rivalry. The Chinese-language Hong Kong poet Leung Ping Kwan tells a story about a proposed book of poems and photographs (the latter by Lee Ka Sing), on the theme of "home," which never saw the light. It was to have been about what happened in China in 1989. Squeezed out of publication space by the publisher's failure of nerve or the

---

24. Louise Ho, "Hong Kong Writing and Writing Hong Kong," in *Hong Kong English*, 173–82, at 175.

25. "Jamming" is in *Local Habitation* (21–23) but unfortunately not reprinted in *New Ends, Old Beginnings*. "Geeleegulu" is glossed in a note as "Double Dutch"; it is the kind of burbling with which infants are sometimes addressed by besotted adults. Varieties of English also jostle in the poems. In "The Australian O," a favourite word is reborn as "heaoaium."

26. Ho, "Hong Kong Writing and Writing Hong Kong", 176.

requirements of the market, Leung's poems were in danger of becoming homeless. But later he worked with the American poet Gordon Osing on producing English versions, so that "these poems of mine, which had found no chance of publication in Chinese, were able to move into what looked like a temporary home in the space provided by a foreign language."[27] It was an important moment in the establishment of Leung's wider reputation, and perhaps it signalled his arrival in international literary space. But to the poet himself it felt like the securing of a home space, so that at the time Lan Kwai Fong, the bar district where they met to talk about the collaboration, became for him something of a local allegory.

> Lan Kwai Fong always makes me think of Hong Kong. The space we have is a mixed, hybrid space, a crowded and dangerous space, carnival-like even in times of crisis, heavenly and not far from disasters, easily accessible and also easily appropriated — by political, economic, and other forces. Is there anything we can do to ensure this remains an open space for all? What appears to be prudence can easily turn into self-censorship; what seems to be free speech can easily infringe upon others' freedom. All sorts of pressures and interpersonal relations keep intervening, affecting how we use words and images to express ourselves and communicate with others. This space that is open to us can all too easily be lost to us. And, without a home that is friendly, stable, and tolerant, we can only drift from place to place lugging with us our words and photographs.[28]

This is home as locality, and it has more than one language.

There is, at least, no official hostility to English in Hong Kong, as there was until recently in Malaysia. Hong Kong government officials and educators speak piously of a wish to create a "biliterate and trilingual" civil service and, eventually, society.[29] In the jittery 1990s, when post-handover postures were being rehearsed, there had been some tendency to decry English as the language of colonial oppression, though much of this disappeared, at least from public discourse, when it became clear that the Chinese central government regarded English as the language of global business. And herein lies the really important factor for the

---

27. Leung Ping Kwan, "The Sorrows of Lan Kwai Fong," trans. Martha P.Y. Cheung and Leung Ping Kwan, in *Hong Kong Collage: Contemporary Stories and Writing*, ed. Martha P.Y. Cheung (Hong Kong: Oxford University Press, 1998), 85–95, at 89. The Leung-Osing collaboration is Leung Ping Kwan, *City at the End of Time*, trans. Gordon T. Osing and Leung Ping Kwan (Hong Kong: Twilight Books, 1992).

28. Ibid., 95.

29. See the written reply of the Secretary of the Civil Service to a question put in the Hong Kong Legislative Council, July 5, 2006. [Available online] [October 29, 2006] Available from http://www.csb.gov.hk/english/info/326.html. Biliteracy in Chinese and English, and trilingualism in Cantonese, Putonghua and English, is the aim.

English-language writer in Hong Kong, for if there is a significant linguistic-ideological rivalry to contend with, it is not with classical written Chinese, Standard Written Chinese, Putonghua, or Cantonese, or even the Great Tradition of English poetry, but with the mighty ambient drone of the variety of English which Michael Toolan has christened Global.[30]

For there is a kind of English that is a prized commodity precisely because it is a-local; it goes everywhere and belongs nowhere, its defining characteristic being not a surplus of associations and affiliations, but an emptiness of these things. This tumbleweed English is entirely instrumental, an English for data and proposals and sales pitches but not for ideas, for negotiating postures and "social talk" but not arguments and conversations. Adrift from location, intellectually weightless and bleached of history, this is a kind of language poorly equipped to help its users pay critical attention to where they are, for they might indeed be anywhere. Michael Toolan characterizes Global as a non-creolizing pidgin, a "second-language language," one whose "locality-free de-culturating" renders it "denatured, artificial, geared to pragmatic or profitable ends."[31] A speedy informational language unbothered by culture or history, uncluttered by nuance, ambiguity or abstraction — anyone who has been into an English-language bookshop in Hong Kong or scanned the advertisements for tutorial schools (or indeed met some Hong Kong students) will know that this is what many want from English. The drowning out of humanistic values by discourses geared to the "informationalization of knowledge" in a fast globalizing economy seemed to Rey Chow — who grew up in Hong Kong in the 1960s and 1970s — to have got off to an early start in the colonized world, in places like Hong Kong, though the process as she sees it is now globally pervasive. "Indeed, on the Chinese mainland itself, the informationalization of knowledge these days includes frenzied attempts at popularizing the English language as information, with words and phrases reiterated by masses like political and/or commercial slogans."[32] The aspirations for financial reward and socioeconomic standing that fuel this desire for instrumental English are not to be despised.[33] But they are part of a situation that "adds value" (ironically enough) to the different kind of language that can produce reflective and humanistic knowledge, a knowledge that is not information but cultural memory, consciousness and conscience. This is what poetry is for.

---

30. See Michael Toolan, "Recentering English: New English and Global," *English Today* [52] 13, no. 4 (1997): 3–10, and "Nation Languages, Local Literatures, and International Readers: A New Indigenization in Native English Writers?" [Available online] [October 29, 2006] Available from http://artsweb.bham.ac.uk/MToolan/nationlanguage.html.

31. Toolan, "Nation Languages, Local Literatures, and International Readers".

32. Rey Chow, "An Addiction from Which We Never Get Free," *New Literary History* 36 (2005): 47–55, at 52.

33. Indeed teachers of literature in English are very aware that the primary motivation of most of their students, and the families who support them, is the enhanced career prospects enjoyed

A place to stand

> Yes, I remember Marvell, Dryden,
> Yeats....

Memory, consciousness and conscience are the themes of much of Louise Ho's work dealing with the recent history of Hong Kong and China, and in particular the poem that starts with the words above, written in the turbulent late 1980s, summoning up "the shadows" of painful events, and asking "how shall you and I / Name them, one by one?" This poem prompted by a national crisis asks difficult questions about remembering, and does so in a local inflection set by Hong Kong and by English. Remembering stands in opposition to repression, which, as Freud understood it, is not so much a forgetting as an inability to name what happened in the past. The interdiction on naming traumatic events may last an unconscionably long time (for example, from 1989 until today); but though they may not be named directly, they cast a shadow, and find other ways of making themselves known. Their shadow, we might say, still takes place. This poem is another episode in Louise Ho's long commentary on the history of her own times and places, stretching back to two poems about the anti-British Hong Kong riots of 1967, and commemorating cultural, demographic, and architectural changes, besides events such as the 1997 handover itself. It is a historical record, the poetry being witness to a changing structure of feeling in a place which has been, whatever else, both unique and exemplary as the site of so many of the shaping forces of modern times. Developments in the mainland at the end of the 1980s were followed closely in Hong Kong, with an attention sharpened by the certain prospect of a return to Chinese sovereignty in eight years' time. So the job of remembering the event, and naming its shadows, is an urgent and very difficult one for the Hong Kong poet. All the more bizarre, then, the opening stanza of this memorial poem.

> Yes, I remember Marvell, Dryden,
> Yeats, men who had taken up the pen
> While others the sword
> That would have vanished
> Were it not for the words
> That shaped them and kept them.

This seems no less than perverse. The solemn mnemonic duty enjoined by the poem's title ('Remembering...') veers off immediately into a different kind of

---

by those who have majored in English studies at university. Not surprisingly, it is not only in Hong Kong and mainland China that this is the case. See Yasmeen Lukmani, "Attitudinal Orientation towards Studying English Literature in India," in *The Lie of the Land: English Literary Studies in India*, edited by Rajeswari Sunder Rajan (Delhi: Oxford University Press, 1993), 156–86. Several of the essays in this volume — whose main title is without deliberate ambiguity as far as I can see — are pertinent to the question of English and education in Hong Kong.

invocation, a naming instead of three canonical English poets, and the revisiting of a truism ("the pen is mightier than the sword") that in context just looks smug: in the end, it seems to say, it's poetry that matters more than political action, because poetry is not ephemeral. It looks as if the poem has already broken the promise of its title and, instead of remembering a concurrence of time and place close to home, it is commemorating Marvell, Dryden and Yeats, in an evasive trope that turns the poem away from its difficult agenda and immediately buries its head in the golden treasury of the English tradition. Scandalously, this poem seems to be asking to be dismissed as proof of the distance between "English poetry" and Hong Kong experience, and the hopeless irrelevance of the former to the latter. But of course it is when we bring these two fields of knowledge together that this opening gambit makes sense. What it affords is not just a "cross-cultural" moment, but one in which Chinese experience is seen *from within* through the optic of English.

Dryden, Marvell and Yeats — two seventeenth-century poets and one twentieth-century one — are no random selections from the canon, but are, as the poem says, writers whose work participated in and interpreted the great public events of their times. John Dryden — English dramatist, satirist, historiographer royal and poet laureate of the Restoration court — was a loyalist to the precarious political authority of Charles II (and later James II) over a country still riven with religious and ideological divisions in the aftermath of the Civil Wars and Cromwell's Protectorate. The political affiliations of Dryden's older contemporary Andrew Marvell were different; he was a friend and assistant of the poet John Milton — himself one of the great political writers in English — and sometime tutor to the family of the parliamentary army commander Fairfax, and a member of parliament during the Cromwellian Protectorate of the 1650s and the Restoration. These men, in the century of the English Revolution, produced some of the most trenchant political poetry in the language, and can stand for later poets as models of possibility — for loyalism, dissent, satire, polemic, tragedy — in the response of the writer to times of political turmoil and rebellion, times too when the publication of a poem might well be not just a political intervention but also a calculated political risk. Marvell's poem "An Horatian Ode upon Cromwell's Return from Ireland" (1650) — the *Oxford Companion to English Literature* calls it "the greatest political poem in English" — while it seems to celebrate Cromwell as a selfless revolutionary hero, has been especially prized for its judicious and even-handed account of both sides in the conflict between Charles I and Parliament, and its famous description of the execution of the King.[34] It was written, in the year after the King's death, to commemorate

---

34. Such is Marvell's mastery of inclusive irony and ambiguity, and so deft is his footwork in the poem, that there is still debate as to just where he stands. For a recent episode in the debate about the Ode, see Peter R. Moore, "The Irony of Marvell's 'Horatian Ode,'" *English Studies* 84, no. 1 (February 2003): 33–56. Marvell attracted William Empson's admiring attention in three of the chapters of *Seven Types of Ambiguity*; see especially 196–204.

Cromwell's return from his campaign of ruthless and bloody repression of opposition in Ireland to the parliamentary cause.

The point of this seventeenth-century excursion is to suggest how English poetry can *work* in a Hong Kong poem, how its history and associations — perhaps the very things that embarrassed Wong Phui Nam — can be mobilized both as a modality, a point of view on things from a certain experience, and as a code.[35] English poetry has a history of thinking about political power and opposition to it, which is activated in the way Louise Ho's poem opens by triangulating Marvell, Dryden and Yeats, thus creating an intellectual location which can be in effect a standpoint, or footing, a *locus standi*. A history inscribed in the words and names of English provides this other place, within the poem, from which its topic — the national political crisis which it adumbrates — can be contemplated. A place to stand enables a way of looking. The complexity — ambiguity indeed — of this poetic history prevents this move being simply an orientalizing trope in which a Chinese experience is to be stuffed into the procrustean model of somebody else's protocols, or condemned to be seen as just repeating actions and responses performed in some other time and place. The third poet invoked, Yeats, shows this most clearly.

The beginning of Louise Ho's poem orients its subject of commemoration in relation to Marvell, Dryden, and Yeats. Marvell and Dryden then disappear from the poem, but Yeats remains a crucial reference point — as he is, in my view, by a long chalk and in many ways the most important English poet (English-language poet, that is, for he was not an Englishman) for Louise Ho. It is important that this poem is cast in the form of talk, and indeed seems to start in the middle of a conversation:[36] it responds and is responsible to an offstage interlocutor, answered in the opening words, addressed later as "My friend," and embraced from time to time in the communal pronoun "we." In the poem that pronoun is a prolocution of the Hong Kong people in general ("it is we, / Who, riding on the crest of a long hope, / Became euphoric") and of the sharers of this conversation in particular ("how shall you and I / Name them, one by one?").

---

35. This leads me to dissent, obviously, from Ackbar Abbas's strange view that "English literature figures in Louise Ho's work, we might say, somewhat like the *Don Quixote* figures in Pierre Menard's." Abbas, *Hong Kong: Culture and the Politics of Disappearance*, 125. If we think of the mobilization of the language of canonical English poetry as switching on or giving access to a kind of knowledge that then operates as another code within the new poem, we might return to "Home to Hong Kong," for example, and note the spooky resonance of the Spanish Steps as not just a tourist destination but a signifying *English* site, that of the death of Keats in 1821 in a house overlooking the Steps; so that the comedy of the globetrotting Chinese poet takes place in the shadow of the tragedy of the exiled English poet, whose name was "writ in water" and who never went home.

36. It takes its place in an interesting little genre of English poems that begin with the word "Yes."

This shows that these reference points, and particularly the recurring "remembering" of Yeats, are not to be taken as just part of the poet's singular experience, but of a shared culture and common language belonging to those educated in English in Hong Kong — a speech community, or more accurately a community of literacy.

Here the aptness of Yeats to the Hong Kong situation is an especially rich one, for Ireland and Hong Kong stand at either end of the history of the dismantling of the British Empire in the twentieth century. Both Irish and Hong Kong writing can be read, with due account of the difference of their circumstances, in ways opened out by developments in postcolonial studies. Yeats, the Irish poet using English, takes as his great theme the revolution through which Ireland lived in his own lifetime. "He rises," as Edward Said finely says, "from the level of personal experience to that of national archetype, without losing the immediacy of the former or the stature of the latter."[37] Yeats's engagement with the Irish predicament could be painful, even violently so, and a critical example is his poem "Easter 1916," about the anti-colonial rebellion at that date in the streets of central Dublin, which was bloodily crushed after six days by British troops, and its leaders later court-martialled and executed. Yeats, himself awkwardly situated as a member of the relatively privileged Protestant Anglo-Irish minority, was no great admirer of the rebellion's leaders, and was unconvinced of the efficacy of direct action at this time in Ireland: nonetheless, he acknowledges the rebellion as a seminal moment, both heroic and tragic, in his country's history, in fact a moment of nation formation. "Easter 1916" keeps returning to this idea of violent transformation. "All changed, changed utterly: / A terrible beauty is born." It is a moment specifically recalled in the Louise Ho poem.

It is in particular to summon up "Easter 1916" that the ghost of Yeats is invoked at the start of this later poem also commemorating fearfully a critical and violent moment in history, and the painful ambiguities of the Yeats poem help to place the complex feeling of Hong Kong Chinese as the events in Beijing unfolded, when an unprecedented political consciousness expressed itself, with demonstrations of up to half a million people on the streets, in solidarity with the Beijing students *and* in a patriotic idiom.[38] For the Hong Kong poet as for the Irish poet in his time, the question is how a poet ought to respond to, name, and remember, a desperate moment in history, arousing painful and divided emotions as it happens, and bringing consequences — like a stone cast into water,

---

37. Edward W. Said, *Nationalism, Colonialism and Literature: Yeats and Decolonization,* Field Day Pamphlet no. 15 (Lawrence Hill, Derry: Field Day, 1988), 23.

38. Steve Tsang gives a figure of over half a million for the demonstrations in Hong Kong on May 21 and June 5, 1989. Tsang, 246, 247. These marches were notable, like the Beijing demonstrations themselves, for patriotic slogans and songs.

in Yeats's image — whose implications will take a long time to ripple out from the centre. The focus of the poem is not so much on China as on Hong Kong itself, and on the way events over the border catalyzed, in the territory divided and uncertain and anxious about its own future, a sense of itself as a single community — what I earlier called a locality.

> Before we went our separate ways again,
> We thought as one,
> We spoke as one,
> We too have changed, if not 'utterly'
> And something beautiful was born.
>
> As we near the end of an era
> We have at last
> Become ourselves....

This moment of becoming does not crystallize into a political resolution (it's hard to see where the agency for such a resolution could have come from for Hong Kong people at the end of the 1980s) but is an awareness that was not fully there before. The problem of this national crisis and its aftermath for people in Hong Kong was a problem of where to stand. "Whoever would not [...] Rejoice at a return / To the Motherland?" On the other hand, events in the capital created a fear of the future that might outweigh even the miseries of alienation and exile (in a phrase remembering a poignant image of homelessness, the figure of Ruth in Keats's Nightingale ode) — "rather pick ears of corn / In a foreign field." Realizing where you are entails realizing who you are, and only then can freedom be a possibility. The first-person pronoun returns at the end of the poem with a newly sharp sense of its modality or *locus standi*, a footing now understood to be precariously narrower than the foot itself. It craves wary walking.

> Ours is a unique genius,
> Learning how to side-step all odds
> Or to survive them.
> We have lived
> By understanding
>
> Each in his own way
> The tautness of the rope
> Underfoot.

The intelligence, poise and integrity of poems like "Easter 1916" and Marvell's "Horatian Ode" have played a part in bringing this predicament into visibility. Nonetheless it is quite specific, a moment of Hong Kong autobiography. The tightrope is an uncomfortable location, yet suited to Hong Kong's "genius" — a predicament, but also a performance, the balances and the turns in which Hong Kong's future will be played out in the open.

I want to end, as I started, with a complete poem. My focus on questions of location, on English, and on Hong Kong identity, has meant I have neglected Louise Ho's aesthetic subjects, yet these, with her satirical themes which I have also not had room for, make up a large portion of her repertory. So I will finish with a poem about a sculpture, "Bronze Horse." (This will not involve a move away from the political, however, any more that we move away from the political if we move from Yeats's "Easter 1916" to his "Leda and the Swan.") The sculpture in question, called "Man, Horse," is a representation of a horse on its back, legs in the air, its neck hanging down and mutating into the torso and legs of a man.[39] It is the work of the Hong Kong artist Antonio Mak (Mak Hin Yeung), who died in 1994, the year in which the poem appeared in *Local Habitation.* Like plenty of other poems in that collection, the poem's relation to Hong Kong's own approaching metamorphosis in 1997 does not need to be spelled out. (Chinese leaders were at pains to reassure Hong Kong people that what they supposed were Hong Kong's favourite pursuits, horse-racing and dancing, would continue in the territory after the transfer of sovereignty.)

"Bronze Horse"

Earth is kind
to fall of sparrow
fall of horse.
Iron ore,
ungiving,
props up
sculpted bronze head
as it breaks its back
on iron pedestal,
its legs
flaying the air.

Tree trunk neck
Sprouts athlete's
Taut thighs
direct downwards
where horse's head
would have arched upwards.
Two motions clash
like trains
into each other's velocity,
two bodies countermining,

---

39. The poem "Bronze Horse" in *New Ends, Old Beginnings* is accompanied by Louise Ho's sketch of the sculpture (74). Photographs of "Man, Horse" and other work by Antonio Mak can be accessed via the Hong Kong Art Archive. [Available online] Available from http://web.hku.hk:8400/~hkaa/hkaa.

        two contraries
        forced into one orbit:
        the unseen body,
        fully in control,
        meets the unseen head,
        losing control,
        at the neck
        of a bronze horse.

Here are brought together two subjects — the horse, and the human figure — with a rich history in sculpture, East and West. The image in monumental form most often carries a meaning of mastery, the horse a symbol of the strength of nature and the rider representing the domination of nature by the human, and hence political or military authority. In Mak's sculpture horse and man are both in trouble, abject, in painful postures, and incomplete. In this grotesque configuration they cannot possibly belong together, yet they do, contradicting each other but constituting a single thing. And at the same time the image has a strange beauty, with its miraculous transition arrested in seamless mid-process, at the moment of the birth of something new. This is a poem of the aesthetic moment, the creation of something still, well-formed and permanent (*aere perennius*, indeed) from a process that is turbulent and violent, horse giving birth to — or consuming? — man or man becoming horse, both of them headless and sightless, unconscious of themselves or each other. This is history in the moment of its making, unable to know itself; Yeats's "uncontrollable mystery upon the bestial floor."[40] The birth of beauty out of conflict and violence — "a terrible beauty" — is a powerful and recurring theme in Yeats, whose "contraries" again haunt this poem: this is another case where the knowledge inscribed in English poetry has helped the Chinese poet to *see* the subject, which is nonetheless an organic expression of its own place and time — Hong Kong, and its own metamorphosis. The poem is entitled "Bronze Horse," but it is not *about* a horse (any more than the sculpture is); it is about a place of fabulous meeting, a contact point of different worlds. Pared down to a minimalist descriptive language, the poem holds its contradictions in balance to be contemplated. There are more ways than one of knowing your place.

Note: *The Incense Tree*, a volume of new and selected poems by Louise Shew Wan Ho, is in preparation with Hong Kong University Press and will be published in early 2009.

---

40. W.B. Yeats, "The Magi." Perhaps also apposite is the question in T.S. Eliot's Epiphany poem, "Journey of the Magi": "Were we led all that way for / Birth or Death? There was a birth, certainly, / We had evidence and no doubt. I had seen birth and death, / But had thought they were different...."

Voices of Hong Kong: The Reconstruction of a Performance in a Teahouse

Bell Yung

Introduction

After the handover to China in 1997, Hong Kong stepped into the uncharted territory of "One Country, Two Systems" on the one hand, and, on the other, "Asia's World City," a recent slogan that is being promoted internationally. These two designations hint at the city's dual aspirations and self-identities. On the one hand, Hong Kong recognizes that it is inextricably a part of China in terms of demography and culture to a significant degree if not completely. On the other hand, it perceives itself as different from other Chinese cities in being more cosmopolitan in outlook, with a natural urge but also a need to reach out to the rest of Asia and the world. The two orientations are certainly not mutually exclusive, yet Hong Kong's identity, self-defined or perceived, is still being debated, molded, and theorized, and is viewed by most as being inseparable from its colonial past, which is generally accepted to be bi-cultural in nature. Thus the co-editors of *Critical Zone* pose the question: is Hong Kong, after 1997, "able to continue to play the role that it has been supposed or expected to play, as a 'meeting place,' 'a contact point' between China and the 'West,' both in popular perception and in the familiar parlance of Hong Kong studies? And if so, in what sense?" To which they reply unequivocally: "Hong Kong needs to understand itself, its history, its present status, and its possibilities."[1] Their

---

1. Q.S. Tong and Douglas Kerr, introduction to vol. 1 of *Critical Zone: A Forum of Chinese and Western Knowledge*, edited by Q.S. Tong, Wang Shouren, and Douglas Kerr (Hong Kong: Hong Kong University Press and Nanjing: Nanjing University Press, 2004), 14.

message is clear: in order to chart one's future, one must know one's past and one's present: what it was and how it came to be what it was; what it is and how it came to be what it is.

But what Hong Kong was and what it is are determined not only by individual and collective memories, by the available "text" broadly defined in the anthropological sense, but also, more specifically, by representations of Hong Kong in the scholarly literature — "Hong Kong studies." This is where being bi-cultural becomes a challenge, because literary representations inevitably diverge as a result of differing perspectives, and, more obviously, the linguistic medium being used — Chinese or English in the current case. Even if writers are bilingual, they may or may not consult textual sources of both languages with equal attention, let alone the anthropological "texts" to be found within both the Western and Chinese sectors that together made and make up Hong Kong. Certainly, the quantity and quality of these literary sources, as well as their scope and depth, may vary depending upon the language being used. Hong Kong's identity may be differently perceived to a not insignificant degree due to the accessibility and the legibility of such texts.

One revealing case is the 2005 bilingual publication by Hong Kong musicologist Yu Siu-Wah with the Chinese title *Yueyou ruci* and the English title *Such are the Fading Sounds*.[2] The book is divided into two parts, "Chinese Music" and "Chinese Music in Hong Kong," within which are short to medium length articles on a great variety of topics organized into chapters. The book makes an admirable attempt to provide parallel Chinese and English versions for every chapter. While the chapters and the section outlines have one-to-one correspondences, it becomes clear that the content of some sections varies greatly between parallel versions; generally the English version is briefer. For example, there are 200 pages of the entire Chinese text, but only 125 pages of English. Equally revealing, though certainly not surprising, is the number of references cited at the back of the book: 173 entries in Chinese and 56 entries in English.

Ackbar Abbas, in his book about Hong Kong cinema, architecture, and writing, states that these topics are "just not recognized to be culture as such. This refusal to see what is there is an example of reverse hallucination...," which Abbas explains is one meaning of Hong Kong's "culture of disappearance."[3] Abbas's observation certainly contains a grain of truth, although perhaps he should qualify it by differentiating the different degrees of "disappearance" between what is documented or revealed in the two linguistic media. But his point is still broadly

---

2. Yu Siu-Wah 余少華, *Such are the Fading Sounds* 樂猶如此 (Hong Kong: International Association of Theatre Critics, 2005).

3. Ackbar Abbas, *Hong Kong: Culture and the Politics of Disappearance* (Hong Kong: Hong Kong University Press, 1997), 6.

valid, for not until the last two decades did many Hong Kong researchers and writers direct their attention anywhere else but towards the city they called home. It was only after 1984, with the signing of the Sino-British Joint Declaration returning Hong Kong to Chinese rule in 1997, that Hong Kongers realized that their future lay in their own hands and that they themselves must learn who they were. Thus areas of representation such as Hong Kong Literature and Hong Kong History, specifically in and about the Chinese sector of Hong Kong, began to flourish, and thus forever after changed the landscape of the city as a new Hong Kong slowly "appeared."

The identification, analysis, interpretation, and representation of these "texts" are obviously necessary if Hong Kong identity is to be defined with some degree of reality. Therefore it is notable when the co-editors of *Critical Zone*, commenting on [Mainland] Chinese academia's view that "Critical theories come and go, but the text remains," state: "The call for a return to the text, therefore, is a strange spasm of the collective intellectual fatigue that ... is developed out of the continuing and doubly belated experience of the overwhelming presence of various kinds of Western 'postology' on the Chinese scene."[4] Whether or not the "text" is defined narrowly as literary, or as broadly anthropological, I wonder if Chinese academia's call to return to the "text" might not so much be the result of being "overwhelmed" by Western theory as it is a simple and prudent realization that text must come before theory, a view which, contrary to what some may believe, is still strongly held by a significant portion of academics in the West despite the flourishing of theory.

It is with such a thought in mind that, when the editors invited me to consider *Critical Zone* as a venue for publishing one of my research projects on the music in Hong Kong, I cautiously agreed because my work loosely fit the goal of the journal, which "is envisaged as an intellectual bridge between China and the rest of the world and as a site of scholarly and critical convergence beyond regional and disciplinary boundaries."[5] More importantly, since several essays in the current issue of the journal are devoted to Hong Kong, my story is one of discovery of "texts," or voices if you will, of and about Hong Kong, voices that have not been adequately represented in the literature, particularly literature in English. The main voice is that of a Hong Kong artist who lived and worked in the city from 1926 until his death in 1979. A secondary one is that of this writer by whom the artist's work is here represented and who, as an outsider, eventually found his way back to Hong Kong to search for and discover what has disappeared.

---

4. Tong and Kerr, Introduction, 6.
5. Tong and Kerr, Introduction, 17.

The blind singer Dou Wun

Dou Wun (Cantonese pronunciation; Putonghua pronunciation is Du Huan) was born into a poor family in 1910 in the village of Jinli, township of Gaoyao, in the prefecture of Shiqing, about fifty miles west of Guangzhou, along the Western branch of the Pearl River.[6] The family made a meager living by tilling a few acres of land. When he was three months old, an accident led to blindness, although he could still sense light and darkness. In 1914, when he was four years old, the river flooded and washed away his family's land; this calamity was compounded in 1917 when his father passed away. Burdened with five children, his mother gave him away to an acquaintance of his father's, a blind man called Wong who made a living by telling fortunes. She thought that her son might learn a blind person's trade, not realizing that Wong was no more than a fraud and a con artist, as Dou, young as he was, quickly realized. No longer able to make a living, and burdened with debt, Wong fled to the metropolitan city of Guangzhou, taking Dou along with him only because Dou's eyesight was a little better than his.[7]

In Guangzhou Dou was abandoned by Wong, and, at age eight, he began several years of eking out a living on his own. He mostly begged for handouts by chanting a few lines of *Muyu* (木魚) songs that he had picked up by ear when he was growing up in the village. He recalled that he was no singer at the time; people took pity on him as a begging child and would give him a few coins; such daily income was enough to keep him alive. After two years of wandering he chanced upon Huanzhu Bridge, where many blind singers congregated to wait for customers. It was obviously a turning point in his young life because for the first time he found friendly and caring company. As Dou described it: "On the bridge scores of blind singers were always sitting, some old, some young, waiting to be hired. When they needed to pee, they had to walk quite a distance through very narrow streets that were crowded with people. Because I could see a little, I would be asked to lead them the way. They also asked for my help when they needed to buy opium. Therefore, I was quite popular and greatly liked because I ran errands for them." Smart, lively, eager to help and to please, Dou soon won the affection of many. It was in that context, through a series of introductions and negotiations, that Dou formally became a disciple of a singer named Sun, whose parents also took to Dou and treated him like a member of the family. For three years Dou learned from Master Sun, and often accompanied him to jobs singing in various

---

6.   Dou Wun's name 杜煥 is Romanized according to Cantonese pronunciation and will be so throughout the essay. Other names and terms will be Romanized according to Putonghua pronunciation unless otherwise noted.

7.   Dou's life story, and direct quotations, were from his autobiographical song "Blind Dou Wun Remembers His Past," recorded in 1975 and 1976, part of which was published as *A Blind Singer's Story: Fifty Years of Life and Work in Hong Kong,* Digital Video Disc. (Hong Kong Museum of History), 2004. More on the autobiographical song later in this article.

Photograph by Rulan Chao Pian

venues. Thus began his training as a *nanyin* (南音) singer and his life of storytelling.

Dou's life journey was drastically altered by larger events, and the decade of the 1920s was a chaotic period in China. Dr. Sun Yat-sen, the founder of China's Nationalist Party (the Kuomingtang) that had overthrown the Qing monarchy in 1911, made Guangzhou his headquarters. When he died in 1925, the city grew in instability as many political factions fought for power. 1925 also saw Guangzhou descend into serious turmoil, swept up by a country-wide fever of nationalism and anti-foreign sentiment. It began on June 19 with a large-scale labor strike in Hong Kong, when reportedly 250,000 strikers left Hong Kong for Guangzhou. Supporting their compatriots, Guangzhou workers also came out on strike, joined by students who marched in support. When British and French gunships fired on the students on June 23, the local event triggered a nation-wide uprising. Dou remembered well: "Guangzhou at the time was quite chaotic. There was often gunfire with opposing forces fighting on the streets. There were curfews, and stores were looted. … Then in the autumn of 1925, there were thousands upon thousands of marchers on the street, which made life for us singers quite impossible, for we were often stuck among crowds and were late to our engagements." Hearing that Hong Kong was relatively calm, he and several fellow singers set out on March 13, 1926, and arrived in Hong Kong after a detour to Macao. Thus began his fifty-plus years of professional life until his death in 1979.[8]

---

8.   He returned to Guangzhou for about two weeks in 1927, as he had promised his teacher Master Sun he would do. Though he does not mention this in his song, it is likely that he brought his mother with him when he returned to Hong Kong. He also spent three months in Macao in 1955.

In Hong Kong, Dou's life and work were intertwined with the larger events in the city. There were happy times: shortly after he arrived he found that his singing was greatly sought after in the many brothels and opium dens in Hong Kong, particularly in the Yaumatei area where he lived. The steady work provided him with a good living and enough money for a young man like him to have some fun. In 1929 he and a fellow singer fell in love and soon were married, producing four children. But the good times, more often than not, were spoiled by personal tragedies and professional calamities that brought misery and despair. Shortly after he began regular engagements in the brothels, the working environment, the easy availability of opium, and his ability to afford it, led him to become addicted to the drug, which plagued him for many decades to come. The outlawing of prostitution in 1934 stripped him of a steady income. None of his children survived beyond a few years; the youngest lived the longest, but died at the age of five in 1940. Later that year his mother, who had joined him in Hong Kong earlier, passed away, followed by the death of his wife the next year. Finally, the Japanese occupation from 1941 to 1945 resulted in extreme hardship, which he had to bear alone.

The end of Japanese occupation brought a brief period of relief to Dou's livelihood. But unbeknownst to him, technology was marching forward and the electronic mass media would soon dominate entertainment. Dou himself recalled how, in 1950, "Science killed us! There appeared something called Rediffusion. My business of singing collapsed completely. … Every night I went out to the street where there used to be many clients, but there were hardly any now." During this period, he met another woman singer, and they decided to live together for convenience because it was cheaper than living separately. But soon afterwards they parted ways. He later discovered a spot in the King George the Fifth Park (in the Western part of Hong Kong island) where interested customers were to be found. But then after two years of steady work there, the park suddenly underwent expansion. In his words, "The 'iron horses' (road barriers) surrounded the park, blocking off pedestrians. … It was truly my period of hopelessness."

However, his luck turned unexpectedly in 1955 when Radio Hong Kong hired him to sing a weekly program of *nanyin* on the air. For almost fifteen years he enjoyed a steady income and through this program he became widely known among *nanyin* aficionados. For example, in the late 1980s I met the writer Lu Jin who specialized in publishing reminiscences of old Hong Kong.[9] I asked him about Dou and played him my recording of Dou's singing; he immediately recalled listening to Dou on the radio two decades earlier, and he also remembered well that as a teenager in the 1930s he had heard Dou in the brothels when his elders took him along on their visits. Another person who fondly remembered Dou's

---

9.   See Lu Jin 魯金, *Rises and Falls in the Performances of Cantonese Operatic Songs* 粵曲歌壇話滄桑 (Hong Kong: Joint Publishing Company, 1994).

singing was Ho Iu-Kwong (a Romanized form according to Cantonese pronunciation which he himself used). The admiration was mutual, for Dou remembered well that he was hired to sing many times throughout the 1960s and 70s at Mr. Ho's home; Dou particularly pointed out how Mr. Ho and his family treated him with respect and kindness, unlike most of his other clients.[10]

But Dou's fortune turned again when in 1970 the radio station suddenly terminated his employment and cancelled the weekly *nanyin* broadcast. He was left desolate and reduced to begging for handouts on a street corner in Mongkok. He was able to survive only because in 1971 the government established a cash relief scheme to assist the very poor, and a kind-hearted person helped him to apply for and obtain assistance, providing him with a meager income.

The early 1970s was a critical period for Hong Kong, for it witnessed the colony's transformation into a truly modern and international metropolis, not only because of the rapid development of industry and the economy, but also owing to the government's progressive policies aimed at building a civil society that offered improved services to its citizenry, including the afore-mentioned cash relief scheme for the very poor.[11] For example, the early 1970s witnessed the first massive construction of modern public housing; the first cross-harbor tunnel began construction in 1970 and was completed in 1972; the goal of free primary education for all was achieved in 1971; the first Hong Kong Arts Festival was created in 1972; and the Hong Kong Arts Centre was established by ordinance in 1974, with the objective to "nurture creativity, and arts and cultural engagement." [12] While the city marched on towards modernity, Dou's songs were left behind in the byways, out of step with the gleaming skyscrapers and the modern educational system.

The writer

My parents emigrated from Shanghai to Hong Kong in 1948, along with many of their compatriots from the Yangzi River Delta region immediately before or after the establishment of the People's Republic. Most of them were well educated, a

---

10. Ho Iu-Kwong 何耀光 was the patriarch of the Ho family, one of the major real estate developers in Hong Kong today. I visited Mr. Ho in 2002 when he was a very healthy 96-year-old; he remembered Dou well and said how very much he had enjoyed Dou's singing. He passed away in October 2006.

11. One reading of the many positive actions taken by the Hong Kong government in the 1970s would see them less as an attempt to create a civil society than as a move to placate the Chinese population and to win their support and loyalty in order to prevent the riots of 1966 and 1967 from happening again.

12. The Hong Kong Arts Centre built its own 14-story building in 1976, which is still a landmark today by the harbor in Wanchai district on the Hong Kong Island.

few quite prosperous; some spoke decent English and most had a cosmopolitan and progressive outlook. The common thread that bound them was a perception of the looming new regime on the Mainland as ruthless and threatening. In our family, my siblings and I were enrolled in Hong Kong's Christian schools even though neither of our parents was Christian; I took piano lessons and one of my younger sisters took ballet classes. We listened to the latest recordings of Beethoven and Chopin, Nat King Cole and Patti Page, and danced to the music of Mambo and Tango. Every weekend the family went to one of the downtown cinemas to see the latest flick from Hollywood. The family's social life revolved around relatives and friends who were also from Shanghai — one reason why even my youngest sister who was only one year old when we left Shanghai continued to speak fluent Shanghainese as she grew up. In short, our lives were not touched very much by the bustling Cantonese culture around us. The only close local contact was through our maid, who we occasionally noticed was listening on the radio to what I realized later must have been Cantonese opera and Cantonese narrative song.

Our main contact with the larger society was through our schools. Even there, the curriculum had little to do with local society. Besides mathematics and science, there was English literature such as *Ivanhoe*, *A Tale of Two Cities*, or an act of Shakespeare, and classical Chinese poetry and philosophical texts that we recited from memory. Geography was about other parts of the world and History simply stopped around 1911; neither touched directly on Hong Kong. My school, run by Irish Jesuits, had a choir that sang Stephen Foster and other selections from the *One Hundred and One Best Songs*, and I was once in a school play called *Queer Street* by some obscure English playwright. I was only vaguely aware that, among the half dozen or so classmates I hung out with, most were also children of Shanghai expatriates like myself, even though we used only Cantonese to converse, and never talked about anything that was particularly related to Shanghai. Still, the fact that we were drawn together must be partially attributed to our shared Shanghainese background. In short, mainstream Cantonese culture was largely absent from our lives.

Many years later when I was working as a graduate assistant in the Music Library of Harvard University, I was asked to catalogue about fifty open-reel audio tapes of Cantonese opera, dubbed from vinyl disks that had been made in Hong Kong, with photocopies of the record jackets containing Chinese lyrics and other documentation. Through the translation and cataloguing process, I began to learn about Cantonese opera, which I eventually chose as my dissertation topic, and which was my first step in re-discovering the "disappeared" culture of my childhood and youth. My choice of dissertation topic brought me back to Hong Kong to conduct fieldwork research in 1972–73 and 1974–75. It was during the second trip that I crossed paths with Dou Wun, an encounter that furthered and deepened my journey of self-discovery. But more importantly, I discovered in Dou Wun a humble and genuine local voice that many older generations of Hong Kongers had heard but had hardly registered as "text."

When I met Dou in 1974, his life was undergoing yet another transformation, just as Hong Kong was. Because of Radio Hong Kong's weekly radio broadcast of his singing for over a decade, Dou's name and music had left an impression on some Hong Kongers. As a result, in 1973, he was "discovered" by a small number of progressive-minded young people with a newly-emerging interest in local culture:[13] he was invited to participate in the second Hong Kong Arts Festival in City Hall, the premier performing space at the time. This was followed in 1974 and 1975 by a series of appearances at the most unlikely places: the Goethe Institute, the Hong Kong University, the Chinese University of Hong Kong, and Saint John's Cathedral in the financial district, where weekly lunch-time recitals were sponsored by the Hong Kong Arts Centre. For Dou, the old performing venues of opium dens, brothels, teahouses and street corners were suddenly transformed into contemporary concert stages and the hallowed halls of academia; his audience were no longer prostitutes and their customers but young intellectuals who had rediscovered an art that they realized was precious but did not quite understand. For Dou, it was simply another chapter in a story of survival.

The Cantonese narratives songs called *nanyin*

Professional storytelling for entertainment has a long tradition in China found in practically all parts of the country. Known as *quyi* (literally "song art") or *shuochang* ("speaking-singing"), the songs were performed by chanting or singing as well as speaking, using the language spoken in the particular region, with distinctive musical characteristics also rooted in that region. Often translated into English as "Narrative Songs," *quyi* tell stories through the medium of poetic verses that are sung, interspersed with prose passages that are spoken. The singer often accompanies himself or herself on a musical instrument, or is accompanied by one or more instrumentalists. Rarely, *quyi* may involve more than one singer. For centuries *quyi* served two major social functions: as popular entertainment in the pre-technological age and as a form of mass education. Before the 20th century the vast majority of the Chinese people were illiterate or semi-literate; *quyi* offered them a view of the wider world, and played a major role in giving the Chinese people a shared sense of history, myths, and mores, thus forging a cultural identity.

Many kinds of *quyi* were sung in the Cantonese-speaking region of southern China. Probably the most important of these forms is the one Dou specialized in, called *nanyin* (Southern Tone), or *naamyam* in Cantonese pronunciation. In performance, *nanyin* was accompanied by a musical instrument such as the *guzheng*

---

13. The President's Report (1973–74) of the Royal Asiatic Society (Hong Kong) writes that "we also hope the Society might be able to do something for young people in Hong Kong who are becoming increasingly interested in local history and culture."

(bridged zither), the *yehu* (coconut-shell bowed lute), or the *yangqin* (hammered dulcimer), together with the percussion instrument *ban* (wooden clappers). The instrument or instruments were played either by the singer himself/herself or by a fellow musician. Other kinds of *quyi* mentioned in this essay are *muyu* (木魚), *longzhou* (龍舟), and *banyan* (板眼).

Some *nanyin* songs are relatively short, taking about twenty minutes to perform; these shorter ones are generally lyrical in nature, expressing thoughts and moods rather than relating a plot-laced story. A common theme in these songs is lamentation over lost love in the houses of pleasure. These songs tend to have a relatively fixed text, very often attributed to a known author of a scholarly bent. Their texts are literary rather than colloquial in style, refined in their choice of words and phrases, and regular in verse structure. Such a *nanyin* song would be sung as a unit in one sitting, with no spoken lines. The best-known example is the song *Ketu Qiuhen* (Wayfarer's autumnal lament), in which the singer yearns for the love of a courtesan whom he has left behind in his wanderings.

Nanyin songs can also be very long, with hundreds or even thousands of lines, requiring dozens or more hours to perform. These songs are usually adapted from well-known works of fiction, legends, or historical events; a popular source is the celebrated Ming dynasty novel *Shuihuzhuan* (variously translated as *All Men Are Brothers, Tales from the Water Margin*, and *The Marshes*). In telling these long stories, the singer alternates between short, spoken passages in prose and longer sung passages in verse. These long songs are normally improvised in the course of performance, even though printed texts might be published for the consumption of readers. By not following a fixed text, the singer gains flexibility in manipulating the story through the addition, elimination, or rearrangement of plot elements. The singer also improvises at a micro level in his or her choice of words and phrases, giving more or less detailed exposition to the plot elements depending upon the amount of time he has available or simply on whim. The singer also improvises the musical material: *nanyin* consists basically of a single short tune, repeated over lines of text with variation. Under the masterful craftsmanship of an experienced singer, the single tune assumes different guises, in part dependent upon the different texts.[14]

In the early part of the 20th century *nanyin* was performed mainly by blind men and women to entertain a paying audience. Common venues for performance included public places such as restaurants, teahouses, brothels, and opium dens; semi-public clubs and gathering places that catered to a particular trade or craft, such as butchers or rice merchants; and private households. A singer would be engaged for a single performance or for repeat performances on a

---

14. For a brief discussion of textual and musical structures, see Bell Yung, "Cantonese Narrative Songs," in vol. 6 of *Garland Encyclopedia of World Music: East and Inner Asia* (China section), eds. Robert Provine, Tokumaru Yoshihiko, J. Lawrence Witzleben (New York: Garland Pub.; Routledge, 2001), 267–273.

regular basis over an extended period of time. The one-time popularity of *nanyin* is testified to by the large number of cheaply printed song texts published during the first half of the last century, copies of which sometimes still surfaced in second-hand bookstores in Hong Kong as late as the 1970s.

Since the middle of the 20th century, *nanyin* has rarely been performed in its traditional context. Rapid changes in society, with the exploding growth of modern entertainment, spelled the death of traditional performing genres such as *nanyin*. The only place it can still be heard live today is on the stage of Cantonese Opera, in which the *nanyin* tunes have been incorporated as a musical resource for dramatic purposes. Yet the stories of *nanyin* embody an ideology which can still resonate for modern Chinese and in which they can still find their roots; moreover, its poetic text captures the liveliness of the Cantonese colloquial language, and its haunting melody finds new audiences, however small.

Reconstructing a performance in a teahouse

I first learned about Dou Wun from a newly met friend, Nishimura Masato, when I arrived in Hong Kong in the fall of 1974. After graduating from college in Tokyo, Nishimura came to Hong Kong in 1970 because of his keen interest in traditional Chinese culture, and particularly local Hong Kong culture, including *nanyin* singing. Introduced by a mutual friend, Perry Link, I met Nishi at the International Research Center on Argyle Street in Kowloon, a place frequented by foreign scholars taking advantage of its book collection. Nishi told me about Dou Wun and *nanyin*, and he took me to hear Dou sing at the Goethe Institute in late 1974. The audience consisted mainly of Chinese students and Westerners. The next time I heard him was at St. John's Cathedral in the early spring of 1975, where the audience consisted almost entirely of office workers from the Central district who found the Cathedral a relatively tranquil place to eat their box-lunches or sandwiches. I knew very little about *nanyin* at the time, having read only the little that had been published,[15] and having heard only the versions of the tune used on the Cantonese operatic stage. But upon hearing Dou, I was immediately struck both by his superb musicianship and by the ethos of storytelling. Instinctively I knew that both the Goethe Institute and St. John's Cathedral were incongruous venues for the sort of stories Dou was telling, and that, however much the audience may have enjoyed his singing, they more likely viewed *nanyin* and

---

15. See Fu Gongwang 符公望, "Longzhou and Nanyin" 龍舟和南音, in *Dialectal Literature* 方言文學 (Hong Kong: Xinminzhu chubanshe, 1949); Xu Fuqin 徐復琴, *The Study of Folk Literature of Guangdong* 廣東民間文學的研究 (Hong Kong: Haichao chubanshe, 1958); and Shi Jun 石峻, "A Preliminary Edition of *Wayfarer's Autumnal Lament*" 〈客途秋帥〉初校, in vol. 4 of *Miscellaneous Documents on Art* 藝林叢錄 (Hong Kong: Commercial Press, 1964), 294–299.

Dou as quaint curiosities from a past era instead of appreciating him as a connoisseur would. Dou himself must have sensed the inappropriateness of the curious venues and the quiet and reverent audiences. What a contrast these must have presented to his old performing environments! How lonely he must have felt as he sang those songs that he had been singing all his life to responsive listeners!

Not long before, Albert Lord had published his now classic *The Singer of Tales* (1960), a must-read for students of oral literature. Lord's study was followed shortly by Robert Scholes and Robert Kellogg's *The Nature of Narrative* (1968), another influential book. Scholars began to recognize the importance of oral composition in storytelling and its high degree of spontaneity, and to realize that such oral creativity, with a long history stretching back to Homeric days, was found in many parts of the world. In the field of music, there was a growing interest in oral composition as well, particularly by scholars of Anglo-American folksongs such as Samuel P. Bayard, Bertrand Harris Bronson, and Charles Seeger (1966).[16] Not coincidentally, a new multi-disciplinary organization called the Conference on Chinese Oral and Performing Literature (Chinoperl) was formed in the United States with a first meeting at Cornell University in 1969, followed by annual meetings that continue until today. Led by the eminent linguist and composer Yuen-ren Chao, the founding members of Chinoperl came from diverse disciplines of literature, music, linguistics, theater, and anthropology.

Strongly influenced by the works mentioned above and by the presentations and discussions at Chinoperl meetings, I encountered Dou's singing with a new appreciation of oral composition and performance. I made the assumption that the environment must inevitably affect the form and content of Dou's performance. Specifically, how he sang must be influenced by his awareness of the audience, or rather, in the venues I heard him sing, by his awareness of the absence of a knowledgeable audience. With these thoughts in mind I decided to record as much of his singing as I could, but to do so in an environment as close as possible to those with which he had been familiar in his earlier life. After his performance at St. John's Cathedral, I approached him and asked if he would be willing to let me record his singing over an extended period of time.[17] He was more than happy to oblige. My challenge was to find a venue in which he could sing and I could record, and to secure funding to compensate him for his time and effort. I wrote a grant proposal to Dr. Frank King, at the time the

---

16. Samuel P Bayard, "Principal Versions of an International Folk Tune," *Journal of the International Folk Music Council* 3 (1951): 44–50; Bertrand Harris Bronson, *The Ballad as Song* (Berkeley, University of California Press, 1969); and Charles Seeger, "Versions and Variants of 'Barbara Allen' in the Archive of American Folk Song in the Library of Congress," *Selected Reports* 1, no. 1. (1966): 120–167.

17. In his autobiographical song, Dou remembered meeting me for the first time at City Hall rather than at the Cathedral.

Director of the Centre of Asian Studies of the University of Hong Kong, to seek funding for this work. Not only was my request immediately granted, but Dr. King also provided me with a member of the Centre staff, Mr. Shiu Koon-shing, to assist me with the project.

Although I had grown up in Hong Kong, I was still a relative outsider to local culture. I wouldn't have known of Dou had I not by good fortune met Nishi. How could I begin to find an appropriate venue for Dou to sing in? It was through my discussions with Nishi that I eventually decided on an old-fashioned teahouse where there were still likely to be old-fashioned customers of the sort who might appreciate *nanyin*. It wasn't easy to find such a teahouse. Although drinking tea (*yam cha* to the Cantonese) while nibbling both savory and sweet delicacies (*dim sum*) such as dumplings and tiny buns was, as it is today, a favorite pastime of local Hong Kongers, by the mid 1970s most of the many teahouses were in fact fancy restaurants that catered to the *yam cha* crowd in the mornings and at lunchtime on weekends. They had contemporary décor, shapely waitresses in tight *cheungsam*, and the latest popular songs piped into the halls. None of these establishments would serve my need.

It took some research, with help from local friends, to find Fu Long Teahouse at 382–386 Queen's Road Central at the corner of Possession Street (Cantonese name Sui Hang Hau), in the Sheung Wan district on Hong Kong Island (the building has since been torn down). According to Zi Yu in his book *Old Hong Kong*, Fu Long Teahouse opened for business in 1897, and by the 1970s it was one of the two or three oldest teahouses in the city.[18] Zi Yu writes that the area near Possession Street at the end of the 19th century was a thriving commercial neighborhood jammed with pleasure-seekers. It was densely populated, with streets lined cheek by jowl with shops, and a concentration of brothels and other houses of pleasure. By the mid-1970s the older buildings in most neighborhoods of Hong Kong had been torn down and replaced by gleaming skyscrapers. Queen's Road Central in the Sheung Wan district was one of the few remaining urban areas that had not been rebuilt; it was narrow and winding, lined on either side with somewhat dilapidated three or four-storeyed buildings. The ground floors were invariably shops, the upper floors residences. Giant shop signs jutted out from the upper floors into the street, seeming almost to touch those opposite. In 1975 Queen's Road Central at Possession Street was still very crowded and filled with shops, but the city's center of activity had moved elsewhere by that time. Fu Long Teahouse and its neighborhood had the look of a forgotten era.

The Fu Long Teahouse was in a four-storey building. The ground floor opening on to the street was the takeout section, where various kinds of dim sum could be bought; the seating areas were on the second and third floors, each one accommodating up to fifty or sixty customers. *Yam cha* and *dim sum* were the

---

18. Zi Yu 子羽, "On the Fu Long Teahouse and Possession Street" 話説富隆茶樓和水坑口, in vol. 1 of *Old Hong Kong* 香港掌故 (Hong Kong: Shanghai shuju, 1979), 137–138.

mainstays in both the breakfast and the lunch periods, catering mainly to those living or working in the neighborhood. The lunch hour was particularly busy, when simple noodle, rice, and *ho fun* (flat rice noodle) dishes were also served. The age of the teahouse was quite apparent from its furniture and general ambience. The fancy but broken rosewood chairs, some of which still had mother-of-pearl decorations on their backs, suggested the elegance of the place in former days. There was no air conditioning; a few electric fans hung from the ceiling or perched on tall stands. Spittoons were still placed beside each table, and tea was served in the old fashioned way in rice-bowl-shaped containers with small lids instead of teacups.

Photograph by Rulan Chao Pian

Most significantly, Fu Long was one of very few teahouses existing at the time in which customers still followed the old tradition of bringing along their tiny songbirds in their ornate cages. As their masters enjoyed tea and read newspapers at leisure, the birds, their cages hung on windowsills, chattered among themselves. During the busiest lunch hours when the rooms were filled, the windows too were almost filled with as many bird cages as there were customers. This custom of bringing pet songbirds to teahouses, like the performance of *nanyin*, belonged to a bygone era, and was fast disappearing amid Hong Kong's fast-paced modernity. The fact that these customers still followed the old tradition convinced me that Fu Long was a place where Dou Wun would find an appreciative audience.

When I first mentioned to Dou that I was arranging for him to sing in a teahouse, his reaction was one of surprise and reluctance. He said that it would be more difficult to sing there than at, say, Hong Kong University, because he had not performed in such a setting for many years. He expected the teahouse customers to know his songs, and this would put him under greater pressure to sing well. This reaction only confirmed my assumption concerning the importance of the environment — that is, the audience — in Dou's creative process. But finally he consented to the location.

The manager of Fu Long Teahouse, Mr. Liao Sen, was surprisingly sympathetic to my rather unusual request. I proposed to him that a singer would perform in his teahouse for about an hour during the busiest lunch time period. There were to be three one-hour sessions per week, for a total of fifteen weeks. I asked Mr. Liao to place a large sign outside of the teahouse announcing the event as a way of attracting the attention of customers. The large red poster read "Dou Wun Performs *Nanyin*, 12 noon to 1:30 pm every Tuesday, Thursday and Saturday." There was of course to be no extra charge to his customers, and nor did Mr. Liao charge me for this intrusion into his regular business. He merely requested that I tip the two waiters for the extra service they were likely to be putting in. I have always regretted not having tried to get to know Mr. Liao better because I was so involved in the project. But I shall always remember his kind and unquestioning support, which enabled me to carry out the project with relative ease.

My assistant Shiu and I set up a performance area in a strategic corner of the teahouse where everyone could see and hear. The table where Dou would place his instrument (the *zheng*) was large enough for us to add three microphones, two connected to an open-reel tape recorder and the third to a small cassette recorder. Dou had his own amplification system consisting of a microphone and a portable speaker—indispensable technology that he used when he sang at the street corner—which added to the clutter on the table. Those were days of relatively primitive technology: our main tape recorder, on loan from the Centre of Asian Studies, was a bulky contraption that used $1/_2$-inch open-reel tapes. Mr. Shiu would haul it to the teahouse and set it up before each session. I took along my own much smaller cassette tape recorder to supplement the open reel-tapes.[19]

On the first day of the series, March 11, 1975, Shiu and I arrived early so as to have everything set up in time. Shortly before noon, Dou came in, accompanied by a woman friend Ah Sou. He carried his instrument in one hand and his personal amplification gear in the other. He quickly set up his instruments, microphone, and speaker, and tuned the sixteen strings on the *zheng*, while at the same time he and I were chatting of this and that. One of the waiters placed a pot of tea and a teacup in front of him. At 12 noon sharp, his public performance began, with a short introduction of both speech and song that went:

---

19. The recording sessions at the Fu Long Teahouse have been reported elsewhere. See Bell Yung, "Reconstructing a Lost Performance Context: A Field Work Experiment," *Chinoperl Papers* no. 6 (1976): 120–143; translated into Chinese by Chen Shouren and Yun-dei Pun and published in *Fieldwork and Research in Chinese Opera* 實地考察與戲曲研究, ed. Sau Y. Chan 陳守仁 (Hong Kong: The Chinese University of Hong Kong Yueju yanjiu jihua, 1997), 297–318. See also Rong Hong Zeng 榮鴻曾 [Bell Yung], "Collecting Contemporary Folk Performing Literature: Singing nanyin in Fulong Teahouse" 當前民間演唱文學的搜集: 富隆茶樓唱南音, *Chinese Studies* 漢學研究 8, no. 1 (1990): 647–654.

[Speaks] Okay! I wish everyone success in all ventures. Your humble servant sang on the radio for many years some time ago. No more now. My songs are very old-fashioned. But hearing them will bring you joy and happiness through the year, and everything will come as you wish. Let me start by singing this old song about the undying love of a man. What is it? It's the very same one that the famous Baak Keui Wing recorded, called "A Man Burning Garments." After hearing it, you'll have success in everything.

(Tuning the instrument)

[Speaks] Okay! I'm going to begin now. Wishing everyone good spirits, prosperous looks with potential for riches.

(Instrumental prelude, in which he plucks the strings of the *zheng* with his right hand and plays the clappers with his left.)
[Sings]

Now I begin my singing; wishing you safety as you go in and out of your house, Men and women, old and young, the entire family together.

After you hear my words, you'll enjoy prospects of wealth and prosperity, For I'll sing how this man falls in love.

First, let me describe this love of his, After hearing it, everything will go your way.

(Begins singing the song proper)

Thus he began the first of his 43 performances at the teahouse that lasted until June 26. After the first 30 minutes, he stopped and took a few sips of tea, and chatted with me for a while. He told me that, during his younger days, he could sing non-stop for several hours; but he didn't have the energy (his word was *jingshen* [精神]) now. The intermission lasted some ten to fifteen minutes before the resumption of the performance. After about another 30 minutes of singing, he ended the day's performance. I would try to keep him for a few more minutes and urged him to have another cup of tea while I asked him about the olden days. Then he would say "Time to go." Holding on to Ah Sou and carrying his various things, they would take a bus to the Hong Kong and Yaumatei Ferry Pier (Cantonese Tung Yat Ma Tau), cross the harbor on a ferry to the Jordan Pier on the Kowloon side, and then walk home. At the time he was living at 996 Canton Road, mezzanine floor (Cantonese *gok lau*).

The teahouse was normally half empty at noon, but quickly filled up within 20 minutes and stayed quite full until shortly after 1 pm. The windowsills would also quickly fill up with birdcages. As soon as the singing began, the little birds would themselves sing even louder, providing quite a sonic backdrop in the teahouse and in the recording. During his performance most of the customers went about their usual business of chatting, reading the newspaper, or admiring the birds, but a few were obviously paying close attention to Dou. Before, in between and after the sessions, some of them would come up to compliment him on his singing, ask him questions, and reminisce about the old days. One of the steady customers even wrote a poem to commemorate a performance. It is true that many customers paid more attention to me because of my obviously out-of-place appearance, and even more attention to the recording machines, than to Dou. But the few who did respond actively to Dou undoubtedly exerted an influence on him. He would begin each session by first wishing the listeners good fortune and happiness, or using other congratulatory expressions appropriate to the day. For example, if it happened to be a day of horse racing, he would wish the audience luck in their betting. Obviously this indicated that Dou was aware of their presence and that he had not lost his professional touch. I believe that such awareness and professionalism, which of course had existed when he worked as a real performer years before, must have been instrumental in the shaping of his songs in 1975.

The entire list of songs, including a few that were not recorded in the teahouse as noted, is as follows:

A Man Burning Garments[20]
A Love-Obsessed Prostitute (also known as A Woman Burning Garments)
King's Farewell to Concubine Yu
Wayfarer's Autumnal Lament
The Haunting of Guang Chang Long, five episodes
Second Sister You Dies
Laments Through the Night by He Hui Qun
Stealing the Poetry Manuscript (an episode from The Jade Hairpin)
The Story of Liang Tian Lai, ten episodes
The Birth of Guan Yin, three episodes
Wu Song Kills the Tiger, 16 episodes
Stealing the Poetry Manuscript, repeat
Killing the Tiger at Jing Yang Gong (an episode from Wu Song Kills the Tiger), repeat
Bi Rong Offers Sacrifices (an episode from The Haunting at the Home of County Magistrate Mei)
Meng Li Jun Has Her Pulse Checked (an episode from Romance in a Second Life)
Returning Home to Mourn His Brother (an episode from Wu Song Kills the Tiger), sung in longzhou style
Slaughtering His Sister-in-Law (an episode from Wu Song Kills the Tiger), sung in longzhou style
The Fight at the Lion's Pavilion (an episode from Wu Song Kills the Tiger), sung in lungzhou style
Drafted into the Army (an episode from Wu Song Kills the Tiger), sung in longzhou style

---

20. The title could be translated as "A Man Mourning His Love." "Burning garments" is to offer sacrifices to a loved one.

Beating the Door God when Drunk (an episode from Wu Song Kills the Tiger), sung in longzhou style
The Eight Immortals Send Birthday Greetings
The Heavenly Official Bestows Blessing
Rotten Big Drum, sung in the banyan style, sung at the home of Nishimura
Second Uncle Chen, sung in the banyan style, sung at the home of Nishimura
Blind Dou Wun Remembers His Past, twelve episodes, the last four of which were sung in 1976 at the Centre of Asian Studies at the University of Hong Kong

The last song was left unfinished when we ended the performance at the teahouse because I had to return to the United States. Eventually, my friend Nishi, who knew Dou well because he was very much involved with the project, completed the recording of the song on my behalf on March 6 and 13 of 1976 at the Centre of Asian Studies. It may also be observed above that, besides *nanyin*, I asked him to sing another kind of Cantonese narrative song called *longzhou* (Cantonese *Longzau*), "dragon boat," which has a different musical style in which the singer accompanies himself on a small gong and a small drum.

In my conversations with Dou, I learned that one kind of song he sang was the type called *banyan* (Cantonese *baan'ngaan*). These songs were risqué in content, often describing sexual acts, and were sung exclusively in brothels. In textual and musical style they were completely different from *nanyin*. Understandably, he absolutely refused to sing these songs at the teahouse because they were completely inappropriate in such a setting. But he agreed to sing them in private. On May 31, I recorded two of his *banyan* songs, approximately two hours total, at the home of Nishimura.[21]

Voices of and about Hong Kong

With the exception of the last item, all the songs on the above list belong to the standard repertory of *nanyin* (and *longzhou* and *banyan*). Of those, *Wayfarer's Autumnal Lament, A Man Burning Garments, A Love-Obsessed Prostitute,* and *Laments Through the Night* by He Hui Qun were widely sung and known to audiences, and the text in each case was relatively stable from one singer to another. These songs are less narratives than emotional outpourings of loss and longing, almost always concerning an illicit liaison between a prostitute and her young lover.[22] The three

---

21. The recording of *banyan* 板眼 was reported in *Chinoperl Papers,* no. 11 (1981) and no. 12 (1983), with the complete translation of one of the two songs, "Rotten Big Drum."
22. These four songs, along with a fifth one *King's Farewell to Concubine Yu,* have been issued as a double CD set called *Naamyam Songs of Love and Longing: Live Recordings of the Legendary Blind Naamyam Singer Dou Wun* at the Fu Long Tea House in 1975, Hong Kong (Chinese Music Archive, Department of Music, The Chinese University of Hong Kong, 1975).

pieces *The Birth of Guan Yin, The Eight Immortals Send Birthday Greetings*, and *The Heavenly Official Bestows Blessing* are ritual songs sung for special celebratory occasions. Their texts are also relatively fixed.

A second group of songs are nationally or regionally known: the Wu Song story is from the afore-mentioned *Shuihuzhuan* and the related novel *Jinpingmei* (The Story of Golden Lotus); the story of Second Sister You is from the novel *Hongloumeng* (Dream of the Red Chamber); *Yuzhanji* (Story of the Jade Hairpin) is a celebrated Ming dynasty drama; and *Zaishengyuan* (Romance in a Second Life) is a Qing dynasty verse epic that has been widely performed in many narrative genres in other parts of the country. The remaining two, *The Story of Liang Tian Lai* and *The Haunting of Guang Chang Long* are regional Cantonese tales.

The songs in this second group shared one thing in common when Dou sang them: they were highly improvisatory. Instead of following a fixed text, Dou exercised great flexibility on two different levels. First, Dou manipulated the story by adding, eliminating, or changing the order of appearance of one or more plot elements. Secondly, on the level of expression, Dou expanded or contracted the time required for performance by his choice of words and phrases, giving more (or less) detailed exposition to plot elements. A good example is *The Story of Liang Tian Lai*, for which I possess a printed version, published in the early 20th century, which has 173 pages and consists of six chapters, each chapter containing eleven to fourteen sections, and each section over a hundred lines. In short, the printed version is itself a lengthy epic of roughly seven thousand lines, plus spoken prose sections interspersed among the verses. When Dou was singing it, I tried to follow the written text but had a difficult time tracking where he was because of his extensive improvisation. After five recording sessions (about five hours), he was still on page 20, only three quarters of the way through chapter one. Extrapolating from that sample, it would take him roughly fifty hours to reach the end of the story.

The improvisatory nature of his performance is further evidenced by what Dou told me one day. When I expressed surprise and admiration at the large number of songs that he claimed to know, his response was something like this: "I don't really know all these songs by memory. Most of them are quite similar to one another, sharing standard episodes like weddings, quarrels, or love scenes. All I need to remember are these episodes, and I use them whenever they are suitable. My singing is like cooking. A chef has a limited amount of ingredients and spices. He mixes them in different ways and sequences, and can produce a very large number of dishes."

Dou's improvisatory abilities became critical when, during his active years as a professional singer, he would often make up a song on the spot based upon some news items he had heard a few hours earlier that day. When I asked him to try doing this at Fu Long Teahouse, he laughingly declined and said that he no longer paid any attention to the news around him. It was then that I came up with the idea of asking him to sing about his own life. I said to him: "Surely you know your own life well, and could make up a new song based on that." After some hesitation, he finally and reluctantly agreed, and that was how "Blind Dou Wun Remembers His Past" came about. The entire song lasted more than six hours, consisting of 1812 lines of text interspersed with many spoken segments, and took four days in the Fu Long Teahouse plus two more one-hour recording sessions in the following year to complete. [23]

Of all the songs recorded in the course of this project, "Blind Dou Wun Remembers His Past" is the most important for several reasons. First, unlike the others, it is an "original" song that no one else sang, or could have sung, before. It reflects Dou's creative genius in his organization of the material, his choice of words and phrases, and his technique of timing. Its originality, and indeed, the unusualness of the content, is shown in the way Dou began each performance at the teahouse. For example, at the very first session of this song, his normal introductory chatter went like this:

> Hello, esteemed listeners, today is Thursday, and here I am again. I shall be taking up another hour of your precious time, to impose upon your fortune-generating ears with my noisy chatter. As to the story, you already know all kinds. So for today, my story will be neither about the past, nor about the present. You'll never guess! And I bet you'll never understand why I'm doing this! There! I'm going to sing about myself! Ha ha. Everything about me, the whats and the whys — nothing will be held back. If I don't sing well, please, esteemed listeners, don't judge me harshly. For this is not your normal song. No singer has ever sung about his own life, isn't that so? So, here I go, giving it a try. Your humble servant is called Dou Wun, that's my name when I sang on the radio, isn't it? Let me give this song a name. I'll call it "Blind Dou Wun Remembers his Past." All right, with your permission, here's my humble offering. Let me sing.

In the three subsequent sessions at the teahouse, his introductory chatter always hinted at the fact that he was a little embarrassed to be singing this song, and was doing so only because he had been cajoled into it. Significantly, for the last two sessions, recorded at the Centre of Asian Studies at the Hong Kong University, he did not begin with such chatter because there was no live audience to whom he felt responsible.

The second reason why this song is particularly important is because it is an autobiographical song by a musician whose life was both ordinary and extraordinary: ordinary because, like many Chinese people of the mid-twentieth

---

23. An excerpt of this song, 164 lines, was translated and published, along with the corresponding recording, as a DVD entitled *A Blind Singer's Story: 50 Years of Life and Work in Hong Kong*. The entire song, both the Chinese text and its English translation, will be published in the future.

century, he lived through displacement, alienation, trials and triumphs; extraordinary because, unlike others, he was the last surviving professional singer of an important genre of music that would never be heard again as it once was, and because he happened to be a talented and experienced story-teller. Since the song was about himself, including episodes of intense emotional upheaval of a personal nature, he performed it with a particular poignancy. The brief sketch of his life story given earlier in this essay was extracted from the song.

Lastly and most significantly for this essay, the song is important because it is about a particular place, Hong Kong, and a particular period of time, from 1926 to 1975. This turbulent period of the city's history is "seen" through the eyes and told through the voice of a lowly citizen and folk artist. Like hundreds of thousands of others, Dou struggled to survive in a rapidly changing city, where the traditional and the modern, and East and West, were in a constant shuffle.

Even though Dou came to Hong Kong half-formed at age sixteen, he fitted in easily because he was born and spent his childhood in a physical environment and a cultural milieu of which Hong Kong had been very much a part for centuries, despite its colonial interlude. The vast majority of Hong Kongers feel a link of kinship with the Pearl River Delta region linguistically, socially, culturally, and often personally. The constant movement of people across the boundary has forged a historical connection between the two regions. The fact that Dou's songs were accepted here is a small but significant indication of these feelings of affinity. His is a personal manifestation of Hong Kong's self identification with the "motherland" to the north, and his voice should be taken as an essential text for our understanding of what the city is and who the people in it are. The story of his life and the stories he sang, in particular the biographical song, are "texts" that validate the "oneness" in the slogan of "One Country, Two Systems."

My path crossed Dou's fortuitously in 1974-75, and I had the opportunity to relay Dou's stories through my perspective. I was also an outsider to Hong Kong, but from a Chinese subculture that was substantially more different from mainstream Hong Kong than Dou's was. Even though I spent my formative years in the colony, the social circumstances were such that I was touched very little by local culture, at least at the conscious level. It was not until I had spent almost fifteen years abroad that I found my way back and discovered the subliminal imprints from my days of youth. I returned after receiving a Western education, and I brought back a personal and professional view of the world that had been molded largely by Western thoughts. If Dou validates "One Country Two Systems," might I not be considered to exemplify the counterpart slogan of "Asia's World City"?

But the main story is Dou's, a voice of China in Hong Kong, and let it be acknowledged that his story has been refracted through my voice, as I was the one who arranged to have him sing in Fu Long Teahouse and pressured him to create the original song of himself and of Hong Kong. More importantly, I am telling his story through the English language, a voice utterly foreign to him and to his world.

Invisible Neighbors: Racial Minorities and the Hong Kong Chinese Community

Kwai-Cheung Lo

Ethnic figure as a kind of absence

Some time ago I wrote a Chinese book on Hong Kong's racial minorities for the Home Affairs Bureau of the Hong Kong Government.[1] Therein racial minorities were defined broadly as people of non-Chinese origin living in the city. I interviewed more than twenty-three people of various ethnicities.[2] Non-Chinese ethnics comprise only about 5 percent of the total population. Because they make up such a small portion, and because of a relatively peaceful interracial environment, racial minorities in Hong Kong have not been considered an issue that arouses the interest or concern of the general public.[3] Local Chinese are

---

1. The book was published in Chinese and is entitled *Colors of Hong Kong: Racial Minorities in the Local Community* 香港・多一點顏色：我們的鄰舍 (Hong Kong: Home Affairs Bureau, 2006). I will make use of some materials from this book to support my arguments in the following.

2. I tend to use the two words *race* and *ethnicity* interchangeably in this essay although, for some critics, analytical distinction is held between the two terms in that *race* is socially defined but on the basis of physical criteria whereas *ethnicity* is socially constructed through cultural characteristics.

3. Only very recently, i.e. by the end of November 2006, the Hong Kong Special Administrative Region (SAR) government has introduced the draft legislation of a race discrimination bill that would cover employment, education, the offering of services and facilities, elections, appointments and participation in social groups. Carrie Lam, Permanent Secretary for Home Affairs, said the government will introduce the bill to make racial discrimination, harassment and vilification unlawful and to prohibit serious racial vilification.

used to see the ethnics as "foreigners" ("ngoi gwok yan" in Cantonese) or "outsiders" ("lao wai" in Mandarin), usually denying their native status, excluding them from the integral part of the community and fundamentally hindering any acts of solidarity with society's "others."

Keeping a safe distance or making the other "out of sight" while being very wary of their proximate existence seems to be the defense mechanism of local Chinese to guard against any over-proximity to the mysterious desire of the other. In a place where over-crowding can easily exacerbate racial antagonism, perhaps pretending not to see the existence of ethnic others may create a more peaceful public sphere. While white people are usually regarded as the symbolic presence of the West, the ethnic is usually defined by a striking absence. As if using the discourse of the fast economic growth to cover up the issue of intensive poverty, Hong Kong always highlights its cosmopolitanism without giving parallel attention to its potential racial tensions. The racial vision of Hong Kong Chinese verges on rendering all the non-white ethnic figures indistinguishable, if not entirely invisible, despite the fact that the bodily markers of racial difference are highly visible to the Chinese eye. Being an entity to be looked at could have posed potential threat to the viewing subject, but the ethnic spectacle is never an object of gaze to the scopic drives of Hong Kong Chinese culture. Such neglect (making the visible unseen), apparently different from the deep-seated psyche fixating on certain racial markers, however, could be a reverse discrimination, though historically it has helped to maintain a temporary racial harmony. Yet it may not be an exaggeration to say that we may grope toward a certain degree of insight if we are able to observe such blindness as a consequence of the unmediated presence of ethnicity in the formation of the Hong Kong subject. In other words, Hong Kong people are blind to what takes place within themselves, and only by turning back upon this blindness, can some knowledge come into being.

This essay focuses not necessarily upon the communities of racial minorities[4] but, from a local Chinese perspective (if not blinded), upon the ethnic dimensions (of which the non-Chinese races are tentatively and strategically homogenized as the "other") and implications of postcolonial subjectivity in Hong Kong since its return to China. During the colonial era, Hong Kong, under British colonial strategic planning, marketed itself as a hybrid conglomerate of both East and West by peddling both an inauthentic Chinese style to the West (when Mainland China was off limits to craving Western eyes) and a superficial version of the West to its

---

4.   For the historical accounts of the minority communities, including mixed-race peoples, in Hong Kong, see, for instance, Cindy Yik-yi Chu, ed., *Foreign Communities in Hong Kong, 1840s–1950s* (New York: Palgrave Macmillan, 2005); Vicky Lee, *Being Eurasian: Memories Across Racial Divides* (Hong Kong: Hong Kong University Press, 2004); Irene Cheng, *Intercultural Reminiscences* (Hong Kong: Hong Kong Baptist University, 1997); Kwok Siu-tong and Kirti Narain, *Co-prosperity in Cross-Culturalism: Indians in Hong Kong* (Hong Kong: Commercial Press, 2003); and Barbara-Sue White, *Turbans and Traders: Hong Kong's Indian Communities* (New York: Oxford University Press, 1994).

Chinese compatriots. The ethnic identity of Hong Kong is actually not a reflexive project of the self but rather a commodified product manufactured for the gaze of outsiders. But what is remarkably dialectical about Hong Kong's ethnicity is that that which begins outside always ends up inside its subjectivity. We have seen projections coming from without pass into the kernel of the subject formation, through which a unique Hong Kong ethnic identity grew and gained strength. The post-1997 nationalist subjectivization (or interpellation, in the Althusserian sense, that constitutes individuals as subjects through the ideological operation of recognition) of Hong Kong is structured around ethnic meanings of Chineseness. However, what has been overlooked in this subjectivization, as Žižek points out in his criticism of Althusser's theory of ideological interpellation,[5] is that there is always a "leftover" that resists such processes of subjectivization but embodies the impossibility of the subject. As an individual living in Hong Kong, I recognize myself as a Chinese subject and consent to be named as such, but there is something more in this subjectivization (i.e. "a Chinese subject, but not quite").

I understand this leftover to be the non-integrated racial minorities that are constitutive of postcolonial subject in Hong Kong. Hence, it is not because we have to fulfill the criteria of political correctness that racial minorities as heterogeneous groups and diverse individuals should be carefully studied; nor is it simply because the wholeness or universality of the community is embedded in particulars or even in particular racial groups, thus necessitating knowing and defining the peripheral or the particular in order to understand the essence of the totality. My understanding of the "residual-ness" of racial minorities in relation to Hong Kong subject formation does not necessarily tie in with the dialectics of the universal and the particular, of the majorities and the minorities, or of the center and the marginal. It is not exactly a contradictory relation of identity and difference, which are related and even converted into a singular substance (as two conflicting sides of the same thing). Instead, the commonalities among Hong Kong Chinese and the minorities, as well as the racial minorities' exteriority or "surplus" to the structure of Hong Kong subjectivity, are articulated through a certain notion of "repetition" — that is to say, a historical repetition from the early colonial era as well as a conceptual repetition in the Deleuzian sense.

Erasing the racial other from past to present

In the early twentieth century, a satirical columnist called "Betty" wrote in the Hong Kong *China Mail* that "the population of Hong Kong as far as I am concerned consists of [her husband] William and about three hundred more,

---

5. See Slavoj Žižek, *The Sublime Object of Ideology* (New York: Verso, 1989), especially "Kafka, Critic of Althusser," 43–47.

none of whom are Chinese."[6] This hyperbolic depiction of general British "not seeing" or indifference to the Chinese presence in the neighborhood might have revealed the typical attitude of the English expatriates or colonizers who ideologically erased other ethnic populations (including Portuguese, Indians, Eurasians, and other Asian peoples) from the landscape of the port city in order to map out their own utopian colonial enclave. Without any doubt, the notion of neighbor is entirely meaningless to colonial domination and imperialist exploitation. The presence of Chinese people in the colony (local Chinese inhabitants were relatively few in number, but there were many who came from the Mainland to seek refuge from disasters) was thus rendered almost invisible in the unilateral racial divide of the British Empire. The symbolic erasure of the Chinese in Betty's account could have been an unconscious desire on the part of British colonials in the face of the overwhelming Chinese majority.[7] Though seemingly arrogant in tone, Betty's satire actually discloses the ruling British minority's fear of the threat of the Chinese population in the colony. Yet in the early colonial days, the British objective was to convert others to their worldview and culture. Perhaps it was wishful thinking on the part of the British colonial to imagine that the alien other could be eliminated precisely by integrating or converting each of them into "one of us." The Chinese differences (not only in terms of physical appearance but also in dress, behavior, eating habits, politics, and religious beliefs) vanished before Betty, who chose to see only the exercise of the colonial separation policy. In other words, power does not have to situate the colonized in the realm of the visible. Making threatening differences unseen is a strategy of colonial control. It is not only the everyday exercise of control that is invisible.[8] Those who are colonized have also been made indiscernible.

The disappearance of ethnic and cultural others in the British imperial account might have found resonance in the consciousness and perception of the Hong Kong Chinese majority in relation to the existence of racial minorities in the postcolonial period. To the colonial-era British, the Chinese remained

---

6. "Betty," *Intercepted Letters: A Mild Satire on Hongkong Society* (Hong Kong: Kelly and Walsh, 1905), 25. She also wrote that her husband William "treated everyone and everything not English with open contempt, and freely expressed the opinion that 'All foreigners were fools, and that if he'd been born a Frenchman he'd have hanged himself as soon as he was old enough'" (6).

7. The ratio of Chinese to non-Chinese people in the late nineteenth century was 95.64 to 4.35. Frank Welsh writes that "[i]t was this great disproportion between the races that gave rise to the most awkward problems. Chinese customs and culture were too strongly marked and deeply ingrained to adapt easily to those of the British." See Welsh, *A History of Hong Kong* (London: HarperCollins, 1993), 253.

8. The invisible power control in everyday life of course refers to Foucault's notion of Panopticon, which put the entire population under constant surveillance while the surveillant authority itself remained unseen.

impenetrable and inscrutable, and thus needed to be converted so that their differences could be made invisible. Such attitudes toward difference mark the relationship between the Hong Kong Chinese and non-Chinese ethnic groups. To make something disturbing and problematic vanish is always a violent political-ideological act. Yet the Hong Kong Chinese majority's general ignorance of other ethnic peoples, apart from the inherited colonial legacy and the Chinese cultural chauvinism that relegates all non-Han to barbarian status[9] ("Han" in the tradition of Sinology is identical to "Chinese," whereas the notion of "Sinicization" always assumes that all racial minorities and foreigners having contact with the Chinese will be inexorably assimilated into the dominant Chinese civilization), may also be attributed to the city's historical search for a voice of its own and a unique local identity.

By no means is it easy to define a "local" identity for Hong Kong since its construction always involves class stratification, gender differences, sexual orientations, and tensions between natives and new immigrants, urban and rural cultures, and Chinese and non-Chinese ethnicities. What we bore witness to at the end of the twentieth century is that if a unique local identity of Hong Kong had ever been constituted, it was never a combination of multiple subjectivities or an outcome of negotiations. In other words, the construction of the Hong Kong identity is not exactly a postmodern identity politics of multiple lifestyles and positions. Instead, it is a particular identity that fights with other particulars for hegemonic representation and claims to articulate universal interests and demands, and engages in struggles and confrontation. Perhaps because of this rule of hegemony, the only universality that Hong Kong society can achieve is a "hegemonic universality" as described by Ernesto Laclau — a universality embedded in or contaminated by a particularity (i.e., local Chinese who claim themselves Hong Kongers) that exerts leadership and maintains its dominance to represent the general interest of society and a certain social order, whereas the particularity of racial minorities has yet to assume a function of universal representation. But this hegemony does not necessarily carry a homogeneous, unitary or totalizing character. That means the voices of non-Chinese ethnic groups have not yet been integrated into the discourse of Hong Kong that has come into being since the transitional period in the 1980s and 1990s. Just as "Han" is considered synonymous with "Chinese," "Hong Kong" is immediately identified as the Chinese majority living in the city. Thus, "Hong Kong literature" usually

---

9. The descendents of the Han dynasty (206 B.C.–220 A.D.) have been generalized as "Chinese" for centuries. Labeling the neighboring non-Han racial and nomadic groups as well as other foreigners as "barbarians" was a Han empire strategy to legitimize their political and cultural superiority. But the concept of Han-Chinese nationality is a modern idea appropriated and advocated by Sun Yat-sen in order to mobilize Chinese people to overthrow the Qing dynasty (1644–1911) and to establish a republic based on the unity of the Han majority and other minorities including the Manchu, Mongolian, Tibetan, and Hui (or Muslim).

means Hong Kong literature written in the Chinese language only, "Hong Kong cinema" refers restrictedly to local film productions either in Mandarin or Cantonese, and so on. Thus the hegemony has not represented the coming together of diverse groups, without establishing a basis of consent.

During the transitional period before the handover, numerous books, journals, documentaries and other cultural forms focusing on the Hong Kong past rewrote or re-imagined its history in order to establish a definite subject position in response to urgent political exigencies. These discourses of Hong Kong, its culture, and its (predominantly Chinese) people usually do not cover or mesh with the histories and cultures of non-Chinese peoples living in the city. Even those authored by minority writers say nothing of the life of the ethnic minority. The example I have in mind is Ackbar Abbas' book, *Hong Kong: Culture and the Politics of Disappearance*,[10] where the multi-ethnic Hong Kong falls entirely into the space of disappearance though the work briefly mentions Hong Kong's English writing. But, by no means do I suggest that a minority writer necessarily can or should speak for his minority group. On the other hand, Gordon Mathews even strongly criticizes Abbas' work for its failure to describe Hong Kong Chinese culture. He writes: "The irony of Abbas' book is that although Hong Kong culture may indeed exist within a space of disappearance, the most striking disappearance is that of Hong Kong from the pages of the book itself.... Hong Kong cultural 'raw materials' are analyzed and refined via Western cultural theory, leaving no space for Hong Kong commentators' own interpretations of Hong Kong culture. The book's bibliographic notes contain remarkably few references pertaining to Hong Kong, and no references at all in Chinese...he brings so little of Hong Kong into the book, his generalizations have an expatriate feel to them; he does not describe Hong Kong, or Hong Kong cinema, architecture, and literature as experienced by most Hong Kong people."[11] At that critical moment of Hong Kong colonial history, the major concern, as expressed by Mathews, is about the underrepresentation of the local Chinese in all the discursive formations of the city. What is needed is more of the local Chinese voices, though this would allow no room for the heteroglossia of other ethnicities.

Perhaps because the Hong Kong Chinese community in these discourses has already been theorized as a hyphenated culture or as a space of in-betweenness, the concepts of hybridity, heterogeneity, and mixture are no longer flexible enough to encompass the multiplicity of the non-Chinese ethnics. The pressing task at that time was to enable the underrepresented and marginalized Hong Kong Chinese to speak and to be heard as a collective alongside the prevailing

10. Ackbar Abbas, *Hong Kong: Culture and the Politics of Disappearance* (Hong Kong: Hong Kong University Press, 1997).

11. See Mathews, "Hong Kong: Culture and the Politics of Disappearance," *The Journal of Asian Studies* 57, no.4 (Nov 1998): 1112–1113.

voices of the British colonizers and the Mainland Chinese authority. What should be constructed for Hong Kong in order to challenge the simple opposition between foreign colonizer and native colonized, or between Britain and China, Rey Chow argues in her essay "Between Colonizers," is "a third space between the colonizer and the dominant [Chinese] native culture, a space that cannot simply be collapsed into the latter even as resistance to the former remains foremost."[12] Nevertheless, it remains unclear whether this "third space" can suspend the totalizing vision of Hong Kong as a unity and bring out the tension between the dominant Chinese and subdominant ethnic minorities within Hong Kong community itself. Perhaps, it is too facile to conclude that privileging the voices of Hong Kong Chinese may imply the re-inscription of a logocentric assumption of cultural solidarity among a heterogeneous people and the rehearsal of a cultural erasure of the marginalized minorities. The failure to articulate the different interests of non-Chinese ethnic minorities, whether or not it is an intentional omission, demonstrates the insufficiency of identity formation and the inadequacy of any discourse on hybridity. But could a liberal, pluralistic inclusionist recognition of the ethnic others lead to the formation of an "all-encompassing" Hong Kong identity without leaving out and discriminating against anyone? As Chow points out elsewhere, this inclusionist, liberalist cultural logic "meanwhile democratizes these [racial hierarchical] boundaries rhetorically with honorable terms such as 'multiculturalism' and 'diversity' and practically by way of the proliferation of enclaves and ghetto."[13]

Is a non-dialectical but equivalent racial relationship possible?

Suffice it to say that the relation between local Chinese and racial minorities as it pertains to Hong Kong subjectivity is not essentially a contradictory or oppositional one. One does not have to negate the other in order to have an identity. However, nor is it true that the notion of Hong Kong subjectivity is driven to reveal and overcome the contradiction by moving to a new, higher concept and to form a synthetic and totalistic entity. If there emerges a new postcolonial Hong Kong subject, it need not be a synthetic unity of local Chinese and racial minorities. Instead of being synthesized or integrated, the minorities are marginalized and remain the other of whom the local Chinese are not fully aware and whom they cannot comprehend, but who will be later recognized as constitutive of the new subject, because, like the local Chinese, they are also one of the particulars fighting for universality, which is itself always a site of contest. What I mean here is that

---

12. Rey Chow, "Between Colonizers: Hong Kong's Postcolonial Self-Writing in the 1990s," *Diaspora: A Journal of Transnational Studies* 2, no.2 (1992): 158.
13. Chow, *The Protestant Ethic and the Spirit of Capitalism* (New York: Columbia University Press, 2002), 29.

the assertion of pure particularity on the part of non-Chinese ethnics without any claim to universalism is no solution to the problem of their invisibility and can only be a self-defeating project.

The Muslim presence in Hong Kong is embodied by a mosque in Kowloon Park in Tsim Tsa Tsui. Despite its occupying sixteen thousand square feet and accommodating up to two thousand Indian and Pakistani worshipers, it does not arouse the attention or interest of the local Chinese. Although the Sikh temple on Queen's Road East is in the very heart of Hong Kong's trademark district, few Chinese citizens can claim familiarity with the customs and lifestyles of South Asians in Hong Kong. A Bengali migrant we interviewed told us that it is difficult to lead an Islamic life in the city, even though there is no apparent prejudice against the religion. Praying five times a day — which is required of Muslims — is hard for Chinese employers to accept since they don't want any disruption of the workday. Public facilities are not designed to accommodate Muslims who are required, before worship, to wash their faces, hands, and arms up to the elbows; rub their heads with water; and wash their feet and ankles. When our Bengali interviewee attempted to do so in a public lavatory by putting his feet in the washbasin, he was embarrassed by the frowns of passersby and was rudely stopped by the janitor. The religious expressions of minorities have for a long time been hidden from the public eye. The difference demanded by religious rituals if seen is considered an unwelcome disturbance to the social order and harmony of the majority.

The Nepalese community leader in Hong Kong's Yau Ma Tei District complained during our interview that their people, because of similarities in facial features, have often been incorrectly taken for Chinese. As a result, their cultural differences and sociopolitical demands have generally been ignored. They once held a press conference to seek public attention for issues that generally have gone underreported. The local media arrived at the venue and one of the reporters bluntly asked where all the Nepalese had gone, when in fact the Nepalese were present. They were there but went unseen. Their invisibility is not unique to contemporary Hong Kong. In the old colonial days, Nepalese soldiers, namely, the Gurkha — a major unit of the British Army stationed in Hong Kong — never mingled with the local Chinese community because of strict military regulations. Some of my Nepalese interviewees were actually born and raised in Hong Kong as their fathers were Gurkha serving in the British colony. However, they could not speak any Cantonese and knew very little of the local society (they were not even permitted to watch Hong Kong local television programs) under the military separatist policy. After 1997, once their fears of political instability evaporated, many Hong Kong–born Nepalese returned to the city to seek out economic opportunities. They came not as returnees to a familiar place, but as strangers who had to learn everything about city life from scratch. The Nepalese also found that there was very little government support available to them, though the government always claims to aim at the betterment of racial integration. For example, very few government departments have interpreters to help the Nepalese apply for necessary documents. Chinese-language education is offered to immigrants only up to sixteen years of age, effectively eliminating chances for adult minorities to learn the dominant language. Many jobs posted by the Labor Department list only the position titles in English; the job descriptions themselves are printed in Chinese. Surveys show that unemployment among the minority community has been as high as 60 percent, compared to a general unemployment rate of about 5 to 6 percent in the society as a whole. Studies also show that racial minorities always earn less than the Chinese, usually work at lower-level jobs, and lack access to resources such as public housing and social welfare.[14]

Under the 2006 "Construction Workers Registration" system, all construction workers in Hong Kong must register and take relevant prerequisite training courses. The vast majority of such courses are conducted in Cantonese and the reading materials are in Chinese; the non-provision of English-language courses puts non-Chinese (mainly South Asian) construction workers at a disadvantage. Non-Chinese real estate agents are in a similar situation, and complain of a severe lack of English-language training materials to use in preparation for required qualification examinations. Moreover, as stated above, it is almost impossible for new non-Chinese immigrants who are over sixteen to receive any public education in Hong Kong. Many non-Chinese ethnics are not hired because of poor Chinese or Cantonese proficiency — if not directly because of their skin color. Because their political sensitivity is sharpened by political conditions in their home country,[15] the Nepalese community has established — in collaboration with local Chinese activists — a pro-democratic Southern Democratic Alliance that seeks to unite South Asians and the local Chinese in a multi-racial Hong Kong and to fight for the rights of racial minorities. With about six hundred Nepalese, Chinese, and Pakistani members to date, the Southern Democratic Alliance supported the electoral campaigns of Chinese councilors who are concerned about minorities' rights — there has never been a minority councilor elected to government office. However, racial minorities who are interested in politics are very rare. Many of them seek to avoid public attention. In my interviews, some even said that they prefer to live on their own terms, free from the scrutiny of the public eye and without being bothered by the authorities. They believe that Hong Kong's blindness to other ethnic groups can provide precisely the space and freedom they need. If they have been ignored by Hong Kong's Chinese majority, they also

---

14. See, for example, *Population Census 2001* (Hong Kong: Census and Statistics Department, 2002); *A Research Report on the Employment Situation of South Asian People in Hong Kong* (Hong Kong: City Univ. of Hong Kong and Unison Hong Kong — For Ethnic Equality, 2003); and *A Study of the Nepalese Community in Hong Kong* (Hong Kong: Society for Community Organization, 2004).

15. In interviews with Nepalese subjects, I was told that Nepalese in general are very conscious of their political rights, and there are more than one hundred political parties in their country.

choose to pay no attention to and have no involvement in local political conflicts and entanglements (let alone voting). Apparently rejoicing in being ordinary and invisible rather than extraordinary and spectacular reveals how deeply the minorities might have agonized over the fact that their looks, languages and cultures differ from those of their neighbors. But the members of minorities interviewed who opt for invisibility are mostly of upper-middle-class status. When non-Chinese in the lower classes usually do not receive public attention and the privileged strata of racial minorities prefer not to be seen, then where do we locate the minorities in Hong Kong? How do we measure their invisibility and silence?

Žižek has reread Kierkegaard's comments on "*You* Shall Love Your Neighbor" in his *Works of Love*[16] by arguing that if to love one's neighbor means equality and if only death erases all distinctions, then the only neighbor we can love is a dead one. "The dead neighbor means," Žižek explains, "the neighbor deprived of the annoying excess of *jouissance* which makes him/her unbearable."[17] Therefore, "the disturbing threat of the [neighbor]'s excessive enjoyment is also eliminated."[18] The Lacanian concept of jouissance or enjoyment is fundamentally related to the Freudian notion of the death drive, inserting the dimension of anxiety into the domain of (sexual) satisfaction. The proximity of the other, or the neighbor, only provokes one's sense of anxiety while one enjoys oneself. The way a neighbor enjoys or lives his/her life is too excessive, traumatic and intolerable. How could a Muslim so devotedly submit him- or herself to praying five times a day in the hectic daily routine? If "the only good neighbor is a dead neighbor," then an invisible and indiscernible neighbor is definitely an ideal one. Then one will not see the disgusting excess emanating from the other and threatening one's own subject position. However, turning one's back on these repulsive leftovers as if they are a hindrance to one's subjectivity, one actually fails to understand that this excess is the very condition of one's subject formation.

A self-proclaimed multicultural cosmopolitan place — Asia's world city — Hong Kong continues to ignore the particularities of non-Chinese ethnic peoples. Before 1997, Hong Kong's Chinese community was desperate to create a subjective identity that would absorb the shocks of the handover, caring little about the similar desires of racial minority groups. Since 1997, Hong Kong has become too preoccupied with reconstituting and transforming itself into a new form of national subjectivity. The drive to assimilate into Chinese nationality and the official promotion of patriotism among the Hong Kong Chinese majority have

---

16. Søren Kierkegaard, *Works of Love* (Princeton, N.J.: Princeton University Press, 1995), eds. and trans. Howard V. Hong and Edna H. Hong.

17. Slavoj Žižek, "The Only Good Neighbor Is a Dead Neighbor!" *Lacanian Ink* 19 (2001): 101. Emphasis original.

18. Žižek, "Introduction," in Slavoj Žižek, Eric L. Santer, and Kenneth Reinhard, *The Neighbor: Three Inquires in Political Theology* (Chicago: Univ. of Chicago Press, 2005), 3.

further rendered racial minority issues imperceptible. Hong Kong's prominent neighbor is now the Chinese Mainland, not the non-Chinese ethnics living with the city's Chinese majority. The call for "neighbor love" is directed to the Mainland Chinese across the border, who have long been despised but are now considered equals to and enjoy the favor of the arrogant Hong Kong Chinese. The non-Chinese neighbors remain an impenetrable and unknowable presence. Unlike those of other colonies, Hong Kong's indistinguishable (hi)stories of ethnic minorities are not the direct upshot of colonial oppression. But the colonial manipulation of a racial divide and hierarchy could lead to mutual disregard for non-whites, engendering and perpetuating the separate concerns of different ethnic groups under the effects of (post)colonialism.

The racial divide or hierarchy is still evidenced in the separate positions held by English-language and Chinese-language media, each of which target different classes and racial readerships in the postcolonial city. The local English-language media upholds and speaks for the liberal, enlightened views of white expatriates and upper-middle class Chinese, advocating the legislation of a new racial discrimination bill and challenging the government to enforce fair treatment for every racial group; but many Chinese-language newspapers and magazines with more parochial, grassroots support still spread derogatory terms for South Asians, Caucasians, Japanese, Filipinos, and Mainlanders in their publications. Common Cantonese slang terms for minorities in Hong Kong include *gweilo* (ghost) for Caucasians, *ah cha* (poor) for Indians and Pakistanis, *ga tau* or *lo baat tau* (carrot head) for Japanese, *bun mui* for Filipina helpers and *hak gwei* (black ghost) for Africans. These racist terms are not hard to find in Chinese-language newspaper columns (also in the headlines) and tabloid reportage even nowadays.[19]

Hong Kong is a "melting pot" in the ironic sense that many non-Chinese ethnics who have lived there for generations are still not considered locals by the community if they cannot speak fluent Cantonese or do not live a Hong Kong–Chinese lifestyle. The obvious assumption is that if you cannot melt and be absorbed into the culture of the majority, you will be seen forever as an outsider and your presence will not be counted. A recent media celebrity, Gill Mohinderpaul Singh (whose Chinese name is Kiu Bo Bo or Q Bobo), a Hong Kong-born Indian, made himself famous overnight by winning in *Minutes to Fame,* a televised singing competition modeled on *American Idol,* and immediately became an object of interest in the local Chinese tabloids. Speaking perfect Cantonese, on camera Singh always declares his love for the Hong Kong-Chinese

---

19. These Cantonese racial slurs are still commonly found today in the headlines of Hong Kong Chinese-language newspapers and magazines. If the race discrimination bill is passed by the Legislative Council, calling names could infringe the law, depending on the context, the tone, how the ethnic feels about it and, ultimately, if s/he goes to court complaining of racial harassment.

culture and lifestyle (he enjoys local snacks like fish balls, hanging out in the lower-class Temple Street area, and singing Cantopop). Though a Sikh, he demonstrates his cultural assimilation by not wearing the usual long hair, beard, and turban. Singh quit his civil servant job (an officer in the Correctional Services Department for 16 years) after winning the contest, and hopes to act full-time on television. He wants to be the most famous Indian actor in the local entertainment industry — for which there is no precedent.[20] But before Singh, another non-Chinese actor made great efforts to turn himself into a local celebrity—Gregory Charles Rivers (whose Chinese name is Ho Kwok Wing), an Australian who speaks perfect Cantonese. He has acted in several Hong Kong movies and dozens of TV dramas. But even after fifteen years in the industry, he has played only minor roles.[21] Indeed, local directors and scriptwriters have had difficulties creating appropriate characters for him in Chinese-oriented dramas.

Representations of non-Chinese ethnic minorities in Hong Kong cinema have never been particularly favorable. Although Fruit Chan's *Little Cheung* (1999) is an exceptional film in that it deals with the subtle relationship between a street-wise Hong Kong kid and his Filipina maid Armi (played by Armi Andres) — whom the boy loves because he has more contact with her than with his parents, who are busy running a local restaurant — the Filipina character is not portrayed as having any depth. But South Asians are usually caricatured or even ridiculed in the Hong Kong culture industry. The most popular South Asian character on Hong Kong television was Maria — a Filipina maid-servant who spoke accented Cantonese and did slapstick comedy — portrayed by Chinese actress Alvina Kong Yan-Yin as part of a variety show in the 1990s. Although this was never clearly stated, the Maria character was assumed to be Filipina, and her face was painted with charcoal, which made her look more like an African American than a South Asian, and was reminiscent of Hollywood's blackface minstrelsy. In other recent Hong Kong films, such as James Yuen Sai Sun's *Driving Miss Wealthy* (2004), in which a Chinese ex-cop pretends to be a Filipino chauffeur in order to protect his boss' daughter, and Wai Ka Fai's *Himalaya Singh* (2005), which is set in India, the main ethnic characters are all played by Chinese actors and actresses. These

---

20. Gill Mohinderpaul Singh has been cast as an Indian yoga master, "Henry," a recurring character in the nightly sitcom *Room Full of Guests* (from March 2006) on TVB; has played minor roles in Hong Kong movies such as *Rob B Hood* (2006), *McDull the Alumni* (2005); and has done voice-over work in the dubbed version of the animated film *Valiant* (2005).

21. Cast in more than forty Cantonese TV series productions since 1989, Rivers also starred in five Hong Kong films and two Chinese musicals. The most prominent character Rivers has ever played in a local movie is in the comedy *Her Fatal Ways IV* (1994) — a popular film series about a Mainland Chinese policewoman — in which he plays John, a Scottish officer in the Royal Hong Kong Police Force, and the love interest of the female protagonist. For a discussion of the film, see Kwai-Cheung Lo, *Chinese Face/Off: The Transnational Popular Culture of Hong Kong* (Urbana and Chicago: Univ. of Illinois Press, 2005).

ethnic characters are present merely for comic relief and the filmmakers have no intention at all of dealing with racial relations in Hong Kong society.

Laclau argues that the only universality a society can achieve is a "hegemonic universality" — a universality that emerges from the struggle among indefinite numbers of substitutable particularities. What unites all these particularities is that "they constitute between themselves a chain of equivalences."[22] In the logic of equivalence, which is based on the structuralist notion of the chain of signifiers, a certain particularity can "universalize" itself or occupy the hegemonic universal position by substituting itself for other particularities. Equivalence means the deterritorialization of a certain social formation by adding to or replacing it with something outside the original context that universalizes by multiplying the positions. But in the hegemony of Hong Kong subjectivity, the possibility of a substitution of one racial particularity for another is not likely to happen. A non-Chinese ethnic individual, participating in the assimilation game or engaging in an equivalent practice, could hardly find a chance to substitute himself for the others in the chain of equivalence, let alone assume his or her own particularity as a function of universal representation. Is this notion of hegemonic universality rendered invalid given the racial situation in Hong Kong? Will racial minorities ever achieve universal representation in Hong Kong? In Evans Chan's *To Liv(e)* (1992), half-Chinese, half-English actress Lindzay Chan is selected as the protagonistic "voice of Hong Kong"[23] to explore the colony's difficulties as it faces the 1997 handover. She is cast not necessarily for her mixed race — an issue which the film avoids — but for her bilingual fluency in Chinese and English; the female protagonist has to read (in voice-over) a series of letters to Liv Ullmann, who denounced the Hong Kong government's deportation of a number of Vietnamese refugees as inhumane but ignored the fact that Hong Kong people might be facing a fate similar to the Vietnamese after the Tiananmen Square crackdown in June 1989.

Retrieving ethnic otherness for the future

Presumably well aware of the socio-cultural limitation or even prevention of their assimilation and representation in Hong Kong, the members of racial minorities

22. Ernesto Laclau, "Constructing Universality," in Judith Butler, Ernesto Laclau, and Slavoj Žižek, *Contingency, Hegemony, Universality: Contemporary Dialogues on the Left* (New York: Verso, 2000), 302.

23. For a detailed discussion of the film, see Gina Marchetti, "Transnational Cinema and Hybrid Identities: *To Liv(e)* and Crossings," in her *From Tian'anmen To Times Square: Transnational China and the Chinese Diaspora on Global Screens, 1989-1997* (Philadelphia: Temple University Press, 2006), 169.

I interviewed seldom show any enthusiasm about integration into the local Chinese community. They lack even any strong motivation to learn the Chinese language (though many can understand Cantonese well enough), and cling to their inherited ethnic identity and diasporic lifestyle. Probably because of their detachment from mainstream society, not only does the Hong Kong Chinese majority see them as other, but the racial minorities themselves, to a large extent, also regard themselves as other and adhere to a marginal position in the community. In a sense, it is a vicious circle — their social marginalization has been internalized and the self-marginalization of the racial minorities further affirms the peripheral position imposed on them. And self-perpetuating marginality has deprived them of the desire to include themselves in the chain of equivalence and aspire to hegemonic universality.

Nevertheless, the relationship between racial minorities and the Chinese community in Hong Kong is not essentially a divide between self and other. Like the Hong Kong ethnic minorities, the Chinese locals are by no means a homogeneous group. The transnational and global experiences of the residents as well as the continuous influx of new immigrants from Mainland China are actually generating fragmentations and even cultural clashes within the (re-) formation of the local cultural identity. I would not go so far to claim that the distinction between minorities and majority has become blurred nowadays, even though a growing number of individuals and groups in Hong Kong society can no longer be easily inscribed in any single ethnic, cultural, linguistic, or religious identity. Racial minorities are not exactly the other for Hong Kong Chinese, who themselves are (un-)consciously positioning themselves or being positioned as "ethnic minority." Race in Hong Kong should be grasped as subjective positions taken up in the symbolic order with regard to the cultural and historical demands of a given society rather than being misunderstood as sheer biological pre-givens.

Enjoying a high degree of autonomy and privilege — as do ethnic minority groups in China[24] — postcolonial Hong Kong is very careful to preserve its own cultural uniqueness and regional characteristics by distancing itself from other Chinese cities on the Mainland. The tie between the Chinese central government and Hong Kong as a Special Administrative Region parallels that between the Beijing government and the racial minorities. To a certain extent, racial minorities in Hong Kong actually mirror the Hong Kong Chinese, reflecting features of the city in its relation to China. In other words, racial minorities in Hong Kong embody the irreducible otherness of Hong Kong Chinese in their relationship

---

24. Emphasizing the equality between ethnic groups and the Han majority and respecting the difference of the ethnic folkways, customs, languages, and religious beliefs, China's minorities policy has also established a system of regional autonomy and adopted a preferential financial policy for ethnic minorities in order to preserve and promote political unity.

with China. It is the otherness that the Hong Kong Chinese subject is aware of but does not want to acknowledge. If Hong Kong constructs its life history in a narrative that addresses China as the Other and defines itself against as well as along with this Other, Hong Kong forgets to account for the racial minorities within its own community that constitute its internal otherness. The core of the Hong Kong subject is partially grounded in this internal otherness, which is an integral part of its colonial legacy. Hong Kong's general blindness to its racial minorities implies that the city remains confused about its own complex historical and cultural components. The connection between Hong Kong racial minorities and Hong Kong Chinese vis-à-vis China involves not only the entanglement between the nation-state and its "minorities" but also the interactive relationships among the "minorities" themselves across national borders. The transnational psychological complex reveals that many non-Chinese ethnics who have lived in Hong Kong for generations still call other places "home," while many local-born Chinese keep their foreign passports and dual citizenships even though they do not seriously consider living abroad. In a way, many Chinese in Hong Kong, like the local racial minorities, still see themselves more as diasporic people than as Chinese nationals with allegiance to the homeland.

The encounter between Hong Kong racial minorities and the local Chinese is a missed opportunity — they mutually fail to notice each other's significance to their subject formation. In short, the neighbors are invisible to each other at a symbolic level. A new sense of postcolonial Hong Kong subjectivity can emerge only by turning upon the city's own internal otherness. This act of turning upon itself could be compared to the repetition compulsion: certain leftovers repressed or obliterated insist on returning to the subject, despite the subject's resistance to them. If the excess of internal otherness has a constitutive role to play in Hong Kong subject formation, it will repeatedly and compulsively come back to haunt the subject, no matter how it has been forgotten. As it pertains to the status of racial minorities in Hong Kong, I prefer to understand the compulsion to repeat positively, as a Deleuzian kind of "repetition" that is not just about how one sees one's mirror image or about how one copies or reflects the other. Rather, it is a repetition that incorporates a difference that gives rise to a certain mutation. It is produced via difference, not mimesis. Indeed the relationship between local Chinese and ethnic minorities cannot be a mimetic one. Insofar as local Chinese are understood to be "minorities" (in relation to Mainland China) and Hong Kong racial minorities are trying to become locals (by engaging in the competition and struggle for hegemonic universality), the process of difference and differentiation transforms the context through which repetition occurs.

What is repeated is not something that already was there but virtual aspects inherent in the context that had been hidden by the historical actualization. Something truly new or something not yet actualized can emerge through such repetition, which dissolves the conventional senses of national and ethnic identity by giving rise to something unrecognizable, indiscernible, and creative. It is generally assumed that the story of Hong Kong ended in 1997.[25] I would say, perhaps, that the story is not yet over if the city can regain the creative impulse that the ex-colony has lost in the historical actualization. That is to say, to connect to what was already in Hong Kong more than to Hong Kong itself — that is, to have access to its excessive core. It is never simply to insert the lost past into the totality of history. On the contrary, it is everything about carving out a piece of the past from the historical continuity or wholeness which is governed by the logic of the reigning power. To "repeat" is not to recognize the way something really was (hence it is not just about how, or it is simply inadequate, to give back the social recognition that racial minorities deserve) but to appropriate a past insofar as it is a failed one, that which has been denied and forgotten in order for a historical continuity to establish itself, and insofar as that past contains the open dimension of the future. Repetition here is an act of freezing and crystallizing the engine of historical movement and also is the moment of appropriating the past by separating the details from its totality. It is a way to re-insert the failed past that has been pushed out of the temporal continuity endorsed by prevalent history back to the synchronic short circuit of signification. But before it can reinstate itself in the chain, what we can see is only the effaced or vanished sign, that is invisible, that takes on its value in the future, a thing that will have been.

---

25. The "end of Hong Kong" after the handover carries double meanings: the postcolonial city was not expected to have a future, in that its freedom and legal system would erode under a Communist regime; and the development of the city is rapidly being overshadowed by the emerging Chinese economy, which is drawing away the international attention that Hong Kong used to enjoy.

Contested Colony: Hong Kong, the 1949 Revolution, and the "Taiwan Problem"*

John M. Carroll

Focusing on a series of diplomatic and political disputes during the 1950s after the establishment of the PRC on the mainland and the Nationalist regime on Taiwan, this article looks at how the Cold War made colonial Hong Kong into a contested and contentious terrain between conflicting visions of Chinese sovereignty — not only between the Communists and the Nationalists but also between Britain and the United States — and between shifting views of the role of the British Empire in the Cold War world. Although Hong Kong was confronted and even defined by its geographical proximity to China, it was also defined by geopolitics on another scale. Hong Kong was a geopolitical space, but it also played a part in the fluid definition of the disputed islands off the PRC's shore, Jinmen and Mazu. A British colony whose geopolitical space before 1949 had been shaped mainly by its relationship with South China and by its position within the

* Earlier versions of this article were presented at the Conference on Taiwan Issues in Columbia, South Carolina, in September 2005, and the Annual Meeting of the Association for Asian Studies in Boston in March 2007. I am grateful to the participants in each panel, especially Carl Dahlman of the University of South Carolina and Elizabeth Sinn of the University of Hong Kong, for their comments. Parts of the article have been published in my *Concise History of Hong Kong* (Lanham, Maryland/Hong Kong: Rowman and Littlefield/Hong Kong University Press, 2007).

British Empire,[1] and which before the establishment of the PRC had little strategic interest for the United States, Hong Kong now became the site of a displaced trans-Atlantic rivalry between Britain and the United States.

The end of the Cold War in the late 1980s and early 1990s has led scholars to reconsider traditional geopolitics, which owed much to the new world order that emerged from the aftermath of World War Two.[2] This geopolitics has been challenged by recent developments and concerns: the "velvet revolutions" in Europe and the collapse of the Soviet Union, the formation of the European Union, the attacks of September 11, 2001, and George W. Bush's "war on terror" and his "axis of evil."[3] But the case of Hong Kong suggests that even as Cold War geopolitics was both shaping and being shaped by the new world order that emerged from World War Two, it already had limitations for understanding these new geopolitical realities. Its emphasis on binary constructs such as East and West, freedom and totalitarianism, and good and evil could obscure the relationships between power, territory, and boundaries, overlooking less obvious tensions such as those between a declining Britain and a rising China, between seemingly steadfast allies Britain and the United States, and among Britain, China, and Taiwan — the last referred to by China as a renegade province hailed by the United States as "Free China," and largely ignored by Britain.[4]

Post-WWII Hong Kong: Saved by the Communist Revolution

Hong Kong is of course not only part of Chinese history but also part of British imperial history. One of the many ironies of British imperial history is that the

---

1. This theme is developed further in my "Colonial Hong Kong as a Cultural-Historical Place," *Modern Asian Studies* 40, no. 2 (2006): 517–43, and in *Edge of Empires: Chinese Elites and British Colonials in Hong Kong* (Cambridge, Massachusetts: Harvard University Press, 2005; Hong Kong: Hong Kong University Press, 2007).

2. For examples of this new geopolitics, see John Agnew, "Mapping Political Power Beyond State Boundaries: Territory, Identity, and Movement in World Politics," *Millennium: Journal of International Studies* 28, no. 3 (1999): 499–521, and *Geopolitics: Re-visioning World Politics*, 2nd ed. (New York: Routledge, 2003); Gearóid Ó Tuathail and Simon Dalby, eds., *Rethinking Geopolitics* (London: Routledge, 1998).

3. Agnew, *Geopolitics*, 1–4. See also Klaus Dodds, "Cold War Geopolitics," and Vladimir Kolossov, "After Empire: Identities and Territorialities in the Post-Soviet Space," both in John Agnew, Katharyne Mitchell, and Gerard Toal [Gearóid Ó Tuathail], eds., *Companion to Political Geography* (Malden, Mass.: Blackwell, 2003), 187–218, 251–70.

4. As Gearóid Ó Tuathail and Simon Dalby argue, Cold War geopolitics "was premised on an extraordinary double irony. It simultaneously denied both geographical difference and its own self-constituting politics" ("Rethinking Geopolitics: Towards a Critical Geopolitics," in Ó Tuathail and Simon Dalby, eds., *Rethinking Geopolitics*, 1).

Communist victory in 1949, which helped end Britain's favored position in China, also enabled Hong Kong to remain a British colony. Had Chiang Kai-shek's Nationalists won the civil war, they certainly would have tried to recover Hong Kong. The rapid loss of Hong Kong to Japan in December 1941 had angered many Nationalists who, having sent their families and money to the supposed safety of colonial Hong Kong, wondered why the British had not accepted Chiang's offers of assistance or trusted local Chinese enough to use them more effectively against the Japanese. With help from Franklin Delano Roosevelt (whose grandfather had been a partner in the American firm of Russell & Co. that traded in south China in the 1840s and whose mother had once lived in Hong Kong), in January 1942 Chiang became the supreme commander of the China-Burma-India Theater. Hoping to use the war to recover Hong Kong and to end the "unequal treaties" and supported by the U.S., in mid-1942 the Nationalists approached Britain to give up Hong Kong or at least the New Territories. In late 1942, Sino-British negotiations began for abolishing extraterritoriality in China and the status of New Territories after the war. At the Cairo Conference in November 1943, Roosevelt would promise to help Chiang recover Hong Kong if he agreed to help Mao Zedong's Communists fight the Japanese.

Fortunately for the British, the Nationalists suddenly aborted their campaign to recover the New Territories, content for the time being with the agreement that China reserved the right to raise the issue at a later date. By early 1943, as the war turned in favor of the Allies, the British Colonial Office resolved to retain Hong Kong after the war. In November 1943, Winston Churchill famously reminded Stanley Hornbeck of the U.S. State Department that he had not become prime minister "to preside over the liquidation of the British Empire." At the Cairo Conference, Churchill informed Roosevelt and Stalin that the British would not try to get any new territory but intended to keep what they already had and would not let anything go without a war — "specifically Singapore and Hong Kong."[5] By mid-1945, Churchill realized that Chiang could not try to recover Hong Kong without support from the U.S., which now considered the continuation of European colonialism in Asia vital to its own interests in the post-war world. The British became even more confident of their ability to recover Hong Kong when the U.S. tried to distance itself, albeit briefly, from Chiang as it became apparent that, already notorious for his corruption, he was stockpiling troops and weapons to fight the Communists after the war.

Although there were loud calls within China for recovering Hong Kong and although he had almost 60,000 troops within 300 miles of Hong Kong when the Japanese surrendered, Chiang realized that Britain would not give up Hong Kong

---

5.   Quoted in James T. H. Tang, "World War to Cold War: Hong Kong's Future and Anglo-Chinese Interactions, 1941–55," in Ming K. Chan, ed., *Precarious Balance: Hong Kong Between China and Britain, 1842–1992* (Armonk, New York: M. E. Sharpe, 1994), 109–110.

easily and that a failure to recover Hong Kong would discredit him in China. Furthermore, Chiang needed the support of both Britain and the U.S. to be a major player in the new world order. Preoccupied with recovering northern China and preventing Communist troops from recapturing Japanese-held territory, he did not want to provoke the communists into entering the race for Hong Kong, especially since their East River guerrillas were closer to Hong Kong than were his own troops. Although Chiang knew he could count on American support against the Communists, he never knew exactly how much the U.S. would support his effort to recover Hong Kong. By the end of World War Two the U.S., concerned about the post-war world order, had softened its stance toward colonialism. Harry Truman was less committed than his predecessor to restoring Hong Kong to Chinese sovereignty, while General Douglas MacArthur, commander of the Allied forces in the South-West Pacific, favored the continuation of the British Empire in East Asia. Instead of recovering Hong Kong, Chiang Kai-shek ended up on Taiwan.

The reaction in Hong Kong and Britain to the Communist victory and the establishment of the PRC in October 1949 was a mixture of anxiety and relief. Most Chinese people in Hong Kong, "fed to the teeth with the corruption and inefficiency of the Nationalist regime," as Governor Alexander Grantham put it, and glad for the civil war to be over, were not especially upset about the establishment of the PRC.[6] Most British officials had realized by late 1948 that the Communists would take power and that British relations with China must change, but the new PRC government did not seem directly to threaten British commercial interests in China. The British were much more concerned about Chinese communists elsewhere: in Malaya, where a guerilla campaign led by local Chinese communists lasted until the early 1950s.

Far from ending Hong Kong's colonial status, the establishment of the PRC gave Hong Kong new prominence, both in the British Empire and across the globe. Despite the Communists' insistence that they had no interest in the short term in recovering Hong Kong, some British officials assumed that it would eventually have to be surrendered to China. Instead, the Communist revolution brought new labor, capital, and energy to a region that had often been eclipsed by Shanghai, the economic center of China. As Wm. Roger Louis writes, when the Communists took control of Shanghai in late 1949, the British realized that "they were witnessing in Hong Kong a demographic as well as an economic revolution that would have profound consequences for the people of the colony and perhaps for the British Empire."[7] From 1946 to the mid-1950s, approximately one million people came to Hong Kong from China — an average of almost three

6. Alexander Grantham, "Hong Kong," *Royal Central Asian Journal* 46 (1959): 122.
7. Wm. Roger Louis, "Hong Kong: The Critical Phase, 1945–1949," *American Historical Review* 102, no. 4 (October 1997): 1056.

hundred people per day. Although in May 1950 the colonial government limited the number of immigrants from the mainland, by the end of the year the influx had increased Hong Kong's population to almost one million. And although in February 1951 the PRC government began to control migration to Guangdong, which in turn lowered immigration to Hong Kong, by 1955 the colony's population was around 2.5 million.

Given that the Communist government of the new PRC was dedicated to ending imperialism worldwide, why was it willing to tolerate British colonialism in the very colony whose cession in 1842 had begun China's "century of shame"? Especially compared with the often disastrous economic, political, and social policies that characterized the first two decades of the PRC, the new Chinese government's policy toward Hong Kong remained consistently levelheaded and sophisticated. Hong Kong had in fact been an important base for the Communist movement throughout the Chinese civil war. In 1947 the Chinese Communist Party (CCP) established its Central Hong Kong Bureau (renamed the Central South China Bureau in early 1949). Through *Xinhua* (the New China News Agency), the CCP spread propaganda within Hong Kong, in China, and among overseas Chinese communities. The CCP trained cadres in the safety of colonial Hong Kong, where it made an "organized and consistent effort" to recruit members from local schools and factories. Nor had the Chinese communists ever shown much interest in Hong Kong. Mao Zedong, who often insisted that Hong Kong was not a priority or even a concern and once referred to Hong Kong as "that wasteland of an island," reportedly told a British journalist in 1946 that neither he nor the CCP was interested in Hong Kong, and that as long as the British did not mistreat the colony's Chinese residents he would not let Hong Kong harm Sino-British relations. In November 1948 Qiao Mu, head of the local branch of the New China News Agency, assured the Hong Kong government that a new communist government would not bother Hong Kong and that it would even allow the colonial government to provide refuge to Nationalist leaders. Although Josef Stalin urged Mao during his visit to Moscow in early 1950 to take Hong Kong because it was full of "imperialist agents," Mao had already decided by January 1949 not to worry about reclaiming Hong Kong and Macau.[8] Thus the Communists reassured the British that they would not try to recover Hong Kong after they took power, ordering their troops not to cause too much trouble as they approached the border.

The Communists' policy toward Hong Kong after their victory was equally pragmatic. As Steve Tsang puts it, for the PRC government the Hong Kong issue was "somewhere between foreign policy and domestic policy."[9] Because the British

8. Sergei Goncharov, John W. Lewis, and Xue Litai, *Uncertain Partners: Stalin, Mao and the Korean War* (Stanford: Stanford University Press, 1993), 40.
9. Steve Tsang, *Hong Kong: An Appointment with China* (London: I. B. Tauris, 1997), 69.

had obtained Hong Kong through the first of the "unequal treaties," which the PRC government quickly renounced, Hong Kong was an internal Chinese matter that would eventually be resolved peacefully though diplomacy.[10] Encouraging nationalism in a colony full of anticommunist refugees would be at best futile and at worst foolhardy, perhaps even pushing local Chinese toward Chiang Kai-shek's Nationalist regime on Taiwan. Alexander Grantham recalled that the PRC government had a hard time agitating Chinese refugees in Hong Kong "for the refugees had fled from the communist paradise, and had no love for the government of China."[11] Even more dangerous, other powers — and the United Nations — might try to intervene if the Communists tried to foment any anticolonial struggles in Hong Kong. Thus even after the outbreak of the Korean War in 1950, the CCP warned communists in Hong Kong to keep a low profile in order to show the colonial government that they were not subversive.

The Communists also realized that a British Hong Kong, however embarrassing, could be of great use to China, as it had been for more than a century: as a way to get rid of undesirables and excess population and as a window to the outside world. (Grantham described Hong Kong as "a peep-hole for the Communists; in fact, it is really their only contact with the free world.")[12] Remittances from overseas Chinese would provide valuable foreign exchange to help rebuild China's war-torn economy, while the colony would be a base for importing goods that China could not produce. Hong Kong proved of great use to the PRC during the Korean War, when scarce goods such as gas, kerosene, and penicillin were smuggled in during the U.S. and UN embargoes. Hong Kong might also be used to push Britain and America apart from each other vis-à-vis their policy in East Asia. Shortly after the outbreak of the war, Zhou Enlai ordered Huang Zuomei, head of the New China News Agency in Hong Kong, to obey the CCP's policy of leaving Hong Kong alone, reminding Huang of Hong Kong's usefulness in overcoming the embargoes and dividing Britain and the U.S. in their China policies.[13] In 1951, Politburo member Peng Zhen explained that taking Hong Kong would both be too difficult and cause problems in China's international relations. Instead, Peng argued, it would be better to maintain Hong Kong's status quo and to use the colony for rebuilding China's war-torn economy.

10. Still, the PRC leadership saw Hong Kong as an important issue that would eventually be resolved. Shortly after the establishment of the PRC, Chinese premier Zhou Enlai informed local Communist activists that although the CCP had no immediate plans to recover Hong Kong, "that does not mean that we are abandoning or retreating from Hong Kong." Recovery of Hong Kong was still "a long-term mission," Zhou insisted, "but you need not worry about it now." Quoted in Tang, "World War to Cold War," 117.
11. Alexander Grantham, *Via Ports: From Hong Kong to Hong Kong* (Hong Kong: Hong Kong University Press, 1965), 158.
12. Grantham, "Hong Kong," 125.
13. Tsang, *Hong Kong*, 71.

It would be "unwise for us to deal with the problem of Hong Kong rashly and without preparation."[14]

This does not, however, mean that the relationship between Hong Kong and the new PRC was always a smooth one. Shortly after closing the border with Hong Kong, the PRC government placed loudspeakers at Lo Wu and Man Kam To (the two main crossing points), blasting criticism of the British and Hong Kong governments. PRC border guards taunted their Hong Kong counterparts, threatening to harm their families once the PRC liberated the colony. A failed tramway strike in Hong Kong during December 1949, provoked by authorities in Guangzhou, showed the colonial government that the new regime was a force to reckon with. In March 1952, a violent confrontation occurred between the colonial police and protesting crowds after Guangzhou delegates of a "comfort mission" on their way to care for fire victims were stopped at the border. One protester was shot dead, more than 100 were arrested, and 12 were deported. After local leftwing newspapers tried to stir up anti-British feelings and some 10,000 sympathizers protested the shooting, the government shut down for six months the pro-Beijing newspaper *Dagong bao* 大公報, which had reprinted an article from the *People's Daily* criticizing the Hong Kong and British governments. In September 1953, Chinese shore batteries fired on a Royal Navy launch on anti-smuggling patrol in international waters, killing seven and wounding five. Although the British government complained, the PRC government never apologized or offered compensation.

Such heated incidents were rare, however, and the governments of China and Hong Kong eventually developed a relationship that was remarkably pragmatic. Knowing, for example, that it might lead to retaliation from the PRC, the Hong Kong authorities persuaded the British government not to use the colony's radio station for spreading anti-Chinese propaganda. As Grantham recalled, "If Hong Kong were to adopt an aggressively anti-Chinese policy against what is the legitimate Government of China, it would suffer for it. Hong Kong is really like a glass-house right out in front, and they do not want big stones thrown through their glass."[15] In December 1948 the British Foreign Office had warned that if the Communists won the civil war, Hong Kong would be like "living on the edge of a volcano."[16] Grantham recalled a rather less alarming image of Hong Kong's position at the edge of the PRC: "The attitude of the Chinese authorities towards Hong Kong was a combination of passive hostility with occasional outbursts of active unfriendliness: rather like a pot on the kitchen stove; the pot being Hong Kong. Normally the pot would be kept at the back of the stove gently

---

14. Quoted in James Tuck-Hong Tang, *Britain's Encounter with Revolutionary China* (London: Macmillan, 1992), 186.
15. Grantham, "Hong Kong," 129.
16. Quoted in Tang, "World War to Cold War," 114.

simmering, but every now and then the cook — the Chinese government — would bring it to the front of the stove when it would boil fiercely. After a while he would move it to the back of the stove again. We never knew when the pot was going to be brought to the boil."[17] Anti-British and anti-colonial campaigns from the mainland were alternated with efforts to woo Hong Kong Chinese by downplaying China's Communist side, such as what colonial authorities called the "Campaign of Sweetness and Light" in late 1955. This, Grantham explained in a speech in 1958, "is the usual Communist technique. First of all there is a period of tension, then there is relaxation, then tension again, and so it goes on, and so it will go on."[18]

British and American attitudes toward the Communist and Nationalist regimes

The emphasis in Cold War geopolitics on the conflict between the Eastern and Western blocs obscures the fact that, often more troubling for Hong Kong than the new political situation across the border, were the conflicting British and American policies toward the two new regimes on opposite sides of the Taiwan Strait, each claiming to be the legitimate government of China. Although they were both determined to contain the spread of Communism, Britain and the U.S. had radically different attitudes toward the PRC. As Grantham put it, "America was imbued with an almost crusading spirit against Chinese communism. Britain, which was just as opposed to communism as was America, did not believe in 'brinkmanship' or in unnecessary provocation."[19] Whereas Britain officially recognized the PRC on 6 January 1950 (a move, recalled Grantham, that was supported by everyone in Hong Kong "except the dyed-in-the-wool pro-Nationalist Chinese"),[20] the U.S. continued to recognize Chiang Kai-shek's Nationalist regime. And whereas some American analysts believed that the Communists might eventually be overthrown with help from a "third force" outside China, most diplomats in Britain and colonial officials in Hong Kong realized that the new regime could not be overthrown. (Grantham explained in 1958 that he did not believe the nominal third force which the U.S. had tried to encourage had "any future whatsoever.")[21] Because the British, who generally saw the new regime on the mainland as Chinese first and communists second, assumed that nationalism would ultimately become stronger than communism in China, they emphasized the need to use peaceful diplomacy to contain

---

17. Grantham, *Via Ports*, 179–80.
18. Grantham, "Hong Kong," 122.
19. Grantham, *Via Ports*, 168.
20. Grantham, *Via Ports*, 169.
21. Grantham, "Hong Kong," 127.

communism and to drive the PRC and the USSR apart. The British faced a dilemma: they needed to forge a good relationship with the PRC — not only for the sake of Hong Kong but also for the sake of British commercial interests in China — yet they also needed to maintain their "special relationship" with the U.S. On the one hand, both Winston Churchill (who was part American) and Harold Macmillan saw Britain's "special relationship" with the U.S. as more important than relations with China and were thus sometimes willing to subordinate Hong Kong to the larger Anglo-American relationship.[22] On the other hand, the British justified recognizing the PRC to the U.S. on the grounds that they had to protect their interests in China and Hong Kong, as well as in Malaya and Singapore, both of which had large Chinese communities. As Grantham explained in a speech to the Council on Foreign Relations in New York in September 1953, returning Hong Kong to China would show that the free world could not withstand the onslaught of Communism. Although there might be little objection in Britain to abandoning Hong Kong, doing so would have great significance in Southeast Asia, whose peoples — the Chinese in particular — were eager to be on the winning side of the Cold War.[23]

Because of their different attitudes toward the PRC, Britain and the U.S. also had widely different views of Taiwan. British officials assumed the island would inevitably become part of the PRC — in 1951 Prime Minister Clement Attlee provoked hostility and resentment in America by declaring that Taiwan should be returned to China — but their American counterparts were determined to keep it from falling to the Communists. Taiwan was an important base for American covert activities toward China: there the Americans maintained a 600-person CIA staff, military intelligence units, and telecommunications-monitoring facilities. Britain worried that once the PRC eventually recovered Taiwan, military equipment supplied by the U.S. would land in Communist hands and might then be used against Hong Kong. The British also knew that Nationalist saboteurs based in Hong Kong received help from the U.S., for the Hong Kong government occasionally discovered American explosives hidden in crowded residential areas. But Britain also realized that the powerful China Lobby and the American determination to contain the PRC guaranteed that the U.S. would continue to supply Chiang. Britain's Labour government supported Harry Truman's decision to intervene during the Korean War, but not his decision to send the U.S. Seventh Fleet to the Taiwan Strait. Although the PRC government said little about Britain sending naval forces to Korea, the British worried that the presence of the Seventh Fleet would jeopardize the safety of Hong Kong and push the PRC closer toward

22. Chi-kwan Mark, *Hong Kong and the Cold War: Anglo-American Relations, 1949–1957* (Oxford: Clarendon Press, 2004), 24.
23. Alexander Grantham, "China as Seen from Hong Kong," speech to the Council on Foreign Relations, 29 September 1953, Hamilton Fish Armstrong Papers, Travels Folder, Mudd Manuscript Library, Princeton University.

the USSR. If a PRC attack on Taiwan led to a conflict between the U.S. and the PRC, the British would be in a bind: supporting the U.S. would harm relations with China and possibly hurt Hong Kong, but not supporting the U.S. would damage Anglo-American relations. Although the U.S. opposed admitting the PRC into the UN, some British officials saw admission as a way to ensure that the PRC did not attack Taiwan.[24] And to achieve a ceasefire in Korea, Britain was willing not only to admit the PRC into the UN but also even to see Taiwan returned to China. The U.S. opposed letting Taiwan go, however, both for strategic reasons and because the loss of Taiwan would undermine American prestige in East Asia.

British and American attitudes toward Hong Kong

Just as they had different attitudes toward the PRC and the Nationalist regime on Taiwan, the Americans and the British saw Hong Kong in dissimilar terms. In the early post-war years most British officials considered Hong Kong to be less important than China. In late 1945, G.V. Kitson, head of the Foreign Office's China Department, offered several proposals for maintaining good relations with China, among them a plan for returning Hong Kong but with Britain continuing to administer the region. Precisely because Britain could not enjoy as favorable a position in China as it had before the war, however, Hong Kong remained important to the British Empire. The colony became the main base for British commercial and industrial interests in East Asia (especially after the end of extraterritoriality in China), for preserving Britain's status as a world power, and for maintaining British prestige and morale (particularly after the humiliating loss of Hong Kong to Japan in 1941). By the late 1940s, Hong Kong became of even greater strategic importance as the center for British commercial operations in China, especially after many British firms moved there from China after 1945, and as a listening post on China. With the insurgency in Malaya and the impending Communist victory in China, holding onto Hong Kong became of great psychological importance: losing the colony would hurt British prestige and undermine the struggle against communism in Thailand, Burma, and Malaya. This strategic usefulness was enhanced by the fact that the cost of retaining Hong Kong was extremely low: after 1948, Hong Kong did not require any financial assistance, although Britain continued to pay for most of the local garrison.

With the establishment of the PRC in 1949 and the outbreak of the Korean War in 1950, Hong Kong became a "reluctant Cold Warrior."[25] Needing American

---

24. Edwin Martin, *Divided Counsel: The Anglo-American Response to Communist Victory in China* (Lexington, Kentucky: University Press of Kentucky, 1986), 156-80; Qiang Zhai, *The Dragon, the Lion, and the Eagle: Chinese-American Confrontations, 1949-1958* (Kent, Ohio: Kent State University Press, 1994), 94–5.

25. Mark, *Hong Kong and the Cold War*, 6.

help to maintain its world-power status, Britain wanted to show the U.S. that it was a loyal and reliable ally, but it also had to keep a low profile to avoid provoking the PRC. At the same time, it had to protect British interests in China and to preserve control over Hong Kong. Britain was less concerned about a direct attack by the PRC than it was about the prospect of Hong Kong being hurt if hostilities between China and the U.S. arose over Indochina, Korea, or Taiwan. The British realized that Hong Kong would be indefensible against an invasion by the PRC — however unlikely — but they were also worried about what they called "the American threat." The U.S. needed allies to contain China, and Hong Kong was the ideal place for gathering intelligence, spreading propaganda, and organizing covert action against China. But the British worried that working too closely with the U.S. and allowing it too much leeway in Hong Kong would provoke the PRC into stirring up trouble in Hong Kong or attacking the colony if war broke out with the U.S. Thus Britain tried simultaneously to persuade the U.S. to help defend Hong Kong and to restrain American policy toward China.

Just as they changed Hong Kong's role within the waning British Empire, the Cold War and the 1949 revolution transformed American attitudes toward Hong Kong. Despite its historical economic interests in Hong Kong, by World War Two the U.S. saw little importance in the colony. American exports to Hong Kong were marginal (comprising less than 1 percent of total U.S. exports) and the region appeared to have little military value (witnessed by the ease of the Japanese invasion in December 1941). The establishment of the PRC and the outbreak of the Korean War, however, forced the U.S. to reconsider Hong Kong's strategic value. And with the escalation of the Cold War, the U.S. saw the potential of using colonies and former colonies to help contain communism.[26] With its proximity to China, good British facilities (including, for example, signals-intelligence posts), and supply of local Chinese talent, Hong Kong was a perfect base for intelligence gathering and China-watching. In late 1949 the CIA established a listening post attached to the U.S. consulate general. When Truman closed the U.S. embassy and consulates in China during the winter of 1949-1950, consular and reporting work shifted to Hong Kong. Under the embargoes imposed on China during the Korean War, the local American consulate was assigned to check imports to and from Hong Kong. During the 1950s this consulate had a larger American staff than any other U.S. consulate in the world. And whereas there were fewer than 1000 Americans in Hong Kong in 1949, there were more than 2000 by 1957. Hong Kong also played an important role in American psychological warfare against China: the United States Information Service (USIS) in Hong Kong produced anti-communist propaganda such as

---

26. Wm. Roger Louis and Ronald Robinson ("The Imperialism of Decolonization," *Journal of Imperial and Commonwealth History* 23, no. 2 [September 1994]: 462–511) argue that the Cold War saved the British Empire, which gradually became an Anglo-American "informal empire" with Britain playing the junior role.

America Today (which after 1952 became *World Today*), *Four Seas*, and a variety of brochures and pamphlets. The colony was also a popular rest-and-recreation destination for the U.S. Navy, as it would be during the Vietnam War.[27]

However, neither the Truman nor the Eisenhower administration considered keeping Hong Kong a British colony to be vital to American national interests. Neither administration saw Hong Kong as the "Berlin of the East" (an image conjured up mainly by the British and Hong Kong governments to draw international support for Hong Kong) or was willing to risk resources or war to defend the colony.[28] At least for Eisenhower, writes Chi-kwan Mark, it was "the British factor, not the significance of Hong Kong *per se*, that mattered." Eisenhower saw Hong Kong not as a military asset but as a "diplomatic bargaining chip" for British help toward Indochina and toward Jinmen and Mazu.[29] Because Britain would not commit to keeping the PRC out of the UN, the U.S. refused to make any promises about defending Hong Kong. And because the U.S. was always more concerned with American domestic politics and the conflict with the USSR than with Hong Kong, "Hong Kong was only a peripheral factor in US global considerations."[30] Thus, writes Mark, Hong Kong became "a colony too valuable to abandon in peace, yet too peripheral to be worth committing scarce resources to for its survival at war."[31]

Nor did the "Berlin of the East" analogy necessarily imply agreement between Britain and the U.S. toward Hong Kong. Indeed, Hong Kong's contested position between the PRC and the Nationalists but also between British and American attitudes toward these two contenders became obvious in December 1949, shortly after the establishment of the PRC on the mainland and the Nationalists on Taiwan, when a dispute arose over the issue of Chinese state properties.[32] The

---

27. Johannes R. Lombardo, "A Mission of Espionage, Intelligence and Psychological Operations: The American Consulate in Hong Kong, 1949–64," *Intelligence and National Security* 14.4 (Winter 1999): 64–81; Cheng Suwei, "America's Hong Kong policy, 1942–1960" 美國的香港政策, 1942–1960, *Historical Research* 歷史研究247, no. 3 (1997): 53–66.

28. Although he was determined not to provoke the PRC government while he was governor, Alexander Grantham frequently emphasized this "Berlin of the East" after he left Hong Kong. In a lecture to the Royal Central Asian Society in 1958, for example, he explained: "By its contiguity with Communist China, Hong Kong provides a contrast between the dictator State of the Communist world with the free States of the free world. It has proved a sanctuary to nearly one million people. In short, Hong Kong is a symbol of the free world not only of the British world but of the free world in the Far East. It has been said with some justification that Hong Kong is really the Berlin of the East" (Grantham, "Hong Kong," 126).

29. Mark, *Hong Kong and the Cold War*, 7

30. Mark, *Hong Kong and the Cold War*, 38.

31. Mark, *Hong Kong and the Cold War*, 1.

32. This account of the airplane dispute is based mainly on Tang, *Britain's Encounter with Revolutionary China*, 187–90; Zhai, *The Dragon, the Lion, and the Eagle*, 105–7; Martin, *Divided Counsel*, 119–22, 139–49; and Mark, *Hong Kong and the Cold War*, 94–9.

dispute centered on the assets of China National Aviation Corporation (CNAC), which although based in Hong Kong was incorporated under Chinese law (the Nationalist government owned 80 percent of its shares, with the remaining shares owned by Pan American Airways) and Central Air Transport Corporation (CATC), an official agency within the Nationalist government. The two firms' assets had been transferred to Hong Kong for safety during the civil war, and some 80 of the CNAC and CATC aircraft (C-46, C-47, C-54, and Convair transport planes purchased under the American Lend-Lease program) were still based in Hong Kong.

On November 9 the general managers and staff of both firms defected to the PRC with 11 of the airplanes. The New China News Agency hailed the defection as an "uprising of the 4000 personnel" of the two companies, and Zhou Enlai declared that the remaining 71 aircraft belonged to the PRC. But the Nationalist government asked the Hong Kong authorities to impound the airplanes so they would not be sent to the PRC, where they might be used to invade Taiwan, while the pro-Nationalist boards and employees of the two companies obtained court injunctions to prevent each other from removing the aircraft. When Nationalist agents in Hong Kong bombed seven of the airplanes before the British government responded, the PRC government accused Britain of not letting the aircraft take off and not protecting them while they were in Hong Kong. To further complicate matters, on December 1 the U.S. government asked the British embassy in Washington if the Hong Kong government could keep the airplanes from falling into the hands of the Communists. On December 10 the Nationalist government announced that all shares of CNAC and CATC had been sold to Civil Air Transport Incorporated (CATI), owned by General Claire Chennault of the legendary "Flying Tigers" and his business partner, Whiting Willauer. Chennault was connected with the pro-Taiwan China Lobby, and CATI, subsidized by the CIA, had been recently formed in Delaware to keep the remaining aircraft from being transferred to the PRC.

When Britain recognized the PRC in January 1950, the PRC government again asked for the remaining airplanes.[33] But CATI, backed by the American government, also asked for them. When the Hong Kong attorney general insisted that the dispute had to be settled by the courts, CATI sent lawyers, among them General "Wild Bill" Donovan, wartime director of the Office of Strategic Services (OSS). Grantham recalled that Donovan "came to see me, and thumping the table, metaphorically if not physically, insisted that the airplanes be handed over to him without further ado, for, he said, if it had not been for the United States Britain would have lost the war. Moreover, he added, if I did not do as he

---

33. Grantham had warned two Pan Am vice-presidents who were on the CNAC board of directors to move the airplanes to Taiwan before Britain recognized the PRC government, but they insisted that there was no room for the airplanes in Taiwan and that moving them would alienate the PRC, where Pan Am hoped to resume operations.

demanded he would make it hot for me with the authorities in London."[34] In late February 1950 the Hong Kong chief justice ruled that the aircraft belonged to the PRC government. However, the U.S. State Department pressured the British government to intervene, threatening that Marshall Aid and the Military Assistance Program would be jeopardized if Britain did not keep the airplanes in Hong Kong. But the British government, fully aware of the implications of this issue for Sino-British relations, worried that not sending the aircraft to China might cause the PRC to organize strikes, riots, and sabotage in Hong Kong or impose an economic embargo on the colony. On the other hand, surrendering the airplanes to the PRC would hurt relations with the U.S. and jeopardize American economic and military assistance to Britain. Republican Senator William Knowland, a vocal supporter of Chiang Kai-shek, warned that the airplanes could be used to attack not only Taiwan but also Japan and Southeast Asia, and accused Britain of helping the spread of communism. Other American senators and congressmen threatened to withhold support for programs that provided economic assistance to Britain.

The British government could not lawfully overturn the Hong Kong ruling that the airplanes belonged to the PRC, but it instructed Grantham to keep them in Hong Kong until full legal proceedings could be conducted. When it became clear that Grantham could not use any statutory powers to keep the aircraft in Hong Kong, the British government told him to do so "by any means" that "did not involve the formal use of statutory powers." The Hong Kong attorney general suggested obtaining an order-in-council from London that would both keep the airplanes in Hong Kong until the matter could be resolved and begin proceedings for a trial. In late April 1950 the British Cabinet issued an order-in-council that kept the airplanes in Hong Kong pending adjudication of ownership and provided right of final appeal to the Privy Council. In the meantime, the Hong Kong government had to prevent further sabotage attempts on the remaining airplanes and to forcefully remove employees who had barricaded themselves on CNAC property and refused to leave.

Worried that the aircraft might be used to invade Taiwan, and faced with the rise of McCarthyism, the Truman administration pressured Clement Attlee's Labour government to reverse the Hong Kong court's decision. Although the British tried hard to avoid any appearance of being under American pressure, in June 1952, following extensive litigation and appeals, the Judicial Committee of the Privy Council ruled that the airplanes were the legal property of CATI but that they not be transferred to Taiwan. The PRC retaliated only with criticism and by nationalizing British-owned public utilities in Shanghai. For Governor Grantham, the new ruling had shown that the British government was "more scared of what the United States might do to Britain, than of what China might do to Hong Kong."[35]

---

34. Grantham, *Via Ports*, 162.
35. Grantham, *Via Ports*, 163.

The "Taiwan Problem"

What British officials referred to as the "Taiwan problem" or the "Formosa problem" frequently posed a threat to Hong Kong and to both Sino-British and Anglo-American relations, thus jeopardizing Hong Kong's security and forcing the colonial government to learn how to coexist within the dangerously fluid space created by the establishment of the PRC on the mainland and the Nationalist regime on Taiwan. Although Chiang Kai-shek's regime had lost credibility in Hong Kong by the late 1940s, pro-Nationalist newspapers in Hong Kong now called for the colony to be restored to the new regime on Taiwan. Throughout the early 1950s the Nationalists conducted guerrilla raids on Communist-held coastal islands and searched and harassed foreign vessels, including British freighters. The Hong Kong and British governments were concerned that Nationalist blockades, mine-laying, and raids near Hong Kong would convince the PRC that the British were involved in such activities, thus provoking the PRC into attacking Hong Kong. Between 1950 and early 1953 the Nationalists regularly searched, detained, or confiscated good from ships trading with China, seventy-five percent of them flying the British flag. In December 1952, for example, Nationalist gunboats attacked the *Rosita*, a British freighter registered in Hong Kong and chartered to a local company with communist connections. The ship's British captain was killed in the attack. The following year Nationalist gunboats attacked the *Rosita* again en route to Shanghai. From 1950 to 1953 the *Rosita* was attacked a total of thirteen times.[36]

During the first Offshore Islands crisis in 1954-1955, the British and American governments disagreed about how to respond to the PRC's bombardment of Jinmen and Mazu, which both revived the question of Hong Kong's security and challenged perceptions and definitions of the islands on the mainland shore. The Eisenhower administration hoped to use defending Hong Kong to pressure the British into supporting the defense of the two islands, but the British considered Jinmen and Mazu part of the PRC and not worth the trouble of defending. However, Eisenhower faced too much pressure from Taiwan and the U.S. military and Congress to let the islands go. Sympathetic toward Hong Kong, Eisenhower assured Churchill that although it would not be popular in the U.S., "we would be at your side" if Hong Kong or Malaya were attacked.[37] But some U.S. officials and, perhaps more important, the American press resented the British position and saw Hong Kong as simply another offshore island that the British expected the U.S. to help them defend. Many U.S. officials and the American public believed that Britain would appease China in order to keep Hong Kong, yet they could not understand why the British did not see Hong Kong as an offshore island.

---

36. Mark, *Hong Kong and the Cold War*, 113–14.
37. Quoted in Nancy Bernkopf Tucker, *Taiwan, Hong Kong and the United States, 1945–1992: Uncertain Friendships* (New York: Twayne, 1994), 202.

The British were especially concerned in early 1955, when the PRC captured the Dachen Islands and the U.S. Congress passed its "Formosa Resolution" authorizing the president to send troops to defend Taiwan, and when Eisenhower threatened to use nuclear arms against the PRC. Although this Anglo-American disagreement and policy dilemma was resolved when Zhou Enlai offered in April 1955 to negotiate with the U.S., even the resolution of the crisis provoked tensions between Britain and the U.S.: with the crisis diffused, the British began to reduce the Hong Kong garrison, which worried American officials that it would have damaging psychological impact on Chinese in Hong Kong and on East Asia in general.

Three additional examples illustrate how "the Taiwan problem" could affect Hong Kong. In July 1954 a PRC fighter shot down a Cathay Pacific airliner over Hainan Island, killing ten people, among them three Americans. When PRC fighters fired on two American airplanes involved in search-and-rescue operations, the American aircraft shot down two Chinese fighters. The PRC government apologized for downing the Cathay Pacific airplane and offered to compensate the British, but it also accused KMT troops of harassing the China coast and the U.S. of using search operations to enter Chinese airspace. Although the U.S. wanted Britain to take a harder line against the PRC, the British tried to downplay the incident, which occurred only a month after the Nationalist navy had seized a Russian tanker, the *Tuapse*. The PRC fighter had apparently mistaken the Cathay Pacific airplane for a Nationalist military aircraft; British officials in Singapore reported that the Chinese airplanes might have been providing air cover for the *Tuapse*, hence the downing of the Cathay Pacific airplane.[38]

In April 1955 the *Kashmir Princess*, a chartered Indian airliner that was supposed to be transporting Zhou Enlai to the Bandung Conference exploded in Indonesian airspace after taking off for Jakarta from Hong Kong's Kai Tak Airport, killing eleven Chinese officials and foreign journalists. Although Zhou was not on board, ostensibly because he had gone to meet Gamal Abdul Nasser of Egypt at the last minute, PRC officials later told Hong Kong government officials that they had some prior suspicions of the plot. Evidence suggests that Zhou had learned about the plot but did not try to stop it, apparently to persuade the Hong Kong government to crack down on a secret ring of Kuomintang agents in Hong Kong. Describing the explosion as a U.S.-Nationalist regime plot, the PRC government demanded that the Hong Kong government capture the Nationalist agents responsible. It was obvious that the plane had been sabotaged and that this must have happened in Hong Kong: examination of the wreckage revealed a time bomb in one of the wings, which could only have been planted by someone with access to the plane while it was at Kai Tak, where the PRC government had requested that the Hong Kong government protect it. The Hong Kong government offered a reward (the highest ever offered in Hong Kong) for

---

38. Mark, *Hong Kong and the Cold War*, 113–14.

the saboteurs and issued a warrant for the arrest of Zhou Zhu, a service technician at Kai Tak who had been bribed by KMT agents to place the bomb, but Zhou escaped to Taiwan on a CATI plane. Although the Hong Kong government was able to deport members of the Nationalist intelligence organization based in Hong Kong, when the British consul in Taiwan demanded that Zhou be returned to Hong Kong for trial, the Nationalist government refused. And because Britain did not recognize the Nationalist regime, it had no extradition treaty to rely on.[39]

In October 1956 clashes between pro-Beijing and pro-Taipei supporters over a Nationalist flag that had been removed from a resettlement block resulted in riots in Kowloon, leading Nationalist sympathizers to loot stores owned by communist supporters. When pro-KMT mobs attacked and killed communist sympathizers, the Hong Kong police responded by firing on the mobs. By the end of the week, almost 60 people were dead and more than 400 had been hospitalized. Neither the British nor the American government was particularly concerned about the 1956 riots (a Parliamentary hearing on the matter later in November lasted only thirty minutes, and the U.S. government was more worried that British defense cuts in Hong Kong and Malaya would mean that the U.S. might have to shoulder Britain's old colonial burdens), but the riots led to tension between the PRC and Hong Kong governments. Although there was no evidence that KMT agents had participated directly in the riots, the PRC government accused the Hong Kong government of absolving the agents who had orchestrated the riots, even charging Britain and Taiwan with being in collusion. Citing this and the sabotage of the CNAC airplanes in 1950 and of the *Kashmir Princess*, the PRC government claimed that the British had been allowing KMT agents to cause trouble in Hong Kong. (When the Hong Kong government published its report on the Kowloon and Tsuen Wan riots in early 1957, it side-stepped the Communist-Nationalist tensions by blaming them on secret societies and refugees.)

In a discussion with the British minister in Beijing, Zhou Enlai criticized the British for allowing KMT agents to use Hong Kong as base for anti-PRC activities, reminding the minister that the PRC did not want to cause trouble in Hong Kong but could easily do so. Zhou also declared that because Chinese residents in Kowloon had lost confidence in the colonial government's ability to protect them, his government had a duty to protect them and would not tolerate more disorders "on the doorstep of China."[40] The PRC government issued similar "reminders" after the British government decided in early 1957 to release and ship back to Taiwan a KMT F-86 Sabre fighter that had landed in Hong Kong in January 1956 to escape PRC fighters.[41] Alexander Grantham, worried about such warnings, was

---

39. Steve Tsang, "Target Zhou Enlai: The 'Kashmir Princess' Incident of 1955," *China Quarterly* 139 (September 1994): 766–82.

40. Quoted in Mark, *Hong Kong and the Cold War*, 70.

41. Steve Tsang, "Strategy for Survival: The Cold War and Hong Kong's Policy towards Kuomintang and Chinese Communist Activities in the 1950s," *Journal of Imperial and Commonwealth Studies* 25, no. 2 (May 1997): 307–10.

concerned that the reduced Hong Kong garrison could not even maintain internal security, let alone defend Hong Kong against an external attack. Grantham asked the British government to expand the garrison, but Harold Macmillan, who was trying to reduce defense costs, thought this would be too costly, especially for maintaining order rather than for defense. Given that Hong Kong had lost any real strategic importance for Britain, whose territorial interests in Asia disappeared with the independence of India, Burma, Malaya, and most of the other former British colonies in the region, the Hong Kong garrison was reduced to a minimal level, and the naval dockyard was closed.

Cooks, stoves, and boiling pots

Few of these incidents had any serious long-term effects on Hong Kong's security. Most officials in Britain and Hong Kong believed that the U.S. would help defend Hong Kong since an attack on the colony would occur only in a global war, and the many American strategic studies, and assurances from Truman and Eisenhower, gave them reason to believe that the U.S. would help defend Hong Kong in the unlikely event of a PRC attack. Alexander Grantham recalled that "although no military alliance or defence pact between the United States and Britain covered Hong Kong, I was, in my own mind, confident that the powerful U.S. Seventh Fleet and the large U.S. Air forces in Taiwan (Formosa), Clark Field in the Philippines, and Okinawa . . . would come to Hong Kong's aid, not to defend a British colony *qua* colony, but because the policy of the United States government was to resist the advance of the Chinese communists in South East Asia."[42] In October 1957, Harold Macmillan and Dwight Eisenhower secretly agreed that in return for Britain's promise — at least for the time being — not to push for China's admission to the UN, the U.S. would help defend Hong Kong in case of an attack by China. (Earlier, in August, Eisenhower had decided that because Britain would not commit to keeping the PRC out of the UN, the U.S. would only help Hong Kong evacuate civilians if the PRC were to attack.)

Nevertheless, these incidents show both the precarious nature of Hong Kong's status and the limitations of Cold War geopolitics for understanding the realities of the post-1949 years. Whereas the establishment of the PRC in 1949 doubtless had an important effect on Hong Kong, both the establishment of the PRC on the mainland and the Nationalists on Taiwan affected Hong Kong in the late 1940s and early 1950s. Communist Chinese authorities frequently reassured — and warned — the British and Hong Kong governments that they would tolerate Hong Kong's status as long as the colonial government cared properly for the local Chinese and as long as Hong Kong did not become a base for anti-PRC subversion.

---

42. Grantham, *Via Ports*, 171.

In October 1955, Zhou Enlai told Grantham in Beijing that the PRC would tolerate Hong Kong as long as the British abided by several "rules of conduct": the colony could not be used as an anti-communist base, no activities aimed at subverting the PRC would be allowed, and the colonial government would protect PRC representatives and organizations. But the uncertain status of the Nationalist regime on Taiwan and the different British and American attitudes toward this regime often threatened to undermine any such reassurances. Hong Kong's history had always been shaped both by developments in China and by its position within the British Empire, but the 1949 revolution complicated this position by adding two new players: Taiwan and the U.S. To borrow Grantham's analogy about pots on kitchen stoves, it was never certain how many pots were boiling or which would boil first.

Babel and Vernacular in an Empire of Immigrants: Howells and the Languages of American Fiction*

Jonathan Arac

Philological criticism is not just the same as close reading. As evidenced through the very different examples of Mikhail Bakhtin and Edward Said, philological care for language and the work of language in human life may operate in the study of discourse practices and patterns that cross the bounds of individual works, even as those patterns are discerned and delineated through scrupulous attention to particular textual moments. Yet sometimes even this may be too close. Despite my suspicions of Franco Moretti's "distant" reading, this essay pursues a case where distance seems the right path.[1]

    This inquiry arises from classroom experience, and it begins from a gross aesthetic judgment on the language of a nineteenth-century novel. To understand

*   My thanks to those who hosted occasions that allowed this line of thought to begin and develop: Douglas Kerr and Q.S. Tong in Hong Kong; Donald E. Pease at Dartmouth; Bruce Robbins at Columbia's University Seminar on Theory of Literature; and J. Gerald Kennedy at Louisiana State University. I learned much from comments by many participants at these events. Thanks too to those whose comments on written drafts heartened, challenged, and instructed me: Rashmi Bhatnagar, Paul A. Bové, Marshall Brown, Lawrence Buell, Amanda Claybaugh, Wai Chee Dimock, James Livingston, Lawrence Rosenwald, and Matt Sandler. Susan Andrade has been indispensable from the beginning of this work.
1.   See Jonathan Arac, "Anglo-Globalism?" in *New Left Review*, n.s. 16 (July-August, 2002), a response to Franco Moretti, "Conjectures on World Literature," *New Left Review*, n.s. 1 (January-February 2000).

the aesthetic problem requires reaching out to issues of immigration over the whole history of the United States. Current debates over immigration now in the twenty-first century evince complex yet striking relationships with issues from the past, in this case especially from the 1840s to the 1920s.

I

The large concern involves both legislative action and public discussion about who shall count as American. At its founding, the US could not claim indigenous immemoriality for any of its members (except the Native Americans, who were originally excluded), so from the start, the nation has given special attention to the various means of making Americans. The use of the English language has been crucial in this process, from very early to right now. The aesthetics of English usage is where I start, in the 1890 novel by William Dean Howells, *A Hazard of New Fortunes.*[2]

This exploration arises from a larger concern with problems of language in American literary history, but the issues obviously bear on current writing as well. I cannot accept what remains, I think, the most established way of thinking about American literary language: to honor and treat as the desired norm what is called *vernacular,* usually without much specification, except that it is not stuck-up school-talk and its great exemplars are Walt Whitman and Mark Twain. Although he is no longer so much referred to, the example of Ernest Hemingway is also crucial in this genealogy; his decorum of terse eloquence was projected back. Even though Ralph Ellison argued against Hemingway's model, and such divergently important novelists as Saul Bellow and John Updike have not honored it in their practice, it continues to guide both everyday book reviewing and the standard pedagogy of creative writing.

Ellison's critique, put forward in his address upon receiving the National Book Award in 1953, set terms that remain powerful. He argued against the Hemingway norm of "understatement" because it "depends . . . upon commonly held assumptions," which had been unavailable to Ellison, since his "minority status rendered all such assumptions questionable."[3] Moreover, Ellison found unpersuasive the claim that such writing captured the "rhythms . . . of everyday

---

2.   William Dean Howells, *A Hazard of New Fortunes* (1890; New York: Penguin, 2001). Page references to this work will appear in the text. The substantial introduction to this edition by Philip Lopate (v–xxix) conveys a vivid appreciation of Howells's "discovery of New York" for the uses of major fiction.

3.   See Ralph Ellison, "Brave Words for a Startling Occasion" (1953) in his *Collected Essays* (New York: Random House, 1995), 152, for all quotations in this paragraph. While criticizing Hemingway, Ellison's total critical position redefined and continued to value the idea of vernacular.

speech." Compared to "the rich babel of idiomatic expression," he found the Hemingway norm "embarrassingly austere."

As a position within scholarly criticism, the first statements of the vernacular thesis date from the early years after World War II. The thesis reduces and simplifies the language values of *American Renaissance*, which praised a combination of realism and "fantastic extravagance."[4] The vernacular perspective, even as invoked by liberal and progressive critics such as Henry Nash Smith and Leo Marx, proves rarely to avoid implications not only of exceptionalism, but even of nativism. So far from having been left behind as part of Cold War ideology, this view has been reanimated by Shelley Fisher Fishkin's *Was Huck Black?*[5] Fishkin herself has become a leader in establishing a more international perspective in the institution of American Studies, but with regard to Twain's language, her book ignores both the contribution of Africa to that which counts as African American and of England to American English.[6]

This essay grows from my long unease with vernacularism, at first somewhat reactively in a 1992 paper on Whitman, then in my 1997 book *Huckleberry Finn as Idol and Target*. Franco Moretti's polemical new millennial manifesto "Conjectures on World Literature" spurred my further thinking about language, and I offer a counter-positive in a recent essay, "Global and Babel." The positive goal seeks a "critical, cosmopolitan, polyglot way of working with the literature of the United States."[7] This goal stands against the exceptionalist cosmopolitanism of American

---

4.   F.O. Matthiessen, *American Renaissance: Art and Expression in the Age of Emerson and Whitman* (New York: Oxford University Press, 1941), 642, discussing the dialect stories of George Washington Harris, which he finds in the spirit of *Moby-Dick*.

5.   See Henry Nash Smith, "The Widening of Horizons," in *Literary History of the United States* (1948), eds. Robert E. Spiller, et al. (3d ed.; New York: Macmillan, 1963), 639–51; and *Mark Twain: The Development of a Writer* (1962); Leo Marx, "The Vernacular Tradition in American Literature" (1958; on Twain and Whitman) in *The Pilot and the Passenger* (1988), 3–17; Shelley Fisher Fishkin, *Was Huck Black? Mark Twain and African-American Voices* (1993).

6.   For Fishkin's current role, see her Presidential address to the American Studies Association, "Crossroads of Cultures: The Transnational Turn in American Studies," *American Quarterly* 57 (2005): 17–58. On her book, see Jonathan Arac, *"Huckleberry Finn" as Idol and Target: The Functions of Criticism in Our Time* (Madison: Univ. of Wisconsin Press, 1997), 207. Fishkin's book was largely inspired by the insights of Ralph Ellison but carries forward his American nationalist emphasis at the expense of his international side. For the interplay of these perspectives in Ellison, see *"Huckleberry Finn" as Idol and Target*, 197–203.

7.   See Jonathan Arac, "Global and Babel: Two Perspectives on Language in American Literature," *ESQ* 50, nos.1–3 (2004): 94–119; "Whitman and Problems of Vernacular," in *Breaking Bounds: Whitman and American Cultural Studies*, eds. Betsy Erkkila and Jay Grossman (New York: Oxford University Press, 1995), 44–61; *"Huckleberry Finn" as Idol and Target*, esp. 154–65; 186–93; 207–10. For the fullest current scholarly demonstration of a critical, cosmopolitan, polyglot American literature, see Wai Chee Dimock, *Through Other Continents: American Literature across Deep Time* (Princeton: Princeton University Press, 2006).

imperial mission. The long history of struggle in American literature between language purity and a messier richness bears on debates, vividly and often bitterly active as I write, concerning the sounds of our future.

The historical ground for a cosmopolitan, polyglot literature arises from the quite distinctive character of the United States, which frames its immigration history. The United States originated as colonies but became an empire immediately upon gaining independence.[8] The motto *e pluribus unum* means that from the start the unitary American people has been plurally heterogeneous: the founding settlements included colonists from several European nations who imposed themselves upon a Native American indigenous population, and who imported many enslaved Africans. Through the nineteenth century, the new nation spread across North America, buying Louisiana and gaining Florida from Spain, and then by war against Spain's successor Mexico conquering Texas and greater California. The self-acknowledged imperial moment around 1900 marked by war against Spain in Cuba and the Philippines has yielded to a neo-imperialism, usually officially unacknowledged. Recently major interpretive overviews by distinguished senior historians have addressed this history: Charles S. Maier, *Among Empires*, and Thomas Bender, *A Nation among Nations*.[9] The *among* in both titles emphasizes a salutary comparative perspective, in contrast to the usual exceptionalism guiding US historiography. Like these works, I hope to address American materials in perspectives that are comparative and transnational.

The struggle between comparatist and nationalist-exceptionalist historiography and criticism of American literary language may be focused through the funniest essay ever written in American literary criticism: Mark Twain's attack against "Fenimore Cooper's Literary Offenses."[10] Twain's own extraordinary accomplishment in *Huckleberry Finn* and elsewhere authorizes an unfair polemic that both marks and helps to make an epochal shift in taste and national self-definition. With Huck, Twain did something quite innovative: he gave over the entire narration of a major work to a near-illiterate speaker of non-standard

---

8.   There are many valuable resources for analysis of the United States as empire, and I forbear full citation, but because it seems too little used by literary scholars, I wish to note the remarkable scholarly accomplishment of the historical geographer D.W. Meinig in his massive four volumes *The Shaping of America: A Geographical Perspective on 500 Years of History* (New Haven: Yale University Press, 1986–2004). This work is fundamentally shaped by an analysis of American imperialism, and it argues, "it is important for Americans to understand more clearly than they do that their nation has been created by massive aggression against a long succession of peoples." See Meinig, *Atlantic America, 1492–1800*, xviii.

9.   Charles S. Maier, *Among Empires: American Ascendancy and Its Predecessors* (Cambridge: Harvard University Press, 2006); Thomas Bender, *A Nation Among Nations: America's Place in World History* (New York: Hill and Wang, 2006).

10.   This 1895 essay is widely available. One standard text may be found in Louis J. Budd's rich selection for the Library of America: Mark Twain, *Collected Tales, Sketches, Speeches, and Essays, 1891–1910* (New York: Literary Classics of the United States, 1992), 180–200.

language, allowing no mediating figure of cultural authority and standard usages to come between the reader and the orally modeled voice of Huck. In his author's "Explanatory" note on the book's language, Twain's point was that he used seven different varieties of American English spoken along the Mississippi, lest any reader "suppose that all these characters were trying to talk alike and not succeeding."[11] Yet the seven varieties all fit within the vernacular model: whether white or black, their speakers all are identified with American locations ("Missouri negro dialect; the extremest form of the backwoods South-Western dialect; the ordinary 'Pike-County' dialect; and four modified varieties of this last"). Things are quite different in *A Hazard of New Fortunes*.

Twain especially objected to the language of Cooper's characters because it was inconsistent (the failure of "trying to talk alike"), but Twain here invokes a model of uniformity within the speech of individuals that is simply untrue to all that sociolinguists have observed and characterized as "code-switching."[12] More largely, Cooper's fiction, cast as it is in the genre of historical romance adapted from the practice of Walter Scott, uses language as an index of social, historical, and political differences between characters, not simply as a marker of geography, which is Twain's concern. Cooper's characters' language differences within English register immigrant, professional, and ethnic variation, as well as regional. In this sense, Cooper's fiction comes much closer to the model of Bakhtin's heteroglossia.[13]

Vernacular serves nationalist language standardization, protests to the contrary notwithstanding.[14] The imperial character of the United States manifests itself far more fully and clearly in Cooper than in Twain and among Twain's contemporaries far more in the work of his friend and literary associate George Washington Cable (Cable and Twain collaborated on a reading tour just as *Huckleberry Finn* was in process of publication). The historical fact of the formation of the United States from populations including major colonizations by France, Spain, and Britain, as well as the importation of Africans and the settlement of

---

11. Unpaginated. See the front matter of the currently best reading edition for the persistence of the vernacularist thesis: Victor Fischer and Lin Salamo, "Foreword" to Mark Twain, *Adventures of Huckleberry Finn* (Berkeley and Los Angeles, Univ. of California Press, 2001), xxv.

12. See definition in David Crystal, *Cambridge Encyclopedia of Language* (Cambridge: Cambridge University Press, 1987), 417: "Changing from the use of one language or variety to another." This comprehends practices both of bilingualism (switching languages) and also of diglossia (switching varieties within one language).

13. See *"Huckleberry Finn" as Idol and Target*, 145–148. See also the outstanding discussion of language in Cooper's *Pioneers* (1823) in David Simpson, *The Politics of American English, 1776–1850*, 156–83.

14. For comparative perspective on questions of the ideology of vernacular in imperial nationalism, see the study by Margaret W. Ferguson, *Dido's Daughters: Literacy, Gender, and Empire in Early Modern England and France* (Chicago: Univ. of Chicago Press, 2003), esp. chs. 2 and 3.

Germans emerges far more clearly in the action and languages of Cable's great and neglected historical romance of 1880, *The Grandissimes,* than it does in *Huckleberry Finn,* despite both novels' being set in territory that shares the same specific political-imperial history before becoming part of the US.

Scholars have claimed that *Huckleberry Finn* addresses the issues of race after Reconstruction,[15] but *The Grandissimes* really does it. Near the start, the flag of the United States of America rises in the heart of New Orleans. The year is 1803, after the Louisiana Purchase, but no reader missed the straightforward allegorical relevance to sixty years later, when the stars and stripes again were raised to mark a transition of political regime after the defeat of the confederacy. And the history of Louisiana meant that the category of free persons of color was already socially important, even while slavery continued. Cable's novel operates in the diverse linguistic registers of Louisianans free and slave; white and black; English, French, and Creole; as well as in a more normative narrative voice, which is, however, largely focalized through a Northerner come South, whose name, Frowenfeld, indicates a German past.

II

It is not the task of this essay to display Cable's language, but Cable's overall practice points to a very different American literature from that of Twain.[16] Eventually, this inquiry will require further thinking about genre forms for historical fiction, keeping in mind that in *Life on the Mississippi* (1883) Twain attacked Scott as savagely as he later did Cooper. *Huckleberry Finn* is itself a historical novel, but not at all in the mode shared by Scott, Cooper, and Cable. Faulkner draws from both Twain and Cable in *Absalom, Absalom!,* but from Cable he draws more of the plot problematic than the language.

In my teaching, I have found a problem that links Cooper and Cable to *A Hazard of New Fortunes*: widely shared canons of prose — the way most of us read now — make their works seem accessible only through labor that makes pleasure impossible. A difficulty all three works share arises from the representation of various modes of nonstandard English. We no longer enjoy practices of language representation that were once widely shared by writers and appreciated by readers.

This preamble has tried to suggest the larger stakes within which I situate the particular analysis of Howells and the problem of language. *A Hazard of New Fortunes* features a compelling time and place. The novel displays New York City

---

15. On *Huckleberry Finn* and politics after Reconstruction, see argument and references in Jonathan Arac, "Why Does No One Care about the Aesthetic Value of *Huckleberry Finn*?" *New Literary History* 30 (1999): 772–73.
16. See the remarkable treatment of language in Cable by Lawrence Rosenwald in *American Literature and Multilingual America* (Cambridge University Press, forthcoming).

in the later 1880s as a new metropolis, a destination for domestic migrants and for worldwide immigration. The framing character Basil March moves from Boston to New York, to edit a new magazine of literature, ideas, and the arts. His perception of New York features his fascinated witness to the new immigrants of the period, coming from southern and eastern Europe — Italy, Russia, Poland, Greece, Hungary, and more — in contrast to the earlier immigration, largely from Ireland and Germany, which had predominated from 1840 to 1880.[17] This variegated population forms for March a valued part of his visual surround. The diverse throng moves him both to social speculation and to aesthetic contemplation, but he and the people who make up the throng are not shown as speaking to each other. He does speak a good deal with one particular member of the old immigration.

In New York, March encounters a mentor from an earlier phase of his life. Back in his native mid-West, before the Civil War, the young and culturally ambitious March had been tutored in German language and literature by Mr. Lindau, a recent German émigré (from "the barricades at Berlin in 1848" [81]), and when they meet again, March finds that Lindau has lost a hand in the war. The aesthetic problem I am concerned with starts from the moment they meet. Here is what Lindau says: "My dear poy. My yong friendt! . . . Idt is Passil Marge — not zo? . . . . It sheers my hardt to zee you" (79).[18] Lindau is a significant character, but every time he speaks, his German-inflected English is rendered in full typographic detailing of his consonant system, in which voiced and unvoiced stops are reversed, and sibilants also differ. There is one important, but rare, exception. When Lindau speaks German, his speech is presented in standard English (169): the convention is that standard English represents standard German, while broken English is transcribed as spoken.[19] When Mark Twain made

---

17. Throughout I rely on the major interpretive synthesis, Aristide R. Zolberg, *A Nation by Design: Immigration Policy in the Fashioning of America* (New York: Russell Sage Foundation and Cambridge: Harvard University Press, 2006).

18. Bruce Robbins has argued in conversation for the live interest of this language, noting, for instance that "hardt" suggests that we may judge Basil hard on his old friend, and that "sheers" for *cheers* suggests the encounter will turn out to cut through Lindau's life, rather than gladdening it. The larger stakes of this claim derive from Robbins's unparalleled exploration of utopian potentials in what had been considered conventional and therefore dead parts of many nineteenth century British novels. See Robbins, *The Servant's Hand: English Fiction from Below* (1986; Durham: Duke University Press, 1993), esp. ch. 2. Against Robbins's Longinian practice of finding great moments, with which I am generally in deep sympathy, in this particular case, I find more utopian potential in considering the total fact of Lindau's language, rather than searching within it as if Howells had written *Finnegans Wake*.

19. This convention plays a crucial role in the dialect writing of Abraham Cahan and, in a later generation, for Henry Roth in *Call It Sleep* (1934). In Cahan, so far as I know it is first used in *Yekl* (1896), so one may imagine an actual influence from Howells's practice to Cahan's, but to establish this requires more inquiry than I have yet performed.

his famous encounter with "The Awful German Language" (1880, Appendix to *A Tramp Abroad*), he was most struck by its grammar, making fun of the systems of case and gender and especially the principles of word order and noun-compounding. But in Lindau's speech, despite a few issues of syntax and idiom, it is the painstaking and consistently depicted sound differences that make reading this character a chore. Lindau's "pathetic mutilation" (81) of body is echoed in the mutilation of his speech.[20]

Howells's representation of Lindau's speech takes place within a larger history of language representation. Dialect writing in the United States had established literary conventions in the nineteenth century.[21] Usually dialect was treated as laughable — either in short genre pieces or else as a component within larger works.[22] Prominent in this set of conventions was the use of "eye dialect,"[23] in which the social superiority of the writer is established by phonetically misspelling words that even the most precise standard speakers would say just as did the dialect speaker (*wuz* for *was; sez* for *says*). But this technique plays no part in Lindau's speech.

Only during Howells's own career, beginning after the Civil War, did an ethnographically serious dialect literature arise, what we call local color. Like Twain's "Explanatory" note it highlighted regional variation among Americans of some generations' standing. Moreover, although local color was more earnestly appreciative than mocking, it too granted superiority to the standard-language speaking reader and writer.[24] There has been some elevation of the dialect speaker, but not yet to the level of seriousness demanded by Erich Auerbach in *Mimesis*, for whom even Dickens remains too far from the tragic seriousness of everyday life that is Auerbach's criterion for the representation of reality he most values. In this case, Howells gives Lindau a full tragic seriousness, except for his language, a problem Auerbach never addresses.

Howells makes it hard to condescend to Lindau. Indeed, when discussing later plans to make a play from the novel, Howells stated of Lindau that he should

---

20. For the best discussion of this topic, see Elsa Nettels, *Language, Race, and Social Class in Howells's America* (Lexington: University Press of Kentucky, 1988), 94–95.

21. See the best recent study of dialect writing in Howells's time, Gavin Jones, *Strange Talk: The Politics of Dialect Literature in Gilded Age America* (Berkeley and Los Angeles: Univ. of California Press, 1999), which still leaves many questions unanswered.

22. The most important antebellum corpus of dialect writing is what is called Southwestern humor. See Jonathan Arac, The *Emergence of American Literary Narrative, 1820–1860* (Cambridge: Harvard University Press, 2005), 32–49.

23. The term was coined by George Philip Krapp, vol. 1 of *The English Language in America*, 2 vols. (1925; New York: Ungar, 1960), 228.

24. See the authoritative interpretive synopsis on regionalism by Richard H. Brodhead in *Cambridge History of American Literature*, ed. Sacvan Bercovitch, vol. 3, *Prose Writing, 1860–1920* (Cambridge: Cambridge University Press, 2005), 45–62, and esp. 55–57.

"almost be the protagonist."[25] March explains that when they had first met, Lindau was editing an antislavery newspaper, struggling with poverty and his wife's illness, "yet he was always such a gentle soul! And so generous! He taught me German for the love of it. . . . . He's one of the most accomplished men! He used to be a splendid musician — pianist — and knows eight or ten languages" (81). With the delight of his "sweet, unselfish nature" (81) at the encounter, Lindau tried to take March's hand with a double clasp, but had to stop because of his missing hand. He explains, "I wanted to gife you the other handt too, but I gafe it to your gountry a good while ago." March is pained at this expression of alienation (the US is *your* country, not *my* country or *our* country), but Lindau explains, "What gountry hass a poor man got, Mr. Marge?" (80). This sharply challenges a common idea that the US was "the best poor man's country."

Lindau remains a character of strong principle and passion. He involves March in moral crisis: Dryfoos, the journal's financial sponsor, is an aggressively antilabor capitalist, and after discovering Lindau's radicalism, he instructs March to fire him. The crisis is provoked by exchanges that occur at a festive banquet for all those involved with the journal, and it hinges on Dryfoos's capacity to understand the German that Lindau speaks to March, believing himself not more widely understood (307-08, 310; 405). (Although Dryfoos has come to New York from the mid-West, his background is Pennsylvania Dutch.) This is the payoff for Howells's establishing Lindau's practice of bilingualism; a reader may recognize that German is not limited to revolutionaries like Lindau and the Haymarket anarchists but is shared by capitalist and radical, spoken on both sides of the class struggle. Lindau is later beaten by police at a streetcar strike where he is vehemently protesting their violence against workers, and he dies from the beating. Lindau is unique in the American literature I know for several decades both before and after: a Union war hero and man of culture yet also an ideologue, foreigner, and, most literally in the strike scene, an outside agitator.

Far more than the timid, confused, and indecisive Basil March, but quite like Howells himself, Lindau challenges the American system of capitalist injustice and inequality. Among established American figures Howells stood alone in his immediate criticism of the judicial miscarriage by which anarchists were convicted, without proof, of capital crimes for the 1886 Haymarket bombing in Chicago. He also came to declare himself a socialist. As the US moved to war against Spain in Cuba and the Philippines, Howells was an anti-imperialist, and from abolitionism in his youth, he was fifty years later in 1909 one of the founding sponsors of the first major national organization to support civil rights for African Americans, the NAACP.

Unlike Lindau, Howells took a Tolstoyan position against violence, but this divergence does not lead the book to reject Lindau except in the two ways fiction

---

25. Everett Carter, introduction to *A Hazard of New Fortunes,* by W.D. Howells (Bloomington: Indiana University Press, 1976), xxv. Vol. 16 of Selected Edition of W.D. Howells.

can make such judgments. First, he suffers and dies; the book shows that his position is literally not viable. But his death is a martyrdom, which carries a positive within the negative. More important, and the point I am pressing on, the book burdens Lindau with a language that no reader of the book enjoys or wants to quote at length. This is an issue I am not aware of Bakhtin's ever addressing in his theory of heteroglossia; in praising and elevating the novel as the underdog genre, Bakhtin leaves some novels out. For Bakhtin, the clash of languages from different social positions should be orchestrated into a higher-level structure, but what if a part refuses to symphonize?

This same problem of language representation besets the other main critic of capitalism in *A Hazard of New Fortunes*, the southern reactionary Colonel Woodburn, who comes with his daughter from Virginia to New York and writes thought pieces for the journal. Howells is more distant from this character's views, but they are recognizable as romantic anticapitalism. I won't quote anything from this character, because the language is both phonologically painstaking and yet unrewarding. This aesthetic shortcoming is anomalous within US literary history. As opposed to the English of German speakers, for which the traditions were at best grotesque, Southern speech had many examples of aesthetically pleasurable crafting, not only in a rich comic corpus, but also in the lyrical portions of *Huckleberry Finn* and at moments in Cable's *Grandissimes*. The reviews of *A Hazard of New Fortunes* cited this failure of Virginia speech. The *Nation* found that "the author's weakness in dialect" called into question "his right to be called an American novelist."[26]

Critics have developed important arguments concerning the compromises of the classical realism that Howells practiced and promulgated as its leading American exponent. Realism contains social struggle in a double sense: it includes it by holding it within bounds. I find a striking instance of this problem in the scene that leads to the first meeting with Lindau. Fulkerson, the culture entrepreneur who brings March to New York, is a Westerner (from what we now call the Midwest) and speaks a language that is at moments more like Mark Twain than anything else in this novel. He tells March about the natural gas fields that provide the wealth for Dryfoos, the financial sponsor of the new journal.

Fulkerson found the boom town exciting not only economically but also morally: "They made up their minds . . . that if they wanted their town to grow they'd got to keep their gas public property. . . . The city took possession of every well that was put down, and held it for the common good. . . . It's a grand sight to see a whole community hanging together and working for the good of all, instead of splitting up into as many different cutthroats as there are able-bodied

---

26. "Mr. Howells's Latest Novel," *Nation* 50 (June 5, 1890): 454. See also "New York in Recent Fiction," *Atlantic Monthly* 65 (April, 1890): 566, which criticizes the "raw" phonetic rendering of Virginia speech: "we would rather have it boiled like that of other human beings."

citizens" (72). But just at this moment, Fulkerson "broke off" and "indicated with a twirl of his head a short, dark, foreign-looking man." He explains: "they say that fellow's a socialist. I think it's a shame they're allowed to come here. . . . They do a lot of mischief shooting off their mouths around here. I believe in free speech and all that, but I'd like to see these fellows shut up in jail and left to jaw each other to death" (72). The book's most voluble talker cannot abide foreigners shooting off their mouths, and this American booster cannot recognize any affinity to socialism in the community property scheme he has just been praising. Socialism, Howells shows but does not say, is Americanism, but there's a problem of communication. And this is the moment in the novel that March first sees Lindau, without yet recognizing him.

We know the many ways realists pull punches, both formally and thematically, to allow works to be published, sold, and read within the very cultures and societies that they are also hoping — or is it only purporting? — to challenge and even to change. It seems that making Lindau's speech inaccessible is one of those ways.[27] Yet evidence from the reviews of *A Hazard of New Fortunes* suggests otherwise, to the surprise of twenty-first century readers. We are used to finding ourselves more socially open-minded than was the nineteenth century, and we are startled to find the opposite true. The several reviewers who mentioned Lindau did so favorably. The *Atlantic* contrasted the failed Virginia speech to Howells's "successful . . . conveyance of Lindau's German-silver English."[28] The *Catholic World* judged that Howells presented Lindau's "sentiments and . . . actions as well as his accent with consummate skill," and it concluded its three-page review by quoting for a full page from a conversation in which Lindau is the major speaker.[29] Even in an adversarial role, realist writers may be so much a part of their own time that their work no longer speaks to the future as powerfully as it does to its own moment, as we witness in our lost capacity to enjoy Lindau.

I still believe in the value of realism — as an impulse motivating fiction, not as a period-limited set of devices. Therefore, I open a different line of speculation, which I find more hopeful. This speculation is more hopeful because it attributes hope to Howells himself. I venture that Howells's aesthetic failure in the language of these characters arises from his belief that American literary English was rapidly

---

27. Let me suggest a strong tendency within recent critical discussion by citing one critic favorably quoting another: Arthur F. Redding quotes Robert Shulman: "Howells uses dialect to disguise Lindau's ideas and distance himself from these opinions he is himself attracted to." See Redding, *Raids on Human Consciousness: Writing, Anarchism, and Violence* (Columbia: Univ. of South Carolina Press, 1998), 93; Robert Shulman, *Social Criticism and Nineteenth-Century American Fiction* (Columbia: Univ. of Missouri Press, 1987), 246.
28. "New York in Recent Fiction," 566. German silver is an alloy of copper, zinc, and nickel and therefore makes quite a good nonbiological term for what is often now called hybridity.
29. "Talk about New Books," *Catholic World* 51 (April, 1890): 120.

changing in ways that would make such speech more, not less, pleasurable in the future. Consider, for evidence, this formulation from an 1895 essay: "A very pretty argument could be made to prove that the tendency of the English spoken among us is towards heterogeneity, rather than homogeneity."[30]

Henry James shared this recognition, though with far more negative affect. Returning to the US after more than twenty years away, James encountered on the Lower East Side what he found an "all-unconscious impudence of the agency of future ravage," which challenged "our language as literature has hitherto known it."[31] James did not fear decline but rather change and loss: "The accent of the very ultimate future, in the States, may be destined to become the most beautiful on the globe and the very music of humanity . . . but whatever we shall know it for, certainly, we shall not know it for English."

Howells worked actively to further that heterogeneity. In the years after *A Hazard of New Fortunes*, Howells took a leading role in bringing to the attention of publishers and readers work produced in varieties of English far from the standard literary language of the time. He supported the careers of the major Yiddish-American writer Abraham Cahan, the dialect writings of the African Americans Paul Laurence Dunbar and Charles W. Chesnutt, and writing by Stephen Crane that represented the language of the New York streets among the underclass of native-born Americans.[32] The new immigration, of which Cahan was a leading instance; the growing place of African Americans in the public world even as the system of Jim Crow racial segregation was also being set in place, these developments Howells understood as changing the United States to important effect that nonetheless produced awkwardness and incomprehension.

---

30. From an 1895 *Harper's Weekly* essay, "Dialect in Literature," in W.D. Howells, vol. 2 of *Selected Literary Criticism* (1886–1897), eds. Donald Pizer et al. (Bloomington: Indiana University Press, 1993). Vol. 21 of Selected edition of W.D. Howells, 223. The recent *Weird English* by Evelyn Nien-Ming Ch'ien (Cambridge: Harvard University Press, 2004) begins to make good on Howells's prophecy with an important difference: she focuses on American English literary writing in which not just the speech of *characters* but the narrative discourse itself is deeply marked by the trace of another language (in the cases she studies, especially Chinese and Spanish).

31. Henry James, *The American Scene* (New York: Harper, 1907), 134; the following quotation comes from p. 135.

32. See the 1896 essays "New York Low Life" and "Paul Laurence Dunbar" in vol. 2 of *Selected Literary Criticism*, 274–81; and from 1900, "Mr. Charles W. Chesnutt's Stories" in *W.D. Howells as Critic*, ed. Edwin H. Cady (London: Routledge, 1973), 295–98. In his critique of Barrett Wendell's *History of American Literature*, Howells emphasized Wendell's total omission of Southern dialect writers Joel Chandler Harris (whose Uncle Remus tales achieved "absolute novelty") and George Washington Cable (whose *Grandissimes* was "one of the few American fictions which may be called great"). See W.D. Howells, vol. 3 of *Selected Literary Criticism* (1898–1920), ed. Ronald Gottesman (Bloomington: Indiana University Press, 1993). Vol. 30 of Selected edition of W.D. Howells, 57.

Howells has never struck posterity as a genius, despite his remarkable career. He rose from Midwestern rural obscurity to a central place in the culture of his time, editing the *Atlantic Monthly* for a decade (1871-80) and then writing a featured editorial column in *Harper's* for nearly thirty years (1886-92; 1900-20). He produced a shelf of novels, three or four of which are sometimes taught. Perhaps the only sign of genius was his capacity while they were all still struggling young writers to discern in such wholly different figures as Mark Twain and Henry James the great authors of his generation. He not only made lifelong intimate friends of both; he also importantly furthered both careers.

Twain and James in turn admired him. Twain found *A Hazard of New Fortunes* a "great book," especially for "the high art by which it is made to preach its great sermon without seeming to take sides or preach at all."[33] William James too called it a "great book" and praised it for "the number of characters, each intensely individual, the observation of detail, the everlasting wit and humor, and beneath it all the bass accompaniment of the human problem, the entire Americanness of it."[34] Henry James read this "prodigious" book with a "rapture" that led him to write several pages about it. Contrasting the subject matter of New York with those subjects he felt himself moved by, James urged Howells to "Go on, go on, even if *I* can't — and since New York has brought you such *bonheur* give it back to her with still larger liberality. Don't tell me that . . . life isn't luxurious to you with such a power of creation. You live in a luxury [of creativity] that Lindau would reprehend . . . and that I am not sure even poor March would be altogether easy about."[35] James links himself and Howells as enjoying the artist's "luxury," against the asceticism shared by Howells's characters.

Howells's example may offer some hope to us who read or teach literature in the United States. He was no genius, but he worked hard to achieve cosmopolitanism at home. It is easier to be cosmopolitan as an American abroad; unlike James, Howells did not expatriate himself. In a review, Howells explains that he had always been blocked by the Hebraic script of Yiddish, but once he read the volume he was reviewing, which put the Yiddish in German Fraktur script as well as providing translations, he saw at once that it was not very different from the German spoken by long-settled Pennsylvania religious communities.[36] What a mentsh. Like Edmund Wilson in the earlier and mid-twentieth century, but like hardly anyone since, Howells reached a wide middlebrow readership with his

---

33. Letter of 11 February, 1890, in vol. 2 of *Mark Twain-Howells Letters: The Correspondence of Samuel L. Clemens and William D. Howells, 1872–1910*, 2 vols., eds. Henry Nash Smith and William M. Gibson (Cambridge: Harvard University Press, 1960), 630.

34. Letter of 20 August 1890, in vol. 1 of *The Letters of William James*, ed. [by his son] Henry James (Boston: Atlantic Monthly Press, 1920), 298.

35. Vol. 3 of *Henry James Letters*, ed. Leon Edel (Cambridge: Harvard University Press, 1980), 283.

36. See the review of Morris Rosenfeld's Yiddish poetry in W.D. Howells, vol. 3 of *Selected Literary Criticism*, 3 vols. (Bloomington: Indiana University Press, 1993), 7.

reviews of current literature, not yet translated into English, written in French, German, Italian, and Spanish.

III

Howells bet wrong. The United States did not grow more polyglot and cosmopolitan. The rise of the US to world power through World War I shut more doors than it opened. As part of war mobilization, German went from being the language most known and studied after English to being prohibited in the schools of many states and locales.[37] After the 1917 revolution that overthrew the Russian Empire, government agencies snooped and harassed all foreign-language publication.[38] Most crucially, in 1924 decades of racist arguments on behalf of purifying the people and culture of the US, arguments that won their first victory in the 1880s by targeting Chinese immigration, succeeded in imposing restrictions that drastically reduced all immigration, especially from southern and eastern Europe. Just when Hitler's policies made refuge abroad urgently imperative for the lives of millions, the US had closed itself to refugees.

It is a stupefying fact that the long presidency of Franklin D. Roosevelt is the absolute nadir of immigration to the United States. In 1932, the number of immigrants admitted was the lowest in over a century — since 1831. The period 1932 to 1945 admitted about the same number as the counterpart period a century earlier, a total of 602,244 for these fourteen years, in contrast to over 10 million for the peak decade of 1905-1914. The Roosevelt era total allowed less than half the number admitted in the single peak year of 1907 (1,285,349), a peak that even a century later now stands as the historically highest.[39] As a result of immigration restriction, the percentage of foreign-born Americans registered by the census dropped from 13.1% in 1920 to 6.9% in 1950, bottoming at 5% in the mid-60s. We still need to rethink the 1960s from this perspective, as the moment of American history with the greatest predominance of native-born population. There is a huge story to tell, of which the following observation is only an iceberg tip: Not until 1965, in harmony with the Civil Rights movement,

---

37. See Marc Shell, "Hyphens: Between Deitsch and America," in *Multilingual America: Transnationalism, Ethnicity, and the Languages of American Literature*, ed. Werner Sollors (New York: New York University Press, 1998), 259 (citing William Beer and James E. Jacobs, eds., *Language Policy and National Unity* [1985]).

38. See the invaluable "Ethnic Modernism," by Werner Sollors, in vol. 6 of *Cambridge History of American Literature: Prose Writing, 1910–1950*, ed. Sacvan Bercovitch, 8 vols. (Cambridge [England]: Cambridge University Press, 1994–), 389.

39. I take these figures from the table of immigration year by year, drawn from *Historical Statistics of the United States*, in Richard B. Morris, ed. *Encyclopedia of American History* (New York: Harper, 1976), 654. The period and decade summations are my arithmetic.

did 'national origin' cease to define who could enter the US.[40] This change opened the way to the new non-European immigration of the later twentieth century and beyond. We now appreciate contemporary "weird English," but we have not recovered the diverse Englishes of the nineteenth century.

Restricting immigration transformed the position of those who had already reached the US from Ireland, Germany, and southern and eastern Europe. With very few more coming to join them, the opportunities and necessity for Americanizing assimilation grew together. The monolingualization that produced the self-understanding of contemporary America dates from this period,[41] and immigrant dialect was cleaned up in the succeeding generation. This is a great success story. It transformed America's aggressively Protestant national self-understanding: By the 1950s Catholic, Protestant, and Jew could be represented all as co-equally American. But the success has limits that we now feel very strongly. We await the process by which Islam will be included in such an understanding, and our current arguments concerning bilingual education are direct inheritances from the debates and decisions that have combined to make Howells's characters' languages more ugly and tedious to us than they were to readers in 1890.[42] It is remarkable that Twain and James, each in his own way so finicky about language, expressed no problem with Lindau.

I wish to read Howells's dialect more hopefully, as ugly prose produced by a hope for the future. Fredric Jameson has argued repeatedly that utopian writing is not fun to read. Utopian writing tries to bring us toward a world radically different from the one we know and that has formed our sensibilities. As a result

---

40. For the current state of work on these connections, see Matthew Frye Jacobson, *Whiteness of a Different Color: European Immigrants and the Alchemy of Race* (Cambridge: Harvard University Press, 1998), as well as his more recent book on the more recent period, *Roots Too: White Ethnic Revival in Post-Civil Rights America* (Cambridge: Harvard University Press, 2006). Even so ambitious and important a synthesis as Gary Gerstle, *American Crucible: Race and Nation in the Twentieth Century* (Princeton: Princeton University Press, 2001), which has a great deal to say about the movement toward the immigration restriction of the 1920s, in its chapter on the 1960s speaks only to the civil rights movement and does not at all discuss the transformation in 1965 of immigration law or, in later chapters, its consequences.

41. The dominance of English is a longstanding tendency within US history, and it will require more research concerning, for instance, the numbers and circulation of newspapers in languages other than English to confirm the hunch I offer in this sentence. I do not mean by this claim that had large immigration continued, immigrants would not have learned to speak English, but I do think that the loss of what we now call heritage languages would have been much diminished, and the result would have been a far greater heterogenization within American English.

42. For the conjunction marked in this sentence, compare Aristide R. Zolberg and Long Litt Woon, "Why Islam Is Like Spanish: Cultural Incorporation in Europe and the United States," *Politics and Society* 27, no.1 (1999): 5–38. Writing before 9/11, they are more positive about the reception of Islam in the United States than I think later developments can sustain.

utopian writing may seem barbaric, off-scale, or even just boring.[43] Howells in his next major novel wrote a full-scale utopia, *A Traveler from Altruria* (1894). In *A Hazard of New Fortunes* I find a small utopia in Howells's anti-capitalist social critics who speak languages that baffle our eyes and jar our ears even as they open our minds by affirming different social principles. Howells, it seems, imagined that if Americans could understand the language of the immigrant as the language they spoke also, so Americans might also recognize his radical ideas as already theirs in a different accent.

The German-Jewish critic Walter Benjamin failed in his migration to New York; he killed himself when blocked at the Spanish border. In his "Theses on the Philosophy of History," Benjamin defines the redemptive task of a properly materialist history.[44] If we cannot "brush history against the grain," then "*even the dead* will not be safe."

Benjamin had in mind anonymous slaves, victims, and workers. Taking Benjamin's perspective allows us to see through an authoritative scholarly tabulation of "National or Linguistic Stocks in the U.S. 1790," drawn from the U.S. Census.[45] It lists English, Scotch, Irish, German, Dutch, French, Swedish, and Spanish. We recognize that it omits all mention of African Americans, who in 1790 made up about one-quarter of the population of the US, and who were carefully censused because even when enslaved their numbers counted for congressional allocation. Moreover, recent scholarship on the forms of racism in the modernist period makes it unsurprising that the computations on which this table relies were done in 1931.[46]

In the light of such scholarship, we may recall a famous characterization of Germanic English speech in *The Great Gatsby*.[47] Gatsby's patron Meyer Wolfsheim

---

43. This is my brief take on much hard thought by Jameson, including his 1977 essay on Louis Marin's *Utopiques*, "Of Islands and Trenches: Neutralization and the Production of Utopian Discourse," in vol. 2 of *The Ideologies of Theory: Essays, 1971–1986: The Syntax of History*, 2 vols. (Minneapolis: University of Minnesota Press, c1988), 75–101; the chapter on Andrei Platonov's *Chevengur* in *The Seeds of Time* (New York: Columbia University Press, 1994), 73–128; and much in *Archaeologies of the Future: The Desire Called Utopia and Other Science Fictions* (London: Verso, 2005), for example, xiii–xvii.

44. Walter Benjamin, *Illuminations* (1968), ed. Hannah Arendt, trans. Harry Zohn (New York: Schocken, 1969). Quotations in this paragraph come from pp. 257, 255, 254. See also Zohn's revised translation, "On the Concept of History," in Walter Benjamin, vol. 4 of *Selected Writings*, 4 vols., ed. Michael Jennings (Cambridge: Harvard University Press, 2003), 392, 391, 390. In the instances cited, the two versions are identical.

45. Morris, *Encyclopedia*, 653, based on analysis produced by the American Historical Association.

46. See Toni Morrison, *Playing in the Dark* (1992), Michael North, *The Dialect of Modernism* (1994), Walter Benn Michaels, *Our America* (1995).

47. F. Scott Fitzgerald, *The Great Gatsby* (1925; New York, Scribner, 2004). Quotations in this paragraph from 70, 71, 69.

is said to have done what in real life the Jewish gangster Arnold Rothstein did — fixed the 1919 World Series. Wolfsheim speaks at moments in the idiom of Damon Runyon's characters (Wolfsheim is a "denizen of Broadway," according to Gatsby; Rothstein was also a model for Runyon's Nathan Detroit), but the mark of Germanic sound-patterns in his speech is inscribed far more economically than in Howells, through a single key sound inserted in two key words. Wolfsheim asks if Nick Carraway is "looking for a business gonnegtion" and then observes that Gatsby "went to Oggsford College in England." (What to make of the *gg*, monogramming the book's title?) Nick Carraway has no truck with the eugenicist racist rant of Tom Buchanan (based on real-life books from Fitzgerald's own publisher Scribner),[48] but Nick's brilliant physical rendering of Wolfsheim is also disgusting: "A small, flat-nosed Jew raised his large head and regarded me with two fine growths of hair which luxuriated in either nostril. After a moment, I discovered his tiny eyes in the half darkness." This is the writer whose prose students love, as I have found in my teaching, even graduate students who themselves come from populations that the 1924 immigration laws hoped to excise from American life. The process of aesthetic nationalization has worked itself deeply into those who care for the literature of the United States, and its undoing can seem strange and painful. My goal, I should make clear, is not reversal but indeed undoing — not new hate but new love.

Benjamin's redemptive mission was directed toward anonymous toilers, not institutionally established cultural figures such as Howells became, but I think the point holds. If Benjamin's messianism seeks that the "past become citable in all its moments," then we must hope for a day when Howells's dialect writing no longer seems too awful to quote. While H.L. Mencken, Sinclair Lewis, and others mocked the defunct "dean" of American letters, treating Howells's death as liberation from Victorian sissification, it was not pure gain to get Wolfsheim for Lindau.[49]

In a visionary spirit comparable to Benjamin's, Northrop Frye argued that the goal of literary knowledge is not to establish a small canon of the very best, but just the opposite: the better reader one is, the closer one approaches the

---

48. For instance, Madison Grant, *The Passing of the Great Race* (1918); Lothrop Stoddard, *The Rising Tide of Color against White World-Supremacy* (1923)

49. See H.L. Mencken, "The Dean" (1919) and Sinclair Lewis's Nobel Prize address, "The American Fear of Literature" (1930), both in *The War of the Critics over William Dean Howells,* eds. Edwin H. Cady and David L. Frazier (Evanston, Il.: Row, Peterson, 1962). Lewis seems to me simply wrong in asserting that Howells "had the code of a pious old maid whose greatest delight is to have tea at the vicarage" (153). Mencken's lead sentence opens an immense and still compelling problematic: "Americans, obsessed by problems of conduct, usually judge their authors, not as artists, but as citizens" (127), but he appeals less when downgrading Howells for being "unequal to any such evocation of the race-spirit" (128) as Mencken finds in Norris or Dreiser.

utopian goal of an "undiscriminating catholicity," in which the imaginative energy in every product of the human mind may be felt and honored.[50] This would be the literary counterpart to a radical democracy in politics, an equality in material goods, and a far wider distribution of opportunities for happiness. I invoke such a project in the name of so ungainly a figure as Howells because the degree of dismissive uninterest we feel for Howells measures our own incapacity to believe in what we do. Our forces as teachers, as readers, as citizens are not strengthened by self-contempt.

---

50. Northrop Frye, *Anatomy of Criticism* (Princeton: Princeton University Press, 1957), 25. According to a younger colleague, Frye "tended to find his fellow-professors ... hide-bound by their hierarchical concept of their discipline which included not only ranking the students, but also ranking the excellence of the authors they taught, and indeed, a snobbish tendency to rank each other according to the degree of 'taste' they displayed." See Germaine Warkentin's introduction to *"The Educated Imagination" and Other Writings on Critical Theory 1933–63* (Toronto: Univ. of Toronto Press, 2006). Vol. 21 of *Collected Works of Northrop Frye*, xxiv–xxv.

Dreaming about the Singularity of the New Middle Ages: Three Provisional Notes on the Question of Imagination

R.A. Judy

> The knowledge which respecteth the faculties of the mind of man is of two kinds; the one respecting his understanding and reason, and the other his will, appetite, and affection; whereof the former produceth position or decree, the latter action or execution. It is true that the imagination is an agent or *nuncius*, in both provinces, both the judicial and the ministerial.*
>
> ο φαντασμα της κοιϖης αισθησεως παθος εστιν **

Is it seriously possible to imagine the world order today, and if so what would it mean to do so? Taken together, the following three provisional notes draw a particular line of inquiry from this question of imagination. The notes are largely expository and aim at exploring the value of imagination in two fields of analysis and speculation — futurist technology theory and international security studies — whose formations are concomitants of the new global information-technology society. The centrality of the technology question in both these fields, which are otherwise radically distinct from one another in conceptual range and methodology, accounts for their having a remarkable degree of topical and even conceptual commonality. The particular commonality concerning this notational

---

* Francis Bacon, *The Advancement of Learning*, ed. William Aldis Wright (Oxford: Clarendon Press, 957) 147.

* * "The image is an affection of the common sense." Aristotle, *De Memoria* 450a, 10–12.

exposition is how both fields seem capable of imagining the present world only as an *integumentum* veiling the underlying dynamics of either an emerging world of technological emancipation, which futurist technology theory designates "the Singularity," or one of resurging barbarities, which international security studies designates as "new medievalism" or "neomedievalism." By acknowledging the ubiquity of the global information-technology society — indeed, making it a principal premise of their respective analyses and speculations — but failing to contemplate the immanence of its events, the methodologies of both fields exhibit an interregnum in thinking, tending to value imagination only where information and intelligence seem inadequate. This disjunction between imagination, information, and intelligence rankles in an era of global information-technology when what is called for is a better understanding of how they interact dynamically, as well as how they have interacted historically. Pursuing such an understanding requires leaving off from Bacon's early modern conception of imagination as *nuncio*.

Note 1: The singularity

The term *singularity* has a nearly identical range in three of today's domains of knowledge. Two of these, mathematics and astrophysics, are established scientific domains with recognized canonical procedures for speculation, making and verifying postulates, as well as establishing facts. In mathematics, a singularity is a point at which a function takes an infinite value. That is a point at which a given mathematical object — meaning a number, function, set, or some sort of space — is no longer "well-behaved." Well-behaved is a mathematics term of art, designating objects that do not violate any assumptions needed to successfully apply whatever analysis is being discussed. The well-behaved object is provable and analyzable to have elegant properties by known elegant means. It is not uncommon in differential calculus, as well as computer science, to refer to not well-behaved objects as pathological. Perhaps the most widely known sense of singularity, however, comes from the domain of astrophysics where a singularity, which is properly understood to be spatial, designates the event in our universe when matter is compressed to infinitely small proportions (a mathematical point) to the extent that gravitational force causes space-time to fold in on itself. Such events are called black holes in popular culture. More precisely, the singularity constitutes the center of a black hole and is made unobservable by the hole's surface. That surface, or "event horizon," is a spherical area whose radius is called the Schwarzschild radius and within which the geometry of space-time profoundly changes. A considerably less than rigorous version of the astrophysics concept of singularity has become a popular commonplace in nearly every corner of the globe, not through the systematic dissemination of education and learning in the professional field of astrophysics, but through the global distribution of such popular television programming as the Star Trek franchise, and numerous commercial films of the space opera science fiction variety. In large measure, this is a factor of a truly planetary system of telecommunications having been realized during the last half of the twentieth century, through which even the most abstract ideas can become commonplace worldwide in a relatively short amount of time; a fact that raises an interesting issue. Does the realization of a public, largely commercial, global telecommunications and information system herald a monumental change in the history of the species, fostering an unprecedented world social order? If it does, then what are the characteristics and protocols of that global society?

A well-known early exponent of such a linkage between the planetary information technology economy and social order was Marshall McLuhan, whose description of the emergent global village from his 1962 book, *The Gutenberg Galaxy*, is often cited as the paradigmatic explanation of how the new information technology is engendering a transformation in human social formations as well as thinking.[1] Besides McLuhan, others, like the mathematician, John Von Neumann, whose work in logical design directly contributed to developments in computer technology that have been a major factor in the advent of the new information technology, also began to speculate about its broad sociological effects. Von Neumann's speculations have played a crucial role in inaugurating a third concept of singularity sometimes called "technological singularity," but generally referred to as "the Singularity." Coinage of neither of these terms is attributed to Von Neumann, but he is credited with introducing the general idea of a technological singularity through his friend and fellow mathematician, Stanislaw Ulam, a figure of considerable distinction himself, having worked with Von Neumann on the Manhattan Project. Reporting on speculative conversations the two mathematicians had during the early years after World War II, Ulam is supposed to have stated in 1958: "One conversation centered on the ever accelerating progress of technology and changes in the mode of human life, which gives the appearance of approaching some essential singularity in the history of the race beyond which human affairs, as we know them, could not continue."[2] This idea subsequently found more public expression in a 1965 article published by the statistician, I.J. Good, in which he predicted an "intelligence explosion" following the creation of the first artificial mind more intelligent than a human's.[3] Good attested that an artificial mind in possession of a formal description of itself would be capable of incremental and additive self-improvements in its own intelligence *ad infinitum*. Another important contribution to the early

---

1. Marshall McLuhan, *The Gutenberg Galaxy: The Making of Typographic Man* (Toronto: University of Toronto Press, 1962). Henceforth cited as *GG*.
2. Stanislaw Ulam, "Tribute to John von Neumann," *Bulletin of the American Mathematical Society* 64, no. 3, May 1958.
3. Irving John Good, "Speculations Concerning the First Ultraintelligent Machine," *Advances in Computers 6* (New York: Academic Press, 1965), 31–88.

development of the technological singularity concept also published in 1965 was Gordon E. Moore's essay, "Cramming More Components onto Integrated Circuits," where he conjectures that the number of transistors fit onto an integrated circuit will double every two years as the cost to produce such chips halves. Following Carver Mead's coinage, that conjecture has become most widely known as Moore's Law.[4] Elaborating on the speculations of Von Neumann, Good, and Moore, the mathematician Vernor Vinge introduced the term "the Singularity" in his 1993 *Whole Earth Review* essay, "The Coming Technological Singularity: How to Survive in the Post-Human Era."[5] Vinge's essay — which was an extended version of the paper he presented at the Vision 21 Symposium sponsored by NASA Lewis Research Center and the Ohio Aerospace Institute in March of that same year — inaugurated a debate about the proximity of this future event that now dominates what is arguably a radically speculative subfield of artificial intelligence theory commonly referred to as futurist technology theory.

Not properly a domain of science in the sense that mathematics and astrophysics are, futurist technology theory is nevertheless a field of knowledge and intellectual activity that has attracted some attention in the more seriously regarded fields of cognitive science, philosophies of mind and technology, and even international security studies. Like that of astrophysics, the concept of technological singularity has also had considerable representation in popular culture in film and the subgenre of science fiction called cyberpunk. As a category of speculative analysis, the Singularity designates a paradigm shift in the way human consciousness is materially manifested — specifically, the shift from the biological to the bioengineered, or cybernetic manifestation of consciousness. A corollary issue is the effect on human civilization in terms of social and political configurations. Given futurist technology theory's sharing with the field of cognitive science John Von Neumann as one of its conceptual progenitors, it is not at all unexpected that the most theoretically ambitious attempts at explaining how the Singularity will mark the shift and its corollary issues have as their underlying problematic theories of the emergence and nature of consciousness. A much discussed exemplary instance of this is Ray Kurzweil's recent elaboration on Moore's Law, as well as the ideas of Good and Ulam, to formulate what he calls the Law of Accelerating Returns; the basic principles of which are meant to describe the relationship between technological development, biological evolution, and sociological configuration.[6] In setting out those principles Kurzweil

---

4. Gordon E. Moore, "Cramming More Components Onto Integrated Circuits," *Electronics* 38, April 19, 1965.

5. Vernor Vinge, "The Coming Technological Singularity: How to Survive in the Post-Human Era," *Whole Earth Review* (Winter 1993).

6. Ray Kurzweil, "The Law of Accelerating Returns." [Available online] [March 7, 2001] Available from http://www.kurzweilai.net/meme/frame.html?main=/articles/art0134.html, published on KurzweilAI.net on. Henceforth cited as LAR.

proceeds from two unproven, and perhaps even un-testable, postulates. One is explicitly stated as the first principle of his law; it is that teleological evolutionary development involves positive feedback, such that every change in a species of life is a solution to the perpetual problem of survival, and every successful solution increases exponentially not just the capacity for future change but also the rate change occurs. The second postulate is implicit in the overall formulation of the principles; it is that the problem of survival is posed to intelligence, such that each solution a species of life achieves is tantamount to a particular material actualization of intelligence in the world. When describing stages in biological evolution, then, we are describing changes in the modality of intelligence's solution to the problem of survival. Kurzweil calls these modalities "paradigms," and he means by intelligence what are called "mental states" in cognitive science and the philosophy of mind. A fundamental issue at stake for Kurzweil in mapping the changing paradigms of intelligence throughout the history of life is what makes something a mental state of a particular type: self-conscious intelligence, or what is more simply and commonly called consciousness.

Kurzweil's Law of Accelerating Returns is predicated on a non-reductive physicalism that pointedly rejects mind-brain identity theory, or type-type physicalism — that is, the view that each and every mental state associated with consciousness is necessarily identified with a specific neural state peculiar to the human brain such that the type of consciousness called human is peculiar and unique to the biological hominid, homo sapiens. In this non-reductive physicalism, Kurzweil adheres to Hilary Putnam's early formulation of (Turing) machine-state functionalism, which holds that the kinds of psychological functions associated with the human brain are identical to the kinds of computational functions of a suitably programmed universal Turing machine (the Singularity). Kurzweil does not deny that what makes human beings as they are involves the body; the biological brain is significant in the Law of Accelerating Returns as a particular physical state in which the particular system of mental states we call consciousness has been manifest. But this, he claims, is a matter of historical, and even political, rather than essential significance.[7] Even then, the material manifestation of the relationship between consciousness and brain has always been technological. When it comes to the question of whether consciousness is fungible, Kurzweil's theory of the Singularity works according to Putnam's idea that *all* mental states are multiply realizable by distinct physical kinds. The propositional formulation of this idea, universally known as the multiple realizability theorem, is: "psychological states are compositionally plastic." Once mental states are described in terms of the role they play in a system, then the system manifest with one type of entity (the biological hominid) could very well be psychologically isomorphic

---

7. LAR.

to a system manifest with another type of entity (a Turing machine) irrespective of differences in physical state.[8]

Viewed according to the neo-Darwinist theory of evolutionary change Kurzweil employs, there is a complex, albeit accidental, relationship between psychological states in a functional system and changing physical states. Consciousness is an effect of the biological hominid as a specific paradigm or method for solving the problem of species survival. The predominate modality of the hominid paradigm is technology such that technology is the "media" by which human consciousness is materially manifested in relation to, but externally from the biological organism. It needs to be borne in mind that the sense of technology at play here is Aristotelian, so that the relationship between conscious intelligence as a dynamic evolving functional system, its material actualization in tools — the latter are otherwise known as "technologies of media" — and the social order of life is irreducible as well as indissoluble. The evolution of technology is the material index of how conscious intelligence is changing the order of human life. Changes in technology, thus, describe the complex relationship between psychological states in an evolving functional system and changing physical states. Kurzweil is not just postulating that technology is a function of biological evolution, however. He is asserting that biological evolution works according to Moore's Law. Because the rate of development of the biological paradigm reflects the exponential rate of technological development the point of paradigm shift will entail the technological forms of intelligence superceding the biological. The Singularity designates the point of this shift when intelligence in life will no longer rely on the wholly biological for its expression, achieving what Kurzweil describes as "technological change so rapid and so profound that it represents a rupture in the fabric of human history."[9]

All of this is quite in keeping with the historical etymology of the word singularity in English (c.f. OED). After all, there is a strong similarity to what the term connotes across the domains of mathematics, astrophysics, and futurist technology theory that really has to do with the extensive range of the mathematical sense of the term. Each domain shares the underlying mathematical sense of singularity as precisely the point at which dominant modes of knowledge fail to work. This perturbance in knowledge is further exacerbated by the fact that the unknowable is representable, as such, but not quite thinkable in the terms of representation. For instance, regarding astrophysics, while we currently possess strong observational evidence for the existence of spatial singularities, the best our most elegant mathematical models can represent are the properties of mass collapsing before imploding into infinity. There are presently no theories capable

---

8. Hilary Putnam, "Functionalism; Cognitive Science or Science Fiction?" in *The Future of the Cognitive Revolution*, eds., David Martel Johnson and Christian E. Erneling (Oxford: Oxford University Press, 1997), 32–44.

9. LAR.

of modeling precisely how a singularity originates or exactly what occurs within the event horizon. We might well say that under such conditions there occurs a profound dissonance between what is imaginable and what can be known. A preeminently common feature of singularity's range as a figure of explanation in all three orders of knowledge, then, is its designating a distinction, or point of departure from the customary understanding of things at which our thinking imagines the relations of parts to the development of the whole, raising the perceived and comprehended details of things to the level of the universal.[10]

Kurzweil's Law of Accelerating Returns is particularly illustrative of this with its overt investment in describing the emergence and nature of consciousness in terms of a functional system that is not determined by any essential object. For instance, his postulating that while the hominid brain is a sufficient condition for the material manifestation of intelligence, it is not absolutely necessary, and even though changes in the physical states with which intelligence is manifest enhance its chances for sustained survival, achieving those states is not its purpose. The implication is that intelligence achieves the human, energizing the plasticity of the organic brain in the activity of abstraction. The force of that activity, however much it is *associated with* the brain, *originates* with intelligence; and its creative agency is traceable in the material record of technological change. Were we to use the phraseology of an older psychology, we might well call this activity "creative imagination" in a quasi Neo-Platonist sense, and take the Singularity to designate the theoretical point at which the activity of creative imagination becomes fully externalized in technology.

The centrality of this sense of a fully externalized technological creative imagination to Kurzweil's argument for the Singularity's advent is perhaps no more evident than in his reverse engineering the human brain thought experiment. Evaluating recent projects in neural computing that he thinks have satisfactorily demonstrated the analogy between the human brain and computer, along with current trends in nanotechnology and biotechnology — specifically positron emission tomography (PET) and functional magnetic resonance imaging (fMRI) that hold forth the prospect of complete high resolution modeling of the human brain and its neural functions — Kurzweil predicts it will soon be possible to reverse engineer the human brain.[11] His thought experiment focuses on two of the scenarios conceivably possible based on the knowledge gained from such reverse engineering. In one scenario, all the relevant physical details, all the neurons and neural activity down to the molecular level of a specific person — the provided hypothetical case is Ray Kurzweil — are scanned using PET and fMRI

---

10. Michael Wedin, *Mind and Imagination in Aristotle* (Hartford: Yale University Press, 1988), 23–63.

11. Regarding this, Kurzweil makes reference to his own work and that of Carver Mead, but strong evidence in support of his claim is also found with Stephen Thaler's so-called "imagination engines."

technologies. Once the resulting massive database of information is "reinstantiated into a neural computer of sufficient capacity, the person who then emerges in the machine will think that 'he' is (and had been) [Ray], or at least he will act that way."[12] In the second scenario, the same information technologies are used; but instead of being downloaded onto a neural computer, the resulting information is used to model nanobot replacements of specific molecular functions. These nanobots then incrementally replace the biological microstructures, progressively constituting a completely, or nearly completely mechanical body, whose macro-physical qualities (its overall physical appearance) will be indistinguishable from the original biological one. Kurzweil's speculations about the Singularity are highly controversial, with even a relatively generous critic like the cognitive scientist Douglas R. Hofstadter considering them wild. Moreover, there are arguable flaws of logic and significant gaps of information in the overall exposition of the Laws of Accelerating Returns that are pronouncedly highlighted in the thought experiment. Both the controversy and the experiment's flaws are beyond the province of this note, which has to do with the way his speculations about the Singularity touch upon the question of imagination in relation to that of human consciousness. In this respect, the aspect of Kurzweil's Law of Accelerating Returns that is most pertinent is his approaching the question of consciousness in terms of personal identity, and how that inclines him to presume the activity of creative imagination will soon become fully externalized in technology.

Both of the thought experiment's hypothetical scenarios seem to embrace a strong supervenience theory of the sort championed by Jaegwon Kim, according to which a supervenient is deducible from the properties of an object's parts. There are two levels of supervenience in the thought experiment. At the first level, the body as a macro-physical object is supervenient to an extremely fluid subvening microstructure at which the actual material content of our bodies is changing constantly and very quickly. In the language of the experiment: "The cells in our bodies turn over at different rates, but the particles (e.g., atoms and molecules) that comprise our cells are exchanged at a very rapid rate."[13] So that any given body is not the same collection of particles it was a month ago. There are, however, what Kurzweil describes as "the patterns of matter and energy" expressed throughout these dynamics.[14] Because these patterns are "semipermanent (that is, changing only gradually)" they are perceived to have continuity, and so identity as a continuous organized life-form. This description implies these patterns are macro-qualities, deducible from a complete knowledge of the properties of all the subvening structure's parts. Kurzweil's aim with this

---

12. LAR.
13. LAR.
14. LAR.

explanation is to establish that we are, in fact, referring to these patterns and not the subvening microstructure when we contemplate the individual human being as a body in the sense of "being a particular kind of sentient spatiotemporal continuant — homo sapiens," as the philosopher Peter Hacker recently put it.[15] Acknowledging the existence of living human beings is currently in relation to particular states of matter (and that means biological microstructures), Kurzweil argues their identity *as* human beings is not necessarily bound up with that, or any other unique physical state. Rather the fundamental identity of the individual human being is the life-form characterized as a self-consciously thinking, rational being.

The second level of supervenience deals with the relationship consciousness has to this life-form. Predictably, consciousness is itself a pattern, but one that is irreducible to the parts of the subvening macro and micro physiology. Like the patterns of matter and energy, it is a special sort of complex supervenient structural property with the same important feature of resistance to dissolution. Apropos the experiment's hypothetical case, this means having a precise mapping of the molecular properties of a specific human's brain and the capacity to produce functionally exact replicates of those properties — either in a neural computer or as nanobot replacements successfully integrated into an existing biological structure — is not only (logically) sufficient for achieving a complex macro-physical object analogous to the human brain, but it is also sufficient for the instantiation of consciousness. Unlike the life-form supervenient, however, consciousness exhibits patterns of behavior that admit no explanation according to the laws of physics alone. Kurzweil lists these patterns as knowledge, skills, and memory, all of which he places under the rubric subjective experience, which he then identifies with the individual person or personality. When he asserts that subjective experience, not objective correlates of that experience, is "the essence of consciousness," which the fully objective view he endorses cannot penetrate because there is no scientifically legitimate method for conclusively determining its presence, this does not mean no explanation at all is possible.[16] There are laws governing the behavior of subjective experience available to rigorous explanation, albeit not according to the fundamental laws of physics. What's more, there is a point of conjuncture at which the explanatory force of these laws meets those of the fundamental laws of physics. In the language of the thought experiment, that point is represented by the person. Kurzweil's premise is that persons, as human beings, are *purported* by bodies. Person, then, is a somewhat broad category of analysis that references a complex of micro and macro-physical, as well as emergent properties, but also much more.

---

15. Maxwell Bennet, Daniel Dennet, Peter Hacker, John Searle, *Neuroscience and Philosophy: Brain, Mind, and Language* (New York: Columbia University Press, 2007), 134.
16. LAR.

Once again, the language of the experiment is crucial here, and it repeatedly identifies personality with self-consciousness and memory. For instance, when first describing the objective question of identity, Kurzweil states: "Objectively, when we scan someone's brain and reinstantiate their personal mind file into a suitable computing medium, the newly emergent 'person' will appear to other observers to have very much the same personality, history, and memory as the person originally scanned."[17] Then: "The new person will claim to be that same old person and will have a memory of having been that person. The new person will have all of the patterns of knowledge, skill, and personality of the original."[18] It can be arguably inferred from such assertions that personality is continuous as far as memory can go, whatever changes of subvening physical state take place. Memory, in this sense, refers to the accumulation of images of oneself as a correlate of all cognitive and perceptual activity identified with the emergent property of consciousness in relation to its subvening physical state.[19] This presumes the capacity to have an accessible image of oneself having engaged in an action in the past as well as the present — in other words, the activity of imagination.

Making memory a basic criterion of personal identity raises numerous problems concerning the relationship between presentation and representation, between perception and apprehension, all of which are important issues in the history of thinking about imagination since Aristotle that continue to occupy current debates in philosophy of mind, neurophilosophy, and cognitive science. Here, I merely wish to gesture towards those issues as important background to Kurzweil's thought experiment and his overall speculation about the Singularity. Keeping our focus on the consideration of memory in his thought experiment, the cumulative images of cognition are transcribed onto the computer software he labels the personal mind file, which contains all the experiences and explanatory regresses constituting the specific aggregate of cognitive events that configure a distinct individual's consciousness. That entire personal mind file software functions as a reduplicated formation, in a way very much like the classical Latin sense of *memoria*. Downloading the personal mind file onto a neural computer does not mean the computer processes the information it contains to arrive at a representation of the person; rather, the computer's neural activity *animates* the information, achieving the aforementioned signs of the person — a

---

17. LAR.
18. LAR.
19. I am fully aware that my use of the term emergent here may be somewhat controversial, especially after I have already referred to consciousness as a complex supervenient structural property. It is the case, however, that the description of consciousness in Kurzweil's experiment suggests a sense of emergent akin to Samuel Alexander's. Cf. Samuel Alexander, *Space, Time, And Deity: The Gifford Lectures at Glasgow, 1916–1918*, 2 vols. (London: Macmillan & Co, 1927).

specific behavior pattern, etc. — indicating a presence of consciousness. Because it is the activity of the Singularity's technology that animates the information recorded on the software, thereby revivifying the person's identity objectively for others — and by conjecture personal identity and consciousness subjectively — we can arguably describe the machine to be commemorating the person. The reasons for this language will be made clearer a bit later. For now, it is important to note that commemoration in such a context has to do with iteration rather than recollection. The technologically reinstantiated consciousness supposedly conceives of itself as the necessary material correlative of the *memoria* from which an authentic sense of identity and purpose is derived. As such, it is a distinct version of the original, with its own variations of behavior patterns. It is a person in the etymological sense of the term, carrying over into English the Latin *persona*, itself a rendering of the Greek προσοπον (*prosopon*), meaning a countenance, outward appearance or manifestation. To be a person according to the description proffered in Kurzweil's thought experiment is to exhibit the qualities that qualify one for the status of a social agent. Those qualities are elements in a public functional system, a discursive economy whose rules are subject to analysis. To quote John Locke's *An Essay Concerning Human Understanding*, Book II, Chapter XXVII of which provides material for a good deal of the scaffolding for Kurzweil's experiment: "person is a forensic term, appropriating actions and their merit; and so belongs only to intelligent agents, capable of a law, and happiness, and misery."[20] Given that manifesting the public qualities of persons is the only objective, non-anthropic biased way to establish the likelihood of consciousness, it will be on the basis of the norms of law that intelligent machines' consciousness must be recognized. Kurzweil correctly characterizes this as "fundamentally ... a political prediction,"[21] highlighting the underlying ethical issues at stake: Allowing the possibility of intelligent machines purporting persons requires adjusting our definition of persons in a way that ultimately undermines the long history in modernity of humanist thought about the nature of intelligence and consciousness, along with the ideologies of social rights engendered by that thinking.

This aspect of Kurzweil's Law of Accelerating Returns recalls what Marshall McLuhan had in mind when he stated in *The Gutenberg Galaxy* and then later in *The Medium is the Massage* (1967) that the global spread of the electronic/digital information technology presages our entering what he called "a new Middle Ages." McLuhan was identifying the current image-based economy of mass telecommunications with the oral-based manuscript economy of Medieval Europe specifically. What he understood the two to have in common is locating the

---

20. John Locke, *An Essay Concerning Human Understanding*, ed. Alexander Campbell Fraser (New York: Dover Publications, 1959), 467.
21. LAR.

animating activity of commemoration in a collective external process. More than thirty years before Kurzweil, McLuhan postulated that the history of the species homo sapiens' development was the progressive externalizing of all its biological functions in technology —beginning with orality as the externalization of self-conscious thinking. He had his acknowledged predecessors in this, chief among whom were Eric Havelock, Walter Ong, Thomas Aquinas, and Aristotle. He shared with the latter two in particular a consideration of imagination's centrality in that history, elaborating from their explanations of *sensus communis* a theory of the new information technologies achieving a completely externalized mechanical capacity of imagination, which is very similar to the one elaborated by Kurzweil about the Singularity. This conceptual legacy and theoretical framework is another way Kurzweil's prognosticating about the Singularity resonates with McLuhan's forecast of a new Middle Ages.

Note 2: The New Middle Ages of international security studies

Highlighting the McLuhanesque aspect of Kurzweil's speculations about the Singularity's imminence, most pointedly the neomedievalist conception of imagination underwriting his theory of portable persons makes it easier to apprehend the conceptual roots futurist technology theory has in common with certain areas of international security studies. One of the more well-known public expressions of the connection between the two fields is the much-cited talk, "Nanotechnology and International Security," given by Mark Avrum Gubrud in 1997 at the fifth biannual Foresight Institute Conference on Molecular Nanotechnology. At the time a researcher associated with the University of Maryland's Center for Superconductivity Research, Gubrud outlined some of the dangers presented by the military applications of nanotechnology entailed in the Pentagon's vision of a "revolution in military affairs." The history of the Pentagon's technological revolution had been outlined at the preceding Foresight Institute Conference in 1995 in a talk entitled "Nanotechnology And Global Security," given by one of the revolution's chief proponents and architects, Retired Admiral David E. Jeremiah who was Commander in Chief of the United States Pacific Fleet from 1987 to 1991, and Vice Chairman of the Joint Chiefs of Staff for Generals Colin L. Powell (1989-1993) and John M. Shalikashvili (1993-1997). *Pace* Admiral Jeremiah's call for technology being placed at the forefront of policy debates, Gubrud draws a direct connection between the Singularity of futurist technology theory and international security, postulating that "as we approach a singularity, rising tidal forces tear at the economic, political and military structure of our world." On the basis of this postulate he prognosticates that the closer we approach the Singularity the greater and more intense will be global conflict and disorder. "An accelerating rate of technical progress can amplify inhomogeneities in the level of development of different nations and even different groups and classes within nations," he states, "upsetting haphazardly constructed military, economic and political balances, and amplifying conflicts of interest and ideology as well."[22] Gubrud goes further, underscoring that adequately addressing the full extent of the linkage between technological development and world-wide transformation in social order requires more serious attention be given to the force of imagination in discerning and understanding security issues.

Although Gubrud's analysis provides an explicit connection between the fields of futurist technology theory and international security studies, it is not a remarkable exhibition of their in-common McLuhan association. Two more recently published analyses better illustrate that association. The first of these is the article, "Globalization's Bastards: Illegitimate Non-State Actors in International Law," by Neal Pollard, a highly regarded analyst in international security studies, which first appeared in a 2002 special issue of *Low Intensity Conflict & Law Enforcement*, which is a highly regarded journal in the field and is now called *Small Wars & Insurgencies*. Edited by Robert Bunker, the entire issue was reprinted under the Routledge imprint in 2005 as the book *Networks, Terrorism and Global Insurgency*.[23] The second illustrative analysis is the article, "The New Middle Ages," by John Rapley, foreign affairs columnist for the *Jamaica Gleaner* and a senior lecturer in the Department of Government at the University of the West Indies, which appeared in the May/June 2006 issue of the Council On Foreign Relations' renowned journal of global current events, foreign policy, and international relations, *Foreign Affairs*. Pollard's article offers an analysis of how the globalization of information technology facilitates, and in some instances even fosters, transnational terrorist and criminal organizations, the occurrence of which he takes to be symptomatic of the tendency towards neomedievalism inherent in the current technology-dependent world political order. Rapley's offers case studies

---

22. Mark Avrum Gubrud, "Nanotechnology and International Security," Fifth Foresight Conference on Molecular Nanotechnology, November 5–8, 1997; Palo Alto, CA.

23. Neal Pollard, "Globalization's Bastards: Illegitimate Non-State Actors in International Law," *Low Intensity Conflict & Law Enforcement* 11, no. 2 (2002): 210–238; and Neal Pollard, "Globalization's Bastards: Illegitimate Non-State Actors in International Law," *Networks, Terrorism and Global Insurgency*, ed. Robert J. Bunker (London: Routledge, 2005), 40–68. All subsequent citations will be referred to the 2005 publication, which will be cited as Pollard. Even in the field of International Security Studies, Pollard is a peculiarity of sorts, with a BA in mathematics and political science, a Masters of Letters in international security studies from the University of St. Andrews, Scotland, and a J.D. cum laude from the Georgetown University Law Center. Besides being an adjunct faculty at the Georgetown University Edmund A. Walsh School of Foreign Service, where he teaches undergraduate and graduate courses on technology and homeland security for the Science, Technology, and International Affairs Program, he is also an Adjunct Professor at the Georgetown Medical Center Department of Microbiology and Immunology, and the Georgetown Public Policy Institute. Before that, having co-founded the Terrorism Research Center in 1996, he advised the governments of the United States, United Kingdom, and Sweden on security matters.

of such organizations as neomedievalisms in precisely Pollard's sense, elaborating Philip G. Cerny's assessment that information technology-driven neomedievalism has generated the new security dilemmas of globalization. Scrutinizing Pollard and Rapley's analyses in tandem will provide occasion to consider the claims for McLuhan's paternal role in the development of international security studies' conception of neomedievalism, as well as the traces of his thinking in Kurzweil's speculations about the Singularity. That consideration in turn affords us the opportunity to evaluate the conceptual framework of McLuhan's thinking, which will both explain how it is that such seemingly diverse fields of knowledge as futurist technology theory and international relations and security studies can think about imagination in so nearly identical a manner, as well as offer something of a corrective to that thinking.

The first thing to consider about Pollard's analysis of the technology question as an issue of international security is how he defines order. Rather than offer his own definition, he invokes the one provided in 1977 by Hedley Bull in *The Anarchical Society: A Study of Order in World Politics*.[24] Bull is generally regarded — along with C.A.W. Manning, Martin Wight, John Vincent, and Alan James — as one of the foundational figures of the so-called English School, whose work has recently seen considerable scholarly reevaluation in the field of international relations. Pollard also makes use of Bull's speculation in the same book about what he called "new medievalism." Because what Pollard states about order and neomedievalism is taken directly from and builds on Bull's work, there is something to be gained by going to the source, not the least of which will be a keener sense of what is at stake in Pollard's amendments and departures.

According to Bull, order refers to a pattern of behavior that sustains the elementary or primary goals of existing social life.[25] The society under consideration is that of the international system, or more precisely, the modern international system of states. In its origin, this was the European system of sovereign states, whose commencement is usually cited as the 1648 Peace of Westphalia but, in fact, emerged progressively in the course of the sixteenth and seventeenth centuries with the dissolution of the Holy Roman Empire as the geopolitical manifestation of *Corpus Christianum*. During the eighteenth and nineteenth centuries, these states became fully articulated as monarchial and, after the American and French Revolutions, liberal nation states. Over that same period of time, the system expanded beyond Europe in colonial conquest to eventually encompass the entire globe, so that by the end of the twentieth century a single worldwide political system was in existence. Throughout the greater part of its history — most assuredly from 1648 to 1946 — the modern international system

---

24. Hedley Bull, *The Anarchical Society: A Study of Order in World Politics*, third edition (New York: Columbia University Press, 2002, c.1977).
25. Bull, 51.

of states has functioned with the conscious presumption of common interests and common values, supposed to rest upon a common culture or civilization, which are what make it an international society of states and not just a system of interacting states. In Bull's account, international society is one of the basic elements of the modern international system; it remains in competition with the elements of a state of war, and of transnational solidarity or conflict.[26] Even though international society is not the sole dominant element in international politics, it has historically been a paramount factor in maintaining order in the system, providing institutions such as international law for making, communicating, administering, and interpreting rules of behavior. One of Bull's chief contentions is that the idea of international society — as it has been articulated by political theorists and historians from Pufendorf to Heeren, as well as, more recently, theorist of international relations such as Martin Wight and himself — conforms to the reality of how statesmen have thought and spoken about the international system. Another crucial point of his analysis is that the successful incorporation of the entire planet into the structures of the modern international system — particularly the expansion of the system to include 140 states, the majority of which are newly formed out of the ant-colonial wars of the mid-twentieth century — has resulted in a situation where there is considerable dissatisfaction with the order provided by international society.

The fact that the European international system's expanding to encompass Africa, Asia, and Latin America has stretched the bonds of the concomitantly European international society to the point of crisis brings Bull to ask: "Is not the international politics of the present time best viewed as an international system that is not an international society?"[27] While concluding that the international society persists, despite the system now encompassing multiple cultures and civilizations, Bull recognizes that the nature and level of the present crisis reveals how "precarious and imperfect" the order provided within modern international society is.[28] This compels him to speculate on what are the most viable possibilities, based on discernable current trends, for an alternative to the current international system whose order is maintained through international society.

That speculation constitutes chapter 11 of *The Anarchical Society.* By no means persuaded that the international system of states is in any imminent danger of collapse, he speculates on four of the most likely alternatives. The first alternative is a system but not a society — this entails the disappearance of the institutions of international law, the mechanisms of diplomatic relations, and the balance of power. The second, states but not a system, requires the total collapse of the regular ordered interaction between states so that the behavior of each is no

---

26. Bull, 49.
27. Bull, 39.
28. Bull, 49–50.

longer a necessary element in the calculations of the other. The third, world government, necessitates the universal abandonment of sovereignty by all current existing states, which would then become subordinate to a centralized world government. Bull acknowledges that the possibility of any of these three warrants consideration, but judges their prospects to be very slim in light of known trends and tendencies in the current world order. The fourth alternative, new medievalism, is given a much more detailed elaboration and takes up the major portion of the chapter, with Bull delineating five tendencies in the current world political order that "provide *prima facie* evidence" of a trend toward this alternative. These are: (i) the regional integration of states, (ii) the disintegration of states, (iii) the restoration of private international violence, (iv) transnational organizations, and (v) the technological unification of the world. In spite of the greater detail of elaboration given to these tendencies, he is no more sanguine about the prospects of this alternative occurring than he is the other three. In fact, he is even more careful in explaining why the prospects for a new medievalism are slim. After enumerating a long list of antecedent anomalies and irregularities that are analogous to the five current tendencies — from the German Empire and the pre 1929 Vatican to the East India Companies and the Barbary Corsairs — all of which the classical theory of world politics has been able to adequately account for in terms of the relation between states, Bull concludes that there is no real cause for alarm. For reasons that will be made clear presently, his conclusion merits full quotation:

> The classical theory has held sway not because it can account by itself for all the complexity of universal politics, but because it has provided a truer guide to it than alternative visions such as that of an imperial system or a cosmopolitan society. A time may come when the anomalies and irregularities are so glaring that an alternative theory, better able to take account of these realities, will come to dominate the field. If some of the trends towards a "new medievalism" that have been reviewed here were to go much further, such a situation might come about, but it would be going beyond the evidence to conclude that "groups other than the state" have made such inroads on the sovereignty of states that the states system is now giving way to this alternative.[29]

The tactical aim of Bull's entire thought experiment on alternatives to the international system is to give serious consideration to current irregularities and anomalies of the system in order to discredit claims that either the system or the society are on the verge of extinction. The greater degree of detail in his account of new medievalism reflects the extent to which that idea was already gaining currency among theorists and so required a somewhat more careful account. This

---

29. Bull, 265.

is borne out by his making use of and explicitly citing Zbigniew Brzezinski's 1970 book, *Between Two Ages: America's Role in the Technetronic Era*, in describing the fifth tendency pointing toward new medievalism: the technological unification of the world. Bull's analysis of the new medievalism, in particular, aims not merely at demonstrating the persistence of international society, but also at indicating the ways in which international relations theory can provide insights to international procedures having the capacity to deal with non-state actors. Above all else, as is stated in the quotation from *The Anarchical Society* just cited, new medievalism is discredited as a category of analysis. It does not yield an adequate account of the current world political order.

The explicitness of that statement does not, however, stop Pollard from citing the five tendencies — he calls them "the five elements of [Bull's] 'new medievalism' world order model" — as "evidence of the decline of states." Nor does it keep him from further stating that the tendencies: "are 'other associations' (to use the medievalists' expression) that are making inroads on the sovereignty and supremacy of a state over its territory, its citizens and its ability to decisively influence world politics. That is, these five elements are evidence of a fundamental shift in power toward NSAs [non-state actors], enabling [them] to move to the 'formal plane.'"[30] The misconstrual of Bull in paraphrase is quite plain. Indeed, it would be hard to imagine a clearer instance of a misreading that does so nice a job of turning the meaning of a text on its head. That which is explicitly discredited as an inadequate analytic concept gets cited as an exemplary analysis of the evidence for new medievalism. The question is: In what interests in this misreading of Bull applied?

On the one hand, Pollard sets out to establish that the proliferation of transnational non-state actors seeking to influence the international system is "enabled and accelerated by the forces of globalization," particularly the accelerating rate of development in information technologies.[31] In pursuit of this, he delineates three types of transnational non-state actors: multi or transnational business corporations, non-governmental organizations (NGOs), and transnational terrorist and criminal organizations.[32] But whereas the first two types are legitimate because they seek to secure a role for themselves within the modern international system, the third is illegitimate because it seeks to destabilize or outright replace the system. This is where the technology-driven international security threat lies. To illustrate this as a constitutive aspect of the dynamics of globalization, Pollard draws an analogy between the way current illegitimate transnational actors, such as al-Qaʻida, have emerged and the way thirteenth century Christian European sovereign rulers authorized the use of force by private armies and mercenaries in order to accumulate power, with the unintended

---

30. Pollard, 47.
31. Pollard, 41.
32. Pollard, 41.

consequence of this privatization of violence being the emergence of rogue forces that these same rulers were compelled to struggle against to reassert order. Although the current devolution of certain aspects of state sovereignty to non-state actors might bear resemblance to structures of power in medieval Europe, the process of devolution is itself entirely a function of globalization, or, as Pollard puts it: "The information revolution is accelerating and exacerbating this 800 year-old trend," with the projection that "governments of all kinds will find their control slipping during the twenty-first century as information technology spreads to the large majority of the world that still lacks phones, computers, and electricity."[33] Determining how the threat posed to international security by transnational terrorism has been generated in the interrelationship between technological development and globalization — with keen focus on the distinctions of infrastructure as well as access and employment of information technologies — is a primary objective of Pollard's analysis. Although meant to bolster that analysis, his misreading of Bull reinforces precisely the problem of inadequate imagination in method that caused the latter to discredit neomedievalism as an analytical category. Nevertheless, Pollard's reading is well within the current post-9/11 trend of invoking Bull's new medievalism speculation as a model for understanding not only the proliferation of networks of Islamist terrorists through the Internet, but also the general security threat posed by illegitimate non-state actors to international society.

Rapley's 2006 *Foreign Affairs* article is another notable example of that trend, generally aligning with Pollard's appropriation of Bull's new medievalism to designate the resurgent political fragmentation and decentralization at the end of the twentieth century that attends an increasingly coherent global capitalism. Rapley adds a qualification to the assessment, however, ascertaining that the designation more aptly applies to the developing world almost exclusively, or at least for the time being almost exclusively. To make his case, he begins by describing the current Jamaican state's devolution of certain aspects of its sovereignty — specifically policing and social services — to what are known in official Jamaican government parlance as "area leaders," but are called locally "dons." These dons' claims of dominion over specific areas and their peoples are enforced through organized gang violence, rudimentary judicial institutions, and social services provided through a patronage system. The revenue for these activities comes from the international trade in illegal drugs, so that what Rapley is describing falls within the ambit of narco-trafficking and is part of a network of transnational non-state actors. The other examples he offers of such arrangements between states and non-state actors are the tribal zone of Northwestern Pakistan, Somalia, the Democratic Republic of the Congo, and Papua New Guinea, in each instance of which large areas officially under the

---

33. Pollard, 46.

sovereignty of the nation state are, in fact, under the dominion of private militia. What is emphasized in Rapley's account about these *imperia in imperio* — "statelets," he calls them — is that they are iterations in a constellation of complex highly localized economies, social systems founded on plural identities functioning in a political system composed of multiple and overlapping authorities, each drawing on an autonomous resource base. As with the *favelas* of Rio de Janeiro, the fact that the nation state is merely one such authority indicates a system in which plurality of order prevails over its centralization; there is a diffusion of sovereignty.

In offering this depiction of neomedievalism as mostly prevalent in the developing postcolonial world, Rapley follows Edward Gibbon in defining the Middle Ages as beginning at the end of the fifth century, with the fall of the Roman Empire associated with the German barbarian invasions, and ending with the rise of modern monarchies in the sixteenth century. The Middle Ages are, thus, construed as a long interregnum in centralized political order, during which Europe's tribes developed ad hoc arrangements to manage the affairs of a suddenly anarchic world. Gibbon's account of the devolution of imperial military and economic power to local arrangements between remnants of the Roman political economic order and Germanic tribal rulers is of particular importance to Rapley. Even more important, however, are those instances where no such arrangements obtained, and tribal rulers created their own political domains, directly controlling land and people through sheer force of arms. These factors enable him to draw a hard analogy between the post-imperial Rome devolution of centralized power to local arrangements and the post-colonial devolution of centralized state power to local arrangements today. On the presumption of that analogy, he provides a descriptive scenario of the new medievalism entailing a new barbarity that while currently at the gates of the imperium, might very well, as happened with Rome, come to prevail throughout the realm. This anxiety accords with Gibbon's depiction of the Germans as the barbarians whose desire to share in the benefits of the empire overwhelmed its system of centralized order, ushering in a new system of decentralized disorder. Rome could not adapt its political structure to sufficiently manage or accommodate the multitudes it attracted. It took centuries before modernity, or more precisely its institutions of science-based technological development, capitalism, worldwide exploration and imperialism, reestablished the centrality, whose highest political manifestation was the international system of nation-states. In lieu of Gibbon's Germanic barbarians, we have the worldwide multitude of stateless immigrants aggregating in zones of societal arrangement beyond nation state sovereignty. The logical inference to be drawn from this scenario is that the threat the new medievalism poses is only in the first instance to the international system. The greater danger is to modernity itself. The devolution of state sovereignty may be more pronounced in the developing world, but it is a global aspect of neoliberalism's economic order, in which the wealthy are so thoroughly integrated into a global network of urban enclaves that they share practically no public consciousness with their immediate local populations. There is indeed, as Rapley remarks, an increasing gap of mind. He is worth quoting on this:

> People everywhere, finally, are leaving behind national symbols and cultures and turning to local and global hybrids. In Dakar, French, the language of the elite, is being displaced by the local tongue of Wolof and hip-hop lingo from the United States. A similar trend is happening in Jamaica, where English is losing ground to the local patois, accompanied by language derived from dancehall reggae and rap. And so the coexistence of local and transnational identities that typified the European Middle Ages has reappeared.

The last remark about coexisting local and transnational identities is most telling. Depicting the genesis of diverse linguistic communities bearing a certain resemblance to the emergence of European vernaculars in the Middle Ages invites a series of questions. In the first place, does the emergence of vernaculars capable of competing with the old imperial languages as discourses of power on the local level amount to the degeneration of those old languages of power globally? In mind here, of course, is the difference between the fate of French and that of English and Spanish — Chinese being an altogether different case, as is Arabic. It is also noteworthy that in the two examples of emergent vernaculars provided — one in the old Francophone zone, the other in that of the British Empire — English, or more precisely a specific form of US-derived urban English is a common thread. Assuming, for argument's sake, that this is a global phenomenon, does this mean that there is a non-elite non-local order of consciousness connecting the various localized ones? This second question suggests that the coexistence of transnational and local identities is not just mapped geopolitically, but is embodied, as it were, in the multitudes themselves. Any serious question concerning the order of consciousness is historically loaded and conceptually vexed; it is most pronouncedly so when language and neomedievalism together come into play. Appreciating the extent to which Rapley's account of neomedievalism is so loaded and vexed requires recalling an aspect of the term's conceptual genealogy generally lost in the way it currently circulates in international relations and security studies.

Even though Bull's 1977 *The Anarchical Society* is frequently cited these days as the earliest analysis of neomedievalism resulting from technology's globalization, that is not the case. Besides the usual issue of disciplinary myopia, the claim for Bull in this respect stems from what he identifies as the fifth feature of the putative trend toward neomedievalism: the technological unification of the world. It is at the very beginning of discussing the technological unification of the world postulate, that Bull cites Zbigniew Brzezinski's 1970 book, *Between Two Ages: America's Role in the Technetronic Era*. Written while Brzezinski was still a professor of international relations at Columbia University, *Between Two Ages* is generally recognized as setting out some of the key concepts that will lead to the formation of the Trilateral Commission. The first chapter, "The Onset of the Technetronic Age," begins with the statement: "The paradox of our time is that humanity is becoming simultaneously more unified and more fragmented."[34] By the fourth chapter, under the heading "Global Fragmentation and Unification," Brzezinski asserts, however:

> Yet it would be wrong to conclude that fragmentation and chaos are the dominant realities of our time. A global human consciousness is for the first time beginning to manifest itself.... During the last three centuries the fading of the essentially transnational European aristocracy and the successive nationalization of the Christian church, of socialism, and of communism have meant that in recent times most significant political activity has tended to be confined within national compartments. Today we are again witnessing the emergence of transnational elites, but now they are composed of international businessmen, scholars, professional men, and public officials. The ties of these new elites cut across national boundaries, their perspectives are not confined by national traditions, and their interests are more functional than national. These global communities are gaining in strength and, as was true in the Middle Ages, it is likely that before long the social elites of most of the more advanced countries will be highly internationalist or globalist in spirit and outlook.[35]

This assessment is clearly the inspiration for the fifth feature in Bull's analysis of the trend toward neomedievalism, which is why he cites it. There is, however, a significant difference between the trajectories of Bull and Brzezinski's analyses. Whereas Bull was focused on how the new image-based electronic and digital technology signaled the dissolution of the social institutions fundamental to the international system, Brzezinski was trying to describe the way in which that very technology signaled the formation of what he calls "a planetary consciousness." The creation of the global information grid, facilitating continuous intellectual interaction and pooling of knowledge among the transnational elites, was enhancing the trend toward a planetary society. Brzezinski was also keen to point out that the same trend involves an increasing gap between these consciously transnational professional elites and the "politically activated masses, whose 'nativism' — exploited by more nationalist political leaders — could work against the "cosmopolitan...."[36] There is some resonance between this assessment and the analysis of the shift occurring in world politics made by James Burnham in his 1941 study, *The Managerial Revolution: What is Happening in the World Now.* Brzezinski makes no reference to Burnham, but takes some care to reference and then

---

34. Zbigniew Brzezinski, *Between Two Ages: America's Role in the Technetronic Era* (New York: Viking Press, 1970), 3.
35. Brzezinski, 58–59.
36. Brzezinski, 59.

dispute Marshall McLuhan's famous metaphor of the "global village," from *The Gutenberg Galaxy*. The problem Brzezinski has with McLuhan's metaphor is that it "overlooks the personal stability, interpersonal intimacy, implicitly shared values, and traditions that were important ingredients of the primitive village"; whereas the emerging planetary society is characterized by "a nervous, agitated, tense, and fragmented web of interdependent relations."[37] Brzezinski finds a more apt metaphor for that society to be the "global city" — a term he takes from Theodore von Laude's 1969 book by that title. Alternative notwithstanding, in citing McLuhan's global village, Brzezinski recalls the first analysis to use the phrase "new Middle Ages" in describing the world-wide social being brought about by global technological unification. By following the recent use of the phrase "new medievalism" or "neomedievalism" in international studies backwards from Pollard and Rapley to Bull, then from Bull to Brzezinski, we arrive at Marshall McLuhan, whose work is fundamental for the current discourse of neomedievalism.

Note 3: Neomedievalism and the question of imagination

The metaphor of the global village in *The Gutenberg Galaxy* is often misconstrued as positive and utopian. McLuhan's primary concern was with mapping the cognitive effects of technological change, and not at all with moralizing about the sociological transformations precipitated by it. Far more important for him than moralizing was the need for adequate descriptive analysis of the correlation between changing technology and cognitive and social transformations. The global village metaphor serves just such a function in describing how the emerging electronic/digital technology of the computer age is displacing the social configuration of classical political liberalism with one of enhanced interdependence and association. The transformation is not direct or immediate but is the eventual consequence of a change in the conceptual foundation of the social order precipitated by the technological event. With respect to liberalism, the fundamental idea is the indelible isolated individual identity as the irreducible element of social order, which in McLuhan's analysis is an effect of typography — *The Making of Typographic Man* is *The Gutenberg Galaxy*'s subtitle. As of yet, there is no cogent grasp of the social configuration concomitant with the new electronic/digital technology, let alone its conceptual foundation, beyond the nebulous idea that information technology will unite humanity in unprecedented ways. Nonetheless, McLuhan detected in the technology-driven trend to bring individuals into more coherent and seemingly organic communities the likelihood for a proliferation of highly localized insular collectivities, brought into "superimposed co-existence" but lacking anything like a universal planetary society — in Kant's sense of one formed in solidarity.

---

37. Brzezinski, 19.

In his reaching for a viable explanation of the correlation between technological development and cognitive interplay in historical socio-political configuration, McLuhan finds particularly significant Karl Popper's account in *The Open Society and Its Enemies* of how discovering the Greek phonetic alphabet launched a visual technology that externalized and abstracted thinking, which facilitated the detribalization of the ancient world, preparing the grounds for democratic open society. It is a principal premise of *The Gutenberg Galaxy* that "the abstracting or opening of closed [tribal] societies is the work of the phonetic alphabet, and not of any other form of writing or technology."[38] In contrast to this abstracting visual technology are what McLuhan refers to it as "audile-tactile" technologies of closed oral societies — the speech, drum, and the ear technologies. Because he identifies the technologies of electric media — chiefly cinema, radio, and television — as also being audile-tactile, he maintains that the emerging electronic age carries the prospect of sealing the entire human family into a single global tribe.[39] Citing the biologist Pierre Teilhard de Chardin's description of the "noosphere" or a technological brain for the world, McLuhan offers an analysis that remarkably anticipates Gubrud's inhomogeneities:

> Instead of tending towards a vast Alexandrian library the world has become a computer, an electronic brain, exactly as in an infantile piece of science fiction. And as our senses have gone outside us, Big Brother goes inside. So, unless aware of this dynamic, we shall at once move into a phase of panic terrors, exactly befitting a small world of tribal drums, total interdependence, and superimposed co-existence.... Terror is the normal state of any oral society, for in it everything affects everything all the time.... In our long striving to recover for the Western world a unity of sensibility and of thought and feeling we have no more been prepared to accept the tribal consequences of such unity than we were ready for the fragmentation of the human psyche by print culture.[40]

What Brzezinski construed as "stability of personality" McLuhan understood to be localized enactments of persona in precisely the classical Latin sense referred to earlier of a countenance, outward appearance or manifestation. The village he has in mind is not the idyllic one of collective solidarity, but rather one in which often competing languages of power call on the same set of human bodies to be the material bearers of their particular story of authenticity. McLuhan's assessment is that audile-tactile technology, whether in oral societies or the electronic/digital, generates a social configuration — as well as an attendant psychological disposition — in which the individual physical human functions as the material prop for a consciousness that, properly speaking, existed only in and through the public utterance.

---

38. *GG*, 8.
39. *GG*, 8.
40. *GG*, 32.

McLuhan's identification of the current electronic/digital technology with audile-tactile technology of Europe's Middle Ages — hence his calling it a new Middle Ages —stems from his extensive engagement with the humanist scholarship on oral societies, most notably Albert Bates Lord's philology-driven comparative history of epic oral composition, *The Singer of Tales* (1960), Walter Ong's *Ramus, Method, and the Decay of Dialogue: From the Art of Discourse to the Art of Reason* (1958), and Eric Havelock's *The Liberal Temper in Greek Politics* (1957) and *Preface to Plato* (1963). One of McLuhan's goals was to establish as a fundamental principle of methodology in the historical analysis of humanity the postulate that any given technological transformation realizes concomitant cognitive transformations, and that the two orders of transformation combined articulate actual human reality. Each and every technology that the human tool-making animal creates is an externalization and extension of one or another human sense organ. As extensions of our senses, all technological tools constitute closed systems, whereas our senses dynamically interrelate with one another in a seemingly open-ended fluidity ratio of interplay. For quite some time — arguably since Kant — when we contemplate this interplay as agency it is termed "imagination." When contemplating the effect of this interplay — the experience of the world as a whole — we habitually term that "consciousness."[41] Whenever a special technological tool extends a specific sense, a rearrangement in the interactions between that sense and the other senses occurs, causing a perceptual reorientation with an attendant conceptual or cognitive shift. The ensuing realignment or shift in the ratio of interplay of our private senses and faculties articulates a change of consciousness and consequently the basis on which we organize our reality, sociologically as well as cognitively. "It is simpler to say," according to McLuhan, "that if a new technology extends one or more of our senses outside us into the social world, then new ratios among all of our senses will occur in that particular culture."[42] In *Understanding Media*, he utilizes Lyman Bryson's phrase "technology is explicitness," to describe this relationship between human senses and technology as one of translation, meaning the "spelling out of forms of knowing ... into amplified and specialized forms."[43] This suggests synaesthesia, both in the psychological sense defined by Frederic W.H. Myers in his 1903 book, *Human Personality and Its Survival Beyond Death*: production, from a sense-impression of one kind, of an associated mental image of a sense-impression of another kind; and the literary sense defined by Hanns Oertel in his 1901 *Lectures on the Study of Language*: the use of metaphors in which terms relating to one kind of sense-impression are used to describe sense-impressions of other kinds. Given McLuhan's acknowledged conceptual indebtedness to Ernest Hans Gombrich's

---

41. *GG*, 5.
42. *GG*, 41.
43. Marshall McLuhan, *Understanding Media: The Extensions of Man* (Boston: MIT Press, 1964/ 194), 56. Henceforth cited as *UM*.

Art & Illusion: A Study in the Psychology of Pictorial Presentation (1960), which borrows and elaborates on Oertel's notion, perhaps greater weight falls on the literary sense of synaesthesia. Grounds for reading McLuhan this way are found in such statements as: "All media are metaphors in their power to translate experience into new forms."[44] The primal instance of humans translating the complex flow of immediate sense experience into retrievable information was the spoken word, which, according to McLuhan, is the first historical occurrence of a corporeal human faculty (cognition) being externalized — assuming speech preceded the visual symbolic representations of systematically coloring objects like shells, stones, and cave walls, or the repetitive shaping of flint tools into uniform symmetrical shapes suited to distinct functions. The question of primacy aside, the main point is that human history is traceable in the history of technological development, in the material record of the species' discovering increasingly dynamic means of translating immediate sense experience and human corporeal faculties into ever more complex and sophisticated systems of abstraction. These externalized extensions of our nervous system, as McLuhan puts it, have reached such a degree of complexity and comprehension that we are now putting our bodies inside them, by means of electric media, setting up "a dynamic by which all previous technologies that are mere extensions of hands and feet and teeth and bodily heat-controls — all such extensions of our bodies, including cities — will be translated into information systems."[45] On this assessment, McLuhan predicts, in a language anticipating Vinge and Kurzweil's theories of the Singularity, that we are moving toward the technological extension of consciousness. Whereas previous technologies were partial and fragmentary, the information technology is total and inclusive. "An external consensus or conscience is now as necessary as private consciousness."[46]

But just what is the nature of the necessity for these extensions of human senses and faculties to have a ratio of interplay — that is, to have a consensus? Even more importantly, what is the nature of the spontaneous interplay supposed to exist within the human brain that the technologies need to emulate? Aristotle's description in *De Anima* of *sensus communis* has considerable influence on McLuhan's conception of external consensus or consciousness both in *The Gutenberg Galaxy* and *Understanding Media*. That influence along with these questions bring us back to the ponderous issue of the nature of consciousness in the world, or more precisely the relation of consciousness to intelligence as well as perception encountered in our exposition of Kurzweil's Laws of Accelerating Returns. We saw that, for Kurzweil — who treats intelligence as a phenomenal force of life manifest in potentially infinite material modalities, rather than an

---

44. *UM*, 57.
45. *UM*, 57.
46. *UM*, 57. Also se *GG*, 5.

essential property of the biological organism, hominid — consciousness is a function of the interrelationship between sufficiently complex biological systems and their emergent properties; a relationship he postulates is translatable based on current trends in a number of information technologies. McLuhan too suggests that this interrelationship is constitutive of consciousness, or more exactly, of self-conscious agency. Only, for him, an analogue of the interrelationship is a necessity for the current technology itself, precisely because it has already achieved the full externalization of human senses. At the end of the sixth chapter in *Understanding Media*, entitled "Media as Translators," he states:

> Our very word "grasp" or "apprehension" points to the process of getting at one thing through another, of handling and sensing many facets at a time through more than one sense at a time. It begins to be evident that "touch" is not skin but the interplay of the senses, and "keeping in touch" or "getting in touch" is a matter of a fruitful meeting of the senses, of sight translated into sound and sound into movement, and taste and smell. The "common sense" was for many centuries held to be the peculiar human power of translating one kind of experience of one sense into all the senses, and presenting the result continuously as a unified image to the mind. In fact, this image of a unified ratio among the senses was long held to be the mark of our rationality, and may in the computer age easily become so again. For it is now possible to program ratios among the senses that approach the condition of consciousness. Yet such a condition would necessarily be an extension of our own consciousness as much as wheel is an extension of feet in rotation. Having extended or translated our central nervous system into the electromagnetic technology, it is but a further stage to transfer our consciousness to the computer world as well. Then, at least, we shall be able to program consciousness in such wise that it cannot be numbed nor distracted by Narcissus illusions of the entertainment world that beset mankind when he encounters himself extended in his own gimmickry.[47]

In equating what he calls here "common sense" with touch, McLuhan recalls precisely Thomas Aquinas's reduction of *sensus communis* to tactility. His seeing the return of that reduction in the advent of Kurzweilian software-based human consciousness might understandably be taken as exemplifying the sort of application of Scholastic thinking to describe modern problems Umberto Eco defined in his 1973 essay, "Dreaming of the Middle Ages," as a particular type of philosophical neomedievalism: *philosophia perennis*, or neo-Thomism.[48] A label that does seem warranted by McLuhan's construal of the cognitive matrix emergent

---

47. *UM*, 60–61.
48. Umberto Eco, "Dreaming of the Middle Ages," in *Travels in Hyper Reality: Essays*, trans. William Weaver (San Diego: Harcourt Brace & Co., 1986) 70.

with electric media as resembling that of the audible-tactile based technologies of medieval Europe. The fact remains, however, *pace* Eco, that the long centuries McLuhan refers to are centuries forward and not backward from Aquinas's 13th century, which means the eight hundred years from then until now. For most of that period, from the 15th century onward, the technology of typography — the technology of the mechanically reproduced book — was ascendant and modernity was under way. And by the last third of the 17th century the association was visual-tactile rather than audible-tactile. A great deal occurs in 17th, 18th, and 19th century thinking that bears on McLuhan's neomedievalism; one more thing beyond the province of a provisional note. All that implicitly taken into account, it will have to suffice here to point out that throughout the eight centuries McLuhan alludes to, beginning with Aquinas on *sensus communis*, every effort to adequately map the relationship between our perceptual and cognitive matrix of interplay and material reality has also had to try and determine the force of that matrix itself in the articulation of intelligence; and this latter attempt has been dogged by the perennial problem of imagination. McLuhan consistently sought to draw a valid analogy between the sort of conceptual and societal transformations occurring with the shift from the primarily oral-based manuscript economy of Medieval Europe to the literate-based print economy identified with European modernity, and those attending the current shift from that very literate-based print economy to the image-based economy of information technology. The imagination question is a fundamental aspect of that effort; McLuhan takes it to be more than merely a corollary to the crisis of the indelible isolated individual identity as the irreducible element of social order precipitated by the globalization of information technology, it is a constitutive feature.

A passing familiarity with the most informative historical scholarship about the nature of oral medieval European societies and the significance of its shift to the book-based knowledge economy of modernity is crucial for grasping on what basis McLuhan draws an analogy between the audible-tactile technology of medieval European society and that of our contemporary information technology. Some of our guides in this are shared with McLuhan: to wit, Albert Bates Lord, Eric Havelock, and Walter Ong. Others followed after him, particularly Paul Zumtor, and Wlad Godzich. One thing that has been learned from these sources is that in oral medieval European societies narratives are collective property. So much stock is placed in storytelling in these societies they are considered narrative-bound. The performance or the telling of stories in oral societies is essentially commemorative, in the precise sense that it is a means of commemoration; which is to say it is a calling to remembrance, or preserving in memory, by some solemn public observance. In an oral society, this refers to a peculiar function of memory, in which stories constitute a vast *memoria*, containing all the sacred texts, all the foundational myth and explanatory regresses — that is, the order of life constituting a specific aggregate of individuals as a distinct collective, as a people distinguishable from all the other such collectives around them. This is a type of mind for which a story told is not cognitively processed for the information it contains, it is told rather to *animate* as many of the constitutive elements of *memoria* as possible. What is valued above all else, even above the semantic force of the narrative, is the way the storyteller's performance achieves this function of animation, in which large numbers of dormant memorial strands are set into motion and vibrate together, thereby revivifying the collective consciousness as such.

There are obvious resemblances between this account of oral society storytelling and that of Kurzweil's technological revivification of personal identity, except that here the *memoria* is collective and is preserved and animated through the full bodied human performance of storytelling. Like the physical individuals and machines in Kurzweil's thought experiment, those gathered at oral society storytelling are the necessary material correlatives of the *memoria* from which any authentic sense of identity and purpose is derived. But unlike in his experiment, where a person is an ontogenetic supervenient emergent property of specific physical states that has been reinstantiated through translation to a computer, they receive their persona in the form of fate from the power residing in *memoria*, which is a power beyond human ken or control.[49] To be a person in this sense is to see oneself as assuming roles that are provided by the larger world of language and not inherent psychophysical properties. Put a bit more carefully, the world of language is encountered as a vast system of parts that one is cast in, and in accordance with whose order one is compelled to assume a role. This is not as voluntaristic as the use of the verb, "assume," suggests. To again follow Ong here, what has just been described as a part is a limited, internally coherent ordering of verbal and nonverbal behavior that achieves specific effects, or at least specifiable ones. There are some grounds for referring to these parts as discourses, each functioning to place its utterer in a position of the subject of that discourse. We might state, then, regarding societies of orality, that a person is the loci in which discourses intersect and produce subject positions. Persons are thus not defined ontologically but discursively, and their aggregate, the community of persons, is equally derived from *memoria* as the treasure trove of discourses. The meaning of existence or life, in the sense of the overall coherence of discursive play, can never reside in the individual member, who is a function of that play; it can only reside at the higher level of the *memoria*, and is made accessible through the animating force of storytelling. There is a resonance of animation here: storytelling animates the dynamic elements of *memoria*, the animated *memoria* thus becomes itself an animating force of meaning. Where the performance of oral society storytelling and technological revivification of personal identity are exactly analogous is in the sense of commemoration.

---

49. This account of commemoration and memoria borrows substantially from Wlad Godzich's 1993 *Surfaces* essay, "The Management of Privatization."

As in the case of Kurzweil's technologically animated person, commemoration in the context of oral society storytelling has to do with iteration and not recollection. But there is something else of importance that goes on in both the situations of Kurzweil's technological and oral society's storytelling animation. Persons are largely heterogeneous from the physical human individual since the latter do not necessarily achieve any coherence in the roles they play. This is also implied in Rapley's depiction of emergent contemporary vernaculars of globalization where the apparent incoherence of definitive social roles contributes to the crisis of proliferating neomedievalism. Yet, in the situation of medieval oral society storytelling, this heterogeneity does not give rise to any anxiety in the way Kurzweil assesses it will with the advent of intelligent self-conscious machines, or Rapley suggests it does with the emergent vernaculars. Quite the contrary, heterogeneity reinforces the belief that one's meaning transcends oneself, residing in a transcendental dimension of *memoria*. The animating activity of storytelling makes *memoria*'s own animating force immanent, but this does not actualize the ultimate meaning or coherence of meaning; it reinforces the promise or faith, if you will, in the capacity of *memoria* to provide that truth. In order to avoid repeating Kurzweil's error by identifying the person of orality with the mind of Descartes, as well as Rapley's of presuming the natural necessity of indelible individual identity, it is crucial to recognize that in the economy of orality the person does not reside somewhere within the physical individual — it is not the external expression of an autogenetic intentionality — rather, it is the articulation of the collective *memoria* that the physical individual embodies through the animating effect of storytelling. Detecting this same sort of articulation to be at play in the information technology engendered global networks of non-state actors and transnational urban vernaculars, may very well be what inclines Pollard and Rapley to view them as neomedievalisms that threaten the international order. That could very well account for why and how the articulations of such persona as al-Qa'ida's get designated as ideological and illegitimate forms of expression.

Bringing our focus back to the scholarly basis for McLuhan's neomedievalism, something Lord, Havelock, and Ong are all concerned with is what happens to the human conceptual and social world when the discursive economy of orality collapses. Once the conventionality, the arbitrariness with which persons or subject positions are assigned to physical individuals is put in real jeopardy, roles can be presumed to be entitlements. When the difference between a subject position and the correlative physical body that purports it is erased, so that specific discourses are held to be natural to those wielding them, there occurs a major transformation of the discursive economy. With that transformation, the function of controlling the animating force of the overall discursive flow devolves to one specific discourse, producing a hierarchization of the economy: only certain specific discursive forms can access authentic meaning. Rather than persons as loci of discursive play, there are individuals with inherently endowed rights and privileges, the integrity of whose now inherent identities is maintained or preserved through a singular overarching discourse of power. The period from the 13th to the 17th century is devoted to this process in which collective *memoria* is progressively replaced by individual consciousness. For McLuhan, the point of critical mass in that process was the invention of the Gutenberg press in the mid 15th century.

Typography's ascendancy as the privileged mode of representing human intelligence was so rapid that by the first decades of the 16th century, it was very apparent there was an emerging new discursive organization producing a new set of social perturbations requiring a new order of management. Instead of the admixture of experiential fact and belief characterizing the person of orality's collective *memoria*, what is present with typographic literacy is the hard differentiation between the subject of knowledge and the subject of experience. Instead of storytelling being the animating activity that brings into play the animating and ordering capacity of *memoria*, imagination becomes the agency of animation, shuttling back and forth between the subject of knowledge and the subject of experience, bringing an inkling of matter to the first and a sense of form to the second. In other words, imagination connects matter and form, being of neither. The problem of imagination presents itself early on after the advent of typography, with the very tendency of that technology to foster a private matrix of consciousness resulting in imagination's appearing as the purely private process of thinking, lacking the substance and permanence of the uncorrupted realm of the *memoria*, making it seem incomprehensible, and groundless. There is a persistent, even if not consistent, effort traceable in the work of Machiavelli, Bacon, Descartes, Spinoza, Hobbes, Locke, Hutcheson, Shaftsbury, Hume, Baumgarten, and Kant to settle and ground what is otherwise unbridled. Neither Hegel nor Freud should be forgotten in this regard; and, as we can see from the most recent efforts of Eric Santers and Slavoj Žižek in their collaborative book, *The Neighbor: Three Inquiries in Political Theology,* to revive a "creaturely" conception of the human, there is still a powerful drive to eliminate the disturbing role of the imagination. McLuhan's preoccupation with *sensus communis* has everything to do with the prospects for imagination. With McLuhan the pertinent question is not how we can imagine the world in a global information technology system, but rather: What are the conditions of possibility for imagination in a global information technology system? Utopian and dystopian visions aside, Kurzweil's postulate that programming algorithms approximate *sensus communis* — now recognized as the agency of imagination — does not settle, but rather gives an added twist to McLuhan's question: What are the conditions and necessities of consciousness in an information age of fragmentation and coexisting identities?

Returning, in conclusion, to Rapley's depiction of coexisting transnational and local identities will provide some sense of both how pertinent and difficult these two questions in tandem are. As stated before, Rapley construes the apparent heterogeneity of the person and the physical human individual entailed in these identities to be symptomatic of the crisis of proliferating neomedievalism. There is a dangerous incoherence of definitive social roles in the fact that the same physical individual can assume contextually the distinctly heterogeneous Wolof and Hip Hop subject positions, as well as the Senegalese, African, and Francophone. In terms of personal identity, Rapley plainly thinks the trend towards neomedievalism is threatening to eviscerate the idea that indelible individual identity is the social order's core element of its political force. Per his depiction of the emergent vernacular speakers, which takes note of the ubiquitous influence of the American urban musical forms Hip Hop and Rap, they are purporting various personas according to local necessities that are in turn animated by a general global activity of dubious political character. We might well call this the activity of the market, whose animating force is a continual flow of images and information that has specific effect, but remains ultimately incomprehensible. The person as a function of hyper-fluid market forces is not analogous to either the persona of oral medieval European society or the indelible isolated individual identity of modernity's book-based economy of knowledge, except that, like them, it is a historical event, both in the sense of being materialist and indexing a fundamental change in the media of imagination. Rapley's depiction, indeed, suggests the market entails a creative capacity that while destructive to the elements of national formation — historically themselves functions of the market's global expansion — also fosters imaginative innovation. There is nothing novel in this idea. Marx recognized capitalism as a revolutionary force. After him, Antonio Gramsci, when contemplating American hyper preponderance (*prepotenza*) in the twentieth century as indicating a transformation in the material bases of modernity, claimed such market-driven force to be a *poesis* and a theory of *poesis*.[50] The situation of coexistence Rapley depicts calls for thinking about the historicity of this *poesis* as a constitutive function of society rather than as an effect of society. Throughout modernity, such thinking has assumed the modalities of historicism and historiography as functions of the state. But, in spite of the state's ongoing effort — of necessity, according to Machiavelli — to manage imagination by generating a totalizing account of the conditions for its possibility, there persist events of its actuality that heat up the circuit of exchange.

The continuity of this effort today is neatly illustrated in the centrality given in the *9/11 Commission Report* to the Janus-like nature of imagination revealed with al-Qa'ida's successful use of commercial jetliners on September 11, 2001 to attack the Pentagon and destroy the World Trade Center. In fact, of the four kinds of failures the *9/11 Commission Report* cites as being instrumental in the United States' vulnerability to such attacks — the other three are policy, capabilities, and management — it holds the failure of imagination as paramount. The

50. Antonio Gramsci, *Quaderni del carcere*, a cura di Valentino Gerratana (Torino: G. Einaudi, 1975.) Edizione critica dell'Istituto Gramsci, v. 1: quaderni 3 §11, 296; quaderni 3 §41, 318.

Commission was so convinced of this it asserts in a section of the report entitled "Institutionalizing Imagination" — which recalls the history of Richard Clarke's efforts from 1996 to get the Pentagon and the Federal Aviation Administration to prepare adequate protocols for an imagined scenario of terrorists using commercial aircraft as guided missiles: "It is therefore crucial to find a way of routinizing, even bureaucratizing, the exercise of imagination."[51] Supposedly a way of better preparing America to defend itself against the asymmetrical warriors threatening global security — which, as both Pollard and Rapley's analysis point out, are spawns of the neomedievalism engendered by globalization — the integration of imagination into the bureaucratic structures and mindset of global security institutions is a positive expression of the robust expectation that technology and imagination will converge into a global system of security and social stability. That is an expectation Kurzweil explicitly shares when he claims that protection against illegitimate uses of the Singularity's technology requires "oversight by regulatory bodies, the development of technology-specific 'immune' responses, as well as computer-assisted surveillance by law enforcement organizations."[52] Such an expectation itself indicates a misapprehension about the nature of imagination. If it becomes possible to absolutely manage imagination globally as a habitual function of security institutions, to both anticipate and then preempt the most unlikely disruptive manifestations of it enabled by the information-driven global economy, then how could there be any truly dynamic thinking in the world? The quandary is about the tension between the possibilities for radical freethinking, spawned by a technology of representing and communicating human thought the necessity of whose media requires decentralization of authority, and the need to secure that very authority as guarantor of that freedom. Stated more succinctly, once the connection is made between the Singularity of futurist technology theory and international security, the real imminently catastrophic dangers posed by the amplified inhomogeneities Gubrud remarks become all that much more apparent. The point is not to account for them in any sort of reductive representational way — as occurs unfortunately with the designations "new Middle Ages" and "neomedievalism," which interpret them according to a discursive economy of radically different material forms. Occurrences like Rapley's coexisting identities are not representations of any thing; they are indexes. And as with any index the task is to think with celerity of flow, moving betwixt but never becoming coincident with any given expression.

---

51. National Commission on Terrorist Attacks upon the U.S., *9/11 Commission Report: Fully Updated with Controversial Third Monograph and Never-Before-Published Progress Reports from the 9/11 Commissioners* (New York: Barnes & Nobles, 2006), 344.
52. LAR.

Part II

Translations

♦ Chinese Nationalism

Modern Chinese Nationalism and the Boxer Movement*

Li Weichao

Nationalism, in its broad sense, refers to an idea or emotion which expresses one's allegiance to one's native land and one's interests. When a nation faces external threats, its glorious past and culture, its courage and wisdom are often appealed to in order to stimulate nationalistic feelings in its members and generate spiritual power to defend the integrity, sovereignty and dignity of the nation. The Burning of Opium at Humen, the Westernization Movement, and the Hundred Days' Reform articulate a history of China's resistance to foreign invasion and its fight for national independence and revival; a history inspired by the nationalistic emotion and strength of China's people. The Boxer Movement was not an organized movement and was ignited by the peasants' spontaneous reactions to the economic infiltrations and religious oppressions of foreign powers; it first took place in Shandong and Hebei after the Reform of 1898 and quickly spread to all parts of the country, representing a surge of grass-root nationalistic feelings. Nonetheless for a long period of time the Boxers failed to gain the recognition and sympathy of the Chinese nationalists; instead their acts were often labeled "narrow-minded nationalism" or "reactionary nationalism." This odd situation was actually determined by characteristics of modern Chinese nationalism, as well as the boxers' superstitious practices and blind anti-foreignism.

* This article was first published in *Social Sciences Journal of Colleges in Shanxi* 山西高等学校社会科学学报, no. 12 (Dec. 2005): 104-106.

The notion of nationalism, in its strictest sense, had been unknown to Ancient China, for allegiance always only flowed to dynastic families or to the Chinese culture in general. Liang Shumin wrote, "In Chinese traditional philosophy, the concept of nation does not exist at all. Ancient Chinese always talked about tianxia (literally, "under heaven," "the world") an unmistakable demonstration of their ignorance of international conflicts, which in turn testifies to the fact that China was not at all nation-like."[1] And a classification of community by dynasty (country) or culture (tianxia) rather than by nation-state or political community could produce nothing more than a "dynastic China" or a "cultural China." Moreover, the legitimacy of a dynasty lies in its status as a representation of the orthodox culture. "It was originally based on cultural unification followed by political unification, with tianxia (the world) replacing the concept of country."[2] The borders of imperial China were never clear. Whatever countries or regions were subjugated culturally or politically to it could be included as members of the Chinese extended family. Qian Mu wrote, "The Chinese definition of nationality is often undistinguishable from that of human race, and their concept of country overlaps with that of the universe or the world. They take nationality or country as a cultural body. For them, a nationality or a country exists only as a cultural entity, and there is no place for 'nationality' or 'country' in the narrow sense."[3] Therefore, old China was marked by a culture-oriented universalism rather than by nationalism. It was not until Western powers had, by blood and fire, disrupted the Chinese dream of a "heavenly empire" that China was forced to substitute the traditional conception of tianxia for an exotic concept of nation. A modern consciousness of nation had not been in existence in China until the Chinese became gradually aware, with the increase of communication and confrontation with other nations, of the importance of forming a national community that served to bind together different races, regions, cultures, and histories.

It can therefore be said that the new-born nationalism in early modern China was a large but empty sign,[4] a rudimentary form of nationalism with excessive affective elements that needed still to be rationalized. When nationalism is in want of an inner spiritual soul, i.e. its role as a catalyst for the modernization of a nation, it becomes an alias for blind anti-foreignism, egomania and an arrogance which itself degenerates into a crude form of anti-Western thought. The Boxer Movement was a typical example of the eruption of such "nationalism." Although the boxers were actually motivated to resist Western invasions, to defend the

---

1. Liang Shumin, "Essential Elements of Chinese Culture" 中国文化要义, in vol. 3 of *Complete Works of Liang Shumin* 梁漱溟全集(Jinan: Shandong renmin chubanshe, 1990), 294.
2. Ibid.
3. Qian Mu, *Introduction to the Cultural History of China* 中国文化史导论(Shanghai: Sanlian shudian [duplicated version], 1988), 19.
4. Xu Jilin, "Modern Chinese Nationalism and Anti-western Thoughts" 中国现代民族主义和反西方思潮, *Mingbo Monthly* 明报月刊, no. 3, 1997.

integrity and dignity of the Chinese people, they resorted to superstitious practices such as sorcery, spells and spirit rapping as a form of their struggle, and rejected indiscriminately everything Western. Their efforts to preserve an agricultural civilization in fact turned their nationalism into a vulgar anti-Westernism which lacked the spirit of modernity and ran counter to modernization. Sun Yat-sen believed that the Boxer Movement was stirred up by the Qing government's "rumors, which caused confusions among the populace, by its evocation of upheavals, which endangered the safety of the country, by its wreaking of disasters, which made the people suffer, as well as by its profuse eulogy of the boxers' virtues."[5] "The anti-foreignism fostered by the Manchurians had reached its pinnacle in the Boxer Upheavals of 1900."[6] Sun's scathing criticism of the boxers' anti-foreignism and obscurantism extended to failing to observe their nationalistic feelings.

The boxers' simple and primitive sympathy for the Chinese people was but a rudimentary form of modern Chinese nationalism. If it was to be elevated to a rational level, it needed to be built into the value system, social system and the code of behavior inherent in the Chinese people. In other words, the boxers' simple and pure emotion for the Chinese nationality had provided only an outer frame for modern Chinese nationalism. But the more important task was to add new content to modern Chinese nationalism and to elevate it from its emotional level to a rational level. This process of change, due to the particularity of Chinese nationalism, was embodied in the transformation of traditional Confucian culture to modern Western culture.

Speaking of modern Chinese nationalism, Fairbank points out that in the beginning of the early modern era China still had kept some non-nationalistic traditions. This means that as long as the rulers of the empire took Confucianism as an all-embracing and universal tool for governing, even when governed by a minority nationality, people would find such governance acceptable. This shows that Chinese culture (or the Chinese way of life) was indeed more essential than Chinese nationalism.[7] Therefore, when Chinese culture collided with a "heterogeneous" Western culture, rising nationalism became a kind of "cultural nationalism." Almost all policies then, such as "using foreign tools to fight off foreign forces," "Chinese culture as system and Western culture as means" and Sun Yat-sen's brand of "nationalism," placed culture in a central position. Theoretically speaking, this was because most species of "nationalism" had taken the key values of the country and the mainstream culture as the very basis of their existence. Here "mainstream culture" refers to the cultural system and value

5.   Sun Yat-sen, "A Letter to the Governor of Hong Kong" 致香港总督书, in vol. 1 of *Complete Works of Sun Yat-sen* 孙中山全集 (Beijing: Zhonghua shuju, 1984), 191–193.

6.   Ibid.

7.   John Fairbank, *The United States and China* 美国与中国 (Beijing: Shangwu yinshuguan, 1987), 74.

system that are dominant in a society, and Confucianism was the mainstream Chinese culture. Since this mainstream culture forms the very basis for the identification of a nation's political and intellectual elite as well as its common people, it plays a significant role in the formation of solidarity and consensus, especially when it has become the central symbol of the nation.

Nationalism as manifested in the Boxer Movement, with the main body of its grass roots participants being peasants, took the traditional "dynastic China" or "cultural China" as the basis of its cultural identification, and maintained the dominant position of Confucian culture as its aim. It is thus conservative in character. However, having experienced the Westernization Movement, the Reform of 1898 and the 1911 Revolution, the Chinese intellectual and political elite, afflicted by the trauma caused by cultural setbacks and nursing an antagonism against mainstream culture, moved a step further from their initial interest in Western material culture to a conscious acceptance of Western cultural values. Yet Confucian culture had also shown its immense strength in resisting a heterogeneous Western culture as well as the powerful historical trend of social reform under way in the early modern era. This gave rise to an anti-traditional element in the formation of early modern Chinese nationalism, which was referred to by some scholars as "a counter-culture nationalism." Its main feature was this: Confucianism, the central symbol of the mainstream culture, was regarded as an obstacle to national progress and therefore a target for demolition.[8] Progressive intellectuals since the 1911 Revolution, under the banners of science and democracy, had taken this critique of the negative aspects of the traditional cultural and political systems as their starting point.

Owing to the boxers' conservative character articulated in their protectiveness of Confucian culture, besides their feudal obscurantism and anti-foreignism, it was only natural that the Boxer Movement was alleged to be the ugliest and worst aspect of traditional culture and became the target of critique for China's intellectual and political elite. Back in 1918, Chen Duxiu regarded the Boxer Movement as "a laughable, stunning, annoying and lamentable historical event." "Though its merit can be hardly recognized, the boxers' thoughts and an increasing number of similar activities have spread to the entire country. Who is to guarantee that the event will not happen again? Who can guarantee that we will not erect yet another monument of humiliation?" Therefore, "if we do not wish the Boxer Rebellion to repeat itself, we must cleanse our country of all the conditions which led to its occurrence."[9] That is to say, we must purge the inherent weaknesses in traditional culture, for China's problems found their very roots in its traditional culture. Here, Chen Duxiu, in his critique, had indeed taken

---

8. Xiao Gongqin, "Nationalism and Ideology in an Era of Transformation" 民族主义与中国转型时期的意识形态, *Strategy and Management* 战略与管理, no. 4 (1994): 4.

9. Chen Duxiu, "The Baron von Ketteler monument" 克林德碑, in *Selected Essays by Chen Duxiu* 陈独秀文章选编 (Shanghai: Sanlian shudian, 1984).

the Boxer Movement as an embodiment of the worst part of traditional culture, failing to see in the movement a kind of "emotional nationalism." Lu Xun held a similar view. He despised the boxers' superstition and obscurantism. He wrote sarcastically, "When the fist is dealt out, it can always hit 'a depth unreachable by guns and cannons.' This happened once in 1900, but sadly, it was a complete failure. How things will work out this time remains to be seen."[10] Such criticism of the boxers' brand of materialism by Chen Duxiu, Lu Xun and others made it clear that the political and intellectual elite of the time had endeavored to infuse modern Western culture into the frame of Chinese "emotional nationalism", in hopes that Chinese nationalism could be rationalized.

But facing increasing national crises, such efforts met serious setbacks, for the imperialist powers, who introduced Western culture to China, had also introduced bloody invasions and cruel exploitations for the Chinese people. As Jiang Menglin put it, "As far as I am concerned, Westerners look like Vishnu, a half-god and half-demon with more than two hands and many faces, who holds in one set of hands a hand light, a boat and a doll, and in another a police club, a pistol and opium. When you see his bright side, he is an angel; when you see his dark side, he is a devil." So while early modern China was studying an advanced Western culture she also had to exert all her efforts to resist imperialist invasion and exploitation. Which of these two tasks was more important? The nationalists' views changed as time and circumstances changed. When external threats to the safety of China did not allow the nationalists to fill the empty frame of "emotional nationalism" at their liberty, but mobilized the nationalists' patriotic feelings to help resist increasingly violent invasions, the kind of nationalistic emotion associated with the boxers' protection of national integrity and independence was re-examined from a new perspective. Those who formerly criticized the Boxer Movement now began to sing the praises of the "nationalistic" spirit of its resistance against imperialist invasion.

In his 1918 speech on "Civil Rights," Sun Yat-sen acknowledged that "the boxers' courage was invincible at the outset." In the Yangcun battle, they fought three thousand soldiers led by Admiral Seymour "fearlessly, to the last drop of blood...Their courage was enthralling and most admirable. It was only after this bloody battle that Westerners realized that China still had some nationalistic thought and a nation like that was unconquerable." Chen Duxiu expressed a similar view in his 1924 article entitled "Two Mistaken Views We Hold of the Boxer Movement." He insisted that the Boxer Movement was an important event in modern Chinese history and likened its importance to that of the 1911 Revolution. He commented, "The whole nation, rather than some rebellious boxers, should be held responsible for the Boxer Movement, no matter whether the event was

10. Lu Xun, "Random Thoughts, no. 37" 随感录，第37篇, in *Collected Essays of Lu Xun: Essays* 鲁迅文集：染文卷 (Heilongjiang remin chubanshe, 1995), 19–20.

deemed a success or a failure." "But for these 'barbarous' boxers, the honor of the Chinese people would not have been defended." "The Boxer Movement was a grand, though tragic, prelude to the history of China's national revolutions."[11] In another essay written several months later, Chen pointed out that the Boxer Movement was one of the four civil movements in the history of the development of the Chinese petty bourgeoisie (the other three being the Hundred Days' Reform, the 1911 Revolution and the May Fourth Movement). "The boxers' renouncing of treaties, their rejection of external forces and Christianity, and their contempt for ermaozi and sanmaozi[12] — imperialists' running dogs — were irreproachable. But their blind faith in supernatural power and rejection of both science and Western culture was where their limitations lay. Nonetheless, these were the inherent weaknesses of agricultural societies, rather than a plausible reason for denouncing the Boxer Movement itself."[13] It goes without saying that Chinese nationalists, e.g. Chen Duxiu and Sun Yat-sen, had taken the event as a constituent part of the Chinese national revolution as well as a manifestation of nationalist spirit. Despite the Boxer Rebellion's inevitable limitations, which included its blind anti-foreignism and superstitious practices, its progressiveness, i.e. its resistance to imperialist invasions, cannot be denied.

That the Boxer Movement was viewed as a constituent part of the Chinese national revolution shows that Chinese nationalism then still remained on an emotional level, that it had only the rhetoric of nationalism, i.e. patriotic sentiments associated with the resistance of foreign invasions. The strategy of infusing Western cultural values into Chinese nationalism was seriously affected by the urge to fight off Western invasions. The neo-nationalist revolution led by the CCP also resorted to nationalistic feelings to encourage the Chinese to battle foreign invaders. Therefore the Boxer Movement received increasing praise. Mao Zedong regarded it as a war against imperialism, saying that it "demonstrated the unyielding spirit of the Chinese to resist imperialism and its running dogs."[14] The Boxer Movement therefore came to be known as an "anti-imperialist patriotic revolution," which played an active role in obstructing imperialist invasions. When China was threatened by foreign powers and during an era in which the revolutionary wheels kept rolling ahead, Chinese nationalism had to undergo the slow process of transformation from an emotional stage to a rational stage. Some nationalists attempted to instill new elements into this emergent nationalism and to disassociate it from the Boxer Movement.

---

11. Chen Duxiu, vol. 2 of *Selected Essays by Chen Duxiu*, 574–5.
12. Offensive terms in late Qing and early Republican eras referring respectively to Chinese converted to Christianity and those who spoke foreign languages or worked for foreigners–translator's note.
13. Chen Duxiu, vol. 2 of *Selected Essays by Chen Duxiu*, 574–5.
14. Mao Zedong, vol. 2 of *Selected Works of Mao Zedong* 毛泽东选集 (Beijing: Remin chubanshe, 1991), 632.

In 1932, at the first anniversary of the "September 18 Event," Hu Shi still thought that "every advance made was inevitably accompanied by the birth of some reactionary forces. Barely had the Hundred Days' Reform achieved any success, the Ci Xi Clique came into power, incurring the 'national humiliation of 1900.'" Of course he accused the boxers of being a part of the reactionary forces in early modern China that had set obstacles to every progressive effort of the time. Behind these reactionary forces was allegedly the old culture, or "our ancestors' sin," whose harmful influences had lasted to that very day. The result of this was demonstrated by "a lamentable statement summarizing thirty years of our revolution: 'Revolution is not yet completed.'" He therefore believed, "The purpose of the so-called 'national salvation' is in fact to cure just these fundamental pains and ailments." "As long as these pains and ailments are not removed, the hope of defeating imperialism and bringing a revival to our nation is only empty talk."[15] His intention was obviously to consolidate Chinese nationalism by replacing the old Chinese culture with modern Western culture. As late as in 1938, Jiang Tingfu, in his book *A History of Early Modern China*, wrote, "The Boxer Rebellion of 1900 represented the total outbreak of all conservative forces in China." He believed, "The Boxer Movement was the third project to save China and its people in the history of early modern China. However this project was anti-Westernization and anti-modernization, which went against the other two. No wonder the boxers were doomed to failure. The heavy price it had exacted was enough to show that reversing the course of history could never be the way to save our nation."[16] What he meant was Chinese nationalism should go beyond the stage of "cultural nationalism" whose primary concern was to protect traditional culture. An anti-Western nationalism would obstruct China's modernization agenda. But other louder voices overpowered Jiang and his associates, and Chinese nationalism, on the eve of the People's Republic, still remained a gigantic but empty sign. After the founding of the People's Republic, it was even harder to imagine how it would be possible, under the influence of the prevalent anti-Western ideology, to construct a modern nationalism. It was not until the Reform and Opening to the Outside World period (since 1978 — translator's note), when the Chinese modernization project was normalized, that Chinese nationalism began to merge itself into the global trend of modernization, marking the birth of an open, non-racial nationalism with its own value system and political system.

In sum, early modern Chinese nationalism constituted only one stage in the modernization process. However, since China's modernization was forced on the country by Western invasion and, moreover, the models for China's modernization

---

15. Hu Shi, "Miserable Memories and Reflections" 惨痛的回忆与反思, in vol. 27 of *The Complete Works of Hu Shi* 胡适全集 (Hefei: Anhui jiaoyu chubanshe, 2003), 418.
16. Jiang Tingfu, *A history of Early Modern China* 中国近代史 (Shanghai: Shanghai guji chubanshe, 2001), 76.

were those Western countries that had invaded China and thus had been colonizers, Chinese nationalism was in direct conflict with modernization itself. Naturally Chinese nationalism should reject world hegemony of all forms, but at the same time it should also draw on various models of modernization, including those of the West. Since the early modern period, China had had sufficient exposure to the value signs and cultural symbols of nationalism; what it really lacked was substantial political content, particularly of a kind related to modernization and public interests. Modern nationalism identifies not only with a certain race or culture, but also, and more importantly, with a nation-state. And a nation-state represents, rather than merely an abstraction of form, sovereignty and law, something substantial, i.e. a common way of life, a social system, and value system. In other words, the identity of modern nationalism is not without its principles and content; it is congruent not only with the borders of a nation-state, but also with its value system and political system. As for what value system and political system will suit China's needs, it is not a simple question of identifying an existing system, but rather a structure that is yet to emerge. So the material content of Chinese nationalism is still in the process of being explored.

(translated by Lin Qinxin)

The Cultural Origin of the Boxer Movement's Obscurantism and Its Influence on the Cultural Revolution*

Wang Yi

[....]

Chinese history in the 20th century was inaugurated by the Boxer Movement. In retrospect, we are not surprised to find that the political twists and turns of the century are closely related to this peculiar inauguration. Not only did this nation-wide movement have decisive influence on the fate of China at that particular historical juncture, but its ways of perceiving the world, mobilizing the masses and its mode of religious belief made a drastic return in the form of "mass movement" during the Cultural Revolution sixty years later.

The cultural goal of the Cultural Revolution was two-fold: it had, domestically, the goal of "eliminating bad elements of all descriptions" and "establishing the absolute authority of 'the red sun,'" and, externally, the goal of obstructing and cleansing all foreign influences under the banner of "beating down imperialism, revisionism, and reactionaries." This pursuit of the Cultural Revolution not only responded to and intensified its domestic cultural goal, but also exerted enormous influence on all important aspects of social life, political, military, diplomatic, and cultural. By comparing the Boxer Movement and the Cultural Revolution, this paper attempts to show why both events' external goal of "liquidating all harmful pests" and domestic goal of "eliminating bad elements of all descriptions" were so closely related with each other and how this relation was rooted in cultural obscurantism.

---

* This article was first published in *Tribune of Social Sciences*, no. 8 (2003), 72–80.

I. The mythologizing of the Boxer Movement and the promotion of its spiritual heritage during the Cultural Revolution

With regard to the concept of foreign cultures, the Cultural Revolution has as its model the Boxer Movement, which swept across China sixty years before. In a long essay entitled "Patriotism or Quislingism?" published in no. 5 of *Red Flag* 红旗 (1967), Qi Benyu, having first blamed the Qing government's treasonable policy toward Western powers and eulogized the Boxer Movement's "anti-imperialist" position, attacks openly the agents of "quislingism" among the communists and the "Chinese Khrushchev." Mao Zedong, in highly appreciative terms, regarded the publication of this essay as the landmark of a new and substantial stage of the Cultural Revolution. In Qi's essay there is one section titled "How to View the Revolutionary Mass Movement during the Boxer Movement" in which he suggests: 1) the Boxer Movement was not only a resistance, in the general sense, to Western powers, but, more importantly, "a battle against imperialism" in the form of "just rebellion" and "mass revolutionary movement"; 2) apart from military struggle against Western powers, other methods adopted by the boxers were: banning foreign goods, attacking embassies, cursing Westerners, taking to the streets, fanatical mass protests and demonstrations which looked like the waves of "a red sea," etc., all of which were assumed to be the most revolutionary and the most divine conduct rather than savage behavior or turbulences; 3) all attacks on the boxers' craze for witchcraft were libels against and distortions of this "revolutionary mass movement;" 4) the difference between revolution and counterrevolution lay in whether one advocated or opposed the Boxer Movement.

Clearly, when Qi Benyu made his comments on the Boxer Movement, he had the on-going Cultural Revolution in mind. As there was a high degree of symmetry in the cultural goal, mode of struggle and historical significance of the two events, eulogizing the Boxer Movement was a necessary measure for upholding the spirit of the Cultural Revolution; conversely, as the Cultural Revolution and this "rebellious mass movement" sixty years earlier shared many common features, the promotion of the boxer spirit would greatly further the Cultural Revolution.

II. The reversal in the assessment of the Boxer Movement since the May Fourth Movement and its cultural orientation

[…]

May Fourth scholars always use the boxers' obscurantism and their fanatic anti-foreignism as counterexamples when promoting the urgency of learning Western science and democracy. In "The Essential Difference between the Civilizations of the East and the West," Li Dazhao, for example, states firmly, "At present our immediate goal is to absorb the advantages of Western civilization so as to make up for the deficiency in Eastern civilization. We should definitely not use the boxers' thoughts and those dying ideas to corrode the rest of the world." In another example, Lu Xun mentioned many times the fundamental opposition between the "boxer bandits" on the one hand and science and social progress on the other. [1] One more example: Chen Duxiu wrote in 1918 a well-known long essay entitled "The Baron von Ketteler Monument" (published in no. 5, vol. 5 of *The New Jeunesse* 新青年), in which he explicates the five cultural causes of the Boxer Movement, with the Movement's inheritance of the primitive cultural spirit of Taoism as one example. "[Taoism] has been the most wide-spread thought in China from time immemorial and a philosophy endemic to the Chinese." "The boxers were the product of a plethora of superstitious practices and heresies in the society. Thus, they always claimed they followed the Great God's will to wipe out all foreigners. " Another immediate cause was the collusion of the conservative elements in the Qing government with the boxers to eliminate supporters of the Hundred Days' Reform.

> At that time, 80 to 90 percent of government officials, due to controversies over reform, wanted to encourage the boxers to fight foreigners. … These officials knew nothing about Western civilization and held fast to the old idea of preserving the egoistic traditional culture that had been passed down from generation to generation. … In their eyes, foreigners who did not know the ethical code and virtues proposed by Chinese saints were not much better than beasts. As for those Chinese who catered to and modeled these beasts, if they did not deserve to be killed, who did? Therefore in 1898 they expelled or executed a bunch of revolutionaries who supported the beasts. This wasn't enough. In 1900, when the boxers, who had faith in the Chinese tradition, i.e. the unification of Confucianism, Taoism, and Buddhism, came out to kill the beasts, these renowned Confucian masters were naturally happy and believed the problem had been finally solved.

Finally, Chen Duxiu warns the people in a serious manner:

> If we want to remove this monument which marks our national humiliation, we should guarantee that the Boxer Rebellion will not happen again, and to insure that the Boxer Rebellion won't happen again, we need to destroy the hotbeds that had nursed it.

---

1. See Lu Xun, *Hot Wind* 热风 33, "What Will Happen after Nora Left Home" 挪拉走后会怎样 (Renminwenxue chubanshe, 1959). Even in his last years, Lu Xun still published essays criticizing the Boxer Movement's rejection of modern civilization. See his "Two or Three Things of which Mr. Taiyan Had Reminded Me" 因太炎先生而想起的二三事, "The Confucius in Modern China" 在现代中国的孔夫子 and so on.

> There are now two roads for us to choose: a bright one which leads to
> science, atheism and the republic, and a dark one which leads to
> totalitarianism, superstition and theocracy. If our people hope that the
> Boxer Rebellion will not happen again, and that the humiliating
> Ketteler Monument will not be erected for a second time, then they
> should know which road to take.

Obviously, Chen Duxiu believes that whether or not the Chinese realize the
fundamental contradiction between the Boxer Movement's cultural origin and
the direction for the process of modern civilization is a vital question. He regards
the question as one decisive for China's future.

The Chinese intelligentsia's general attitude toward the Boxer Movement
underwent a fundamental change in 1924, when those intellectual radicals who
wrote for *The New Jeunesse* became divided in their appraisal of the event. While
some stuck to their earlier critical attitude, others talked about the Movement in
positive terms. On September 3, 1924, Chen Duxiu published "Two Mistaken Ideas
We Hold about the Boxer Movement" in no. 81 of *Guide* 向导, a journal edited
by the Central Committee of the Chinese Communist Party. In it, he not only
sings the praises of the Boxer Movement, a drastically different opinion from what
he had written six years earlier in "The Baron von Ketteler Monument," but also
rejects in radical terms the critique of the boxers' obscurantism in ideological
circles[2] :

> The Boxer Movement is a momentous historical event in modern
> China. Its significance equals that of the 1911 Revolution. But the
> general public ... holds two mistaken ideas about it. First, they detest
> the boxers' anti-foreignism. They see only the boxers' anti-foreign
> activities but fail to see the causes of the activities: the bloody oppression
> of foreign armies, diplomats and missionaries and the indignation of
> the oppressed... They accuse the boxers of supporting the Qing
> government and rejecting foreign powers, but they forget that China
> today is still a society under the yoke of patriarchy, feudalism and
> theocracy! Inevitably, the boxers were stubborn, superstitious and
> savage, but since the whole world (of course including China) is in a
> stubborn and savage state, why should we only accuse the boxers, whose
> acts constituted, in a sense, a part of the national resistance
> movement?... Having read the history of China's diplomatic relations
> and the history of its commerce, I can no longer deny that the Boxer
> Movement is a tragic prelude to the history of China's national
> revolution.

After the splitting of the May Fourth intellectuals, it was only natural for Chen
Duxiu, considering the political circumstances and his position as the leader of

---

2. Vol. 2 of *Selected Works of Chen Duxiu* 陈独秀文章选编 (Sanlian shudian, 1984), 574–5.

the Communist Party, to have shown a significantly different attitude toward the Boxer Movement. What is worthy of our notice is his essay's peculiar reasoning. First, he attributes the criticism of the Boxer Movement to the critics' blindness to the oppression of China by foreign powers. Chen's accusation obviously does not agree with basic facts. Those May Fourth intellectuals who bitingly criticized the Boxer Movement, like Chen himself, were at the same time deadly enemies of imperialist oppression. To neglect this basic fact results in an absolute logic: those who denounced the Boxer Movement were ignorant of the atrocities committed by imperialists. (During the Cultural Revolution, this logic naturally becomes: any objection to the boxer-like radical anti-foreignism was equal to quislingism). Conversely, because of the existence of the imperialists' oppression, even the "savagely anti-foreign" and "chronically superstitious" boxers could still be an army of justice as well as the precursors to resistance in resisting the oppression of foreign powers under modern social conditions. (During the Cultural Revolution, this logic underwent a new exegesis: because of the existence of international oppression, the boxer-like "rebellion against imperialism, revisionism, and reactionaries and their agents within the Party" became the only righteous conduct.) Second, although in this article Chen Duxiu still uses terms such as "superstition," "savagism," and "horror" to describe the Boxer Movement, he holds that any means, fair or foul, to curb those most wicked enemies was justifiable and therefore should not be blamed. Following Chen Duxiu's lead, Li Dazhao, in an article titled "History of the British Empire's Invasion of China" published in 1925 right after the "5/30 Event," showed a similar change in attitude. Though he still criticizes the Boxer Movement for "its incorrect judgment of situations, its anti-foreignism... and its worship of such gods as the Monkey King and Guan Yu," his narrative focus shifts to the idea that "the Boxer Movement is a nationalist revolution ... provoked by the prevalent indignation of the Chinese after the imperialist powers invaded northern China."[3] Contrary to this change in attitude, liberal thinkers such as Hu Shi still insisted on the *The New Jeunesse* intellectuals' critique of the Boxer Movement; moreover, in a firm and unyielding manner, they took Chen Duxiu and his followers to task for changing their stance.[4]

Since the 1920s, the Boxer Movement received an increasingly higher appraisal; such a high evaluation of the movement reached its extreme from 1949 to the Cultural Revolution and was instilled in the minds of millions of the Chinese people. For instance, in 1958 when Mao Zedong took "large-scale peasants' revolutionary movement" as the model of the people's commune, he explicitly eulogized "the Boxer Movement in the late Qing dynasty," and issued this full-

---

3. Vol. 2 of *Collected Works of Li Dazhao* 李大钊文集 (Renmin chubanshe, 1984), 802.
4. Wang Yi, "Different Appraisals of the Boxer Movement since May Fourth and their Respective Cultural Orientations" ‘五四’以来对义和团运动的不同评价及其文化导向 in *The Open Times* 开放时代 no. 4, 1998.

length commentary to the Sixth Plenary Session of the Eighth Committee of the CCP as a guideline for the nation-wide campaign to promote the "people's commune" system. In official historians' "authoritative" description, even the limited criticisms of the Boxer movement's obscurantism by Chen Duxiu and Li Dazhao in the 1920s had disappeared. Moreover, in their depiction of the event this kind of obscurantism was "gloriously" justified as a "revolutionary weapon." As Jian Bozhan, a leading historian then, puts it, perhaps against his own will:

> Beneath such religious superstition (of the Boxer Movement) lies the real revolutionary enthusiasm. Given the fact that the boxers evoked deceased or non-existent figures as the object of their worship for the sake of transfusing the power of these gods to their own bodies, a power used to defeat their ferocious enemies…, the boxers' hatred for the Christian church as well as their narrow-minded xenophobia, as expressed in their struggle against foreign invaders, were understandable, for what they fought against were nothing other than "wolves in sheep's clothing."[5]

However, the tragic irony was that historian Jian Bozhan, who depicted the boxers as having "real revolutionary enthusiasm beneath their religious superstition" for the sake of pleasing the top leaders of the country, was later swallowed up by a similar "craze for revolution" during the Cultural Revolution and, like countless other victims, took his own life.

III. A total eruption and spread of obscurantism during the Boxer Movement and its recurrence in the Cultural Revolution

As the indigenous Chinese culture was challenged to an unprecedented degree in early modern times, and after the Reform of 1898 was brutally repressed, the Boxer Movement could only resort to conservative cultural forms and local religious forces for the purpose of resisting Western oppression.

[…]

All the religious elements in the cultural system were activated fully so as to display its consecrated qualities and its mode of operation, in the hope of defending it and resisting the invasion of Western culture. Among the major religious modes of behavior thus activated, there were several which were most in line with those of the Cultural Revolution: 1) an absolutely antagonistic attitude toward foreign races and foreign cultural elements (particularly toward national

---

5. Jian Bozhan, "The Boxer Movement" 义和团运动 (February 24, 1958), in *Selected Historical Writings of Jian Bozhan* 翦伯赞历史论文选集 (Renmin chubanshe, 1980), 328–333.

cultural reform under foreign influences); 2) an unconditional worship of gods and all holy ways in which divine power could be used to eliminate all devils; 3) the fanatical mode of mass movement, and the mutual reinforcement between this fanatical socio-cultural/cultural-religious atmosphere and people's pattern of behavior and thinking; 4) unscrupulous hunting down of and merciless crackdown on heresies. Let's look at them one by one.

First, hostility to and rejection of heterogeneous cultures. Anthropological studies show that in a primitive community, alien cultural elements are considered harmful to its own cultural system and to the divinity of its totem. As a result, the more influential a foreign culture is, the more vigorously the defense mechanism of the native cultural elements will be activated in a tribal society. Conversely, the indigenous culture of a tribal society will not treat alien cultural elements as something normal, but will rather treat them as apparitions endowed with evil forces. It was just this kind of primitive cultural thinking that drove the boxers to wipe out all "foreign devils" and obliterate everything foreign, for they could not see the complex relationship between the invasion and oppression of Western powers and the advances of world civilization. Such a rejection of anything foreign is virtually a kind of, to borrow a popular term of the Cultural Revolution, "total elimination."

> After all properties of the Christian churches had been burned, foreign goods in shops run by foreigners were either destroyed or looted by the poor... News also came that after those converted to Christianity were killed, students who read foreign books would follow their fate. This terrified the students; people who owned foreign books lost no time to burn them.[6]

> The boxers' goal was to reject everything foreign: foreigners, foreign religions, foreign goods, foreign clerks, foreign tools... Even foreign buttons on clothes were torn off and replaced with old-fashioned ones.[7]

This kind of "total rejection" is based on the cultural notion that everything foreign must be evil. One familiar example is the boxers' perception of photography, a foreign technology, as witchcraft: the camera would suck out the eyes of a person before his picture was taken. Another example is: the boxers' reason for burning down "offices of foreign affairs" in the Qing government and the School of Combined Learning (Tongwenguan) was that "these places were saturated with demonic aura, and the School of Combined Learning had plenty of foreign books. They must all be burned. And those who spoke foreign languages were traitors and should be put to death."

6. Yang Dianhao, "Historical Events of 1900" 庚子大事记, in *A Chronicle of 1900* 庚子记事 (Zhonghua shuju, 1978), 86.

7. "Anti-Imperialist Movement in Ningjin County" 宁津义和团反帝运动, in *Historical Materials of the Boxer Movement* 义和团史料(Zhongguo shehui kexue chubanshe, 1982), 973.

[...]

The boxers' cultural concept and mode of conduct experienced a resurgence during the Cultural Revolution. This is demonstrated not only by the red guards' hatred for and extirpation of all the "smuggled goods" of "feudalism, capitalism and revisionism" and their continuous and merciless suppression of the so-called "slavish comprador philosophy" and "traitor's political line," but also, more importantly, by the fact that underneath the surface of this conduct the deeper cultural motive was the same as those of primitive societies and of the Boxer Movement. That is, the introduction of anything not endemic to one's own country was assuredly poisonous, laden with evil portent, capable of shaking the foundation of the sacred cultural system, and therefore treasonous.Clearly, the cultural essence of this kind of absolute, extremist and supernatural exclusionism far exceeds the boundaries of any racial conflicts or cultural difference in a normal rational society. Rather, it bore resemblance to the kind of taboo against foreign culture characteristic of tribal societies. Liang Qichao, commenting on the Boxer Movement, wrote, "China has long been known for its exclusionism. Slaughtering foreigners, destroying churches, attacking embassies, killing diplomatic ministers... these are examples of barbaric exclusionism... they treated them as thieves. Foreigners in China are bound to seclude themselves from Chinese society, a consequence being that we cannot benefit from their cultural wisdom... Therefore the most ardent exclusionism is found in the most savage society. In a patriarchal and tribal society, strangers are treated as enemies."[8]

Second, the similarities between the Boxer Movement and the Cultural Revolution in terms of their modes of operation: their worship of divinities and their determination to "eliminate evils of all descriptions." The degree of enthusiasm for one's own native religion is proportionate to both the extent to which the native religion is affected by a foreign religion and the degree of the natives' hostility to foreign peoples. That this important cultural principle of clannish times should come to the foreground in the Boxer Movement was due to the unprecedented cruelty of Western invasion and the inflow of Western culture on an unprecedented scale. When someone asked him "if he could guarantee the boxers' success," Xu Tong, Grand Secretary in the Qing government as well as the firmest advocate of the Boxer Movement, replied succinctly, "The boxers are deities, whereas foreigners are devils. For deities to fight devils there is no chance of losing!"[9]

It is obvious that most superior divinity was what guaranteed the boxers' victory over "foreign devils." Therefore, the boxers elicited the help of all sorts of deities, including Buddhist and Taoist gods and a multitude of local gods and

---

8.   Liang Qichao, "A Comment on Exclusionism" 排外平议, in *Selected Writings of the Late Qing* 晚清文选, ed. Zheng Zhenduo (Shenghuo shudian, 1937), 469–470.

9.   Hu Sijing, *Selected Writings: On the Donkey Back* 驴背集, in the series vol. 2 of *The Boxer Movement*, eds., Jian Bozhan et al (Shanghai renmin chubanshe, 1961), 507.

demigods from folklore, historical tales and legends such as Xiang Yu, Zhao Yun, Huang Tianba, Mu Guiying, the Monkey King, the Pig King, inviting them to descend to the world. Because of the prevalence of such fanatical worship, "business in joss stick shops was one hundred times better than in peaceful times. In broad streets and small lanes, both the noble and simple burned joss sticks every night. In the capital city incense was often out of stock."[10] The degree and scale of the boxers' mobilization of local religions was much greater than any other rebellious movements in Chinese history. This testifies again to the degree to which a people's worship of gods is unavoidably proportionate to the degree of the "devils'" oppression of them and the degree of their own enthusiasm for wiping out "evils of all descriptions."

During the Cultural Revolution, the same kind of cultural mechanism, which had provoked religious fanaticism among the boxers, revealed to a full extent its "magic power" once again. On the surface, it may appear that almost all forms of religious practice had been abolished since 1949. Yet the religious tradition and psyche of a people, which has been formed little by little through thousands of years, cannot be eradicated completely in less than two decades, particularly when the traditional mode of production remains in most parts of its society. Just as the Cultural Revolution's attack on the devils, e.g. "the purge of all vermin," was most virulent, so too its yearning for the highest and "invincible" gods was most vehement. [The red guards'] religious enthusiasm is different from the boxers' religious fanaticism only in that its expression, which is reactivated from the socio-cultural system, needs to be channeled into the worship of the top leader, or "the Sun on which the growth of all things depend,"[11] as the gods and demigods in traditional religions such as Guan Di, the Jade Emperor, the Zhen Wu Emperor, the Eight Immortals had virtually ceased to exist after 1949. [...]

[...]

Third, the fanatical mode of mass movement, and the mutual reinforcement between such fanatical socio-cultural/cultural-religious atmosphere and people's pattern of behavior and way of thinking. Based on primitive beliefs, the whole society had taken the fanatical "mass movement" (e.g. collective exorcism, collective worship of totem) as the most sacred action to which everybody should devote himself. It is obvious that this kind of nation-wide movement would, in turn, greatly reinforce people's primitive beliefs. During the Boxer Movement, the inner mechanism of the obscurantist culture had displayed its most potent and fullest manifestations, while the cultural sediment it left on the belief system and on the national psyche was bound to exert direct influence on the Cultural Revolution.

---

10. Yang Dianhao, *A Chronicle of 1900*, 26.
11. See my article " 'The Growth of All Things Depends on the Sun' and the Primitive Form of Worship" '万物生长靠太阳' 与原始崇拜, in *Young Thinkers* 青年思想, no. 1 (1999).

Qi Benyu deemed the Boxer Movement as the grandest "mass movement" in history, which was certainly an accurate description of its cultural nature. What then are the most prominent characteristics of the Boxer Movement as a mass movement? I believe it includes the following important aspects:

1. Almost everyone could not help but be involved in this nation-wide movement. Unless they joined the mainstream activities, they would not survive. In fact, they would lose completely their abilities to act if they did not follow the pack:

> Everywhere people burned the joss sticks so as to kill the devils. Everybody spoke with the same voice... [...] Everybody, young or old, male or female, wrapped their heads with red headbands and burned joss sticks three times a day...If this rule was not observed, then the Cowherd wouldn't come down to the world to save the people from the disaster... If joss sticks were not burned, people wouldn't be protected from foreign guns and cannons... [...][12]

The kind of nation-wide mania (i.e. everybody was a boxer, "everything was red," every family worshipped gods, rumors spread by word of mouth, people flocked like ants) during this "mass movement" was to become a most familiar scene during the Cultural Revolution.

2. This form of social practice, religious in nature, is so powerful that it defines and regulates people's ways of behavior, life, and thinking. For example, "All jinrick-shaws must have red covers. Women had to wear red scarves; otherwise, they would be considered indecent and sentenced to death. Men wore a piece of red cloth in the front of their garments, to show their faith in the boxers."[13] [...] Everybody in the society had strictly to abide by the code of conduct prescribed by the "mass movement," or he would be severely and divinely punished. This recourse to divine power and "mass movement" for the compulsory integration or shaping of a mode of social behavior was to become the most popular practice in the Cultural Revolution. Among the most popular slogans then were: "You are either a revolutionary or a counter-revolutionary;" "Stand out if you are for revolution, or go on, scram!" In the "Song of Rebellion" sung by the red guards, there were such words as, "He who dares speak ill of the Party shall be sent at once to hell." From these examples we can get a glimpse of the astringent process of disciplining.

3. Laden with a religious spirit, and having mobilized the whole nation's religious ardor, the "mass movement" had an extraordinary social effect. The following are a couple of scenes in this movement:

---

12. Zhong Fang Shi, "Memories of 1900" 庚子纪事, in *A Chronicle of 1900*, 15–27.
13. Long Gu Shan Ren, "A Review of Poetry, 1900" 庚子诗鉴, in *Historical Materials of the Boxer Movement*, 73.

When foreign ships, several li in length and width, approached, all the chief did was to point his finger at them. And then cannons were fired and the ships sank. In Japan, a fifty-li street was burned to ashes by Hongdengzhao (young woman boxers, normally in red – translator's note). As the boxers arose in foreign countries as well, foreigners could hardly protect themselves, let alone cross the vast ocean to invade China.[14]

[...] ...The robes, hats, and tools of the gods in Buddhist and Taoist temples were all stolen by them [the boxers]... They said these divine belongings were capable of protecting them from knives and swords, for even foreign guns couldn't penetrate them...There were those who wore divine clothes, hats, held divine apparatuses or clay dragons and tigers taken from arhat temples. There were those who took bamboo cages where they put stolen cats (they viewed these cats as divine dragons and tigers which could change their size at will and could devour corrupted officials, despotic landlords, foreigners as well as readers of foreign books). One could not bear to look at such fatuity and pitiful scenes.[15]

In a "mass movement" mobilized by religious ardor, such as the Boxer Movement, the Great Leap Forward and the Cultural Revolution, the more imaginativeness and creativity its participants' self-sacrificial enthusiasm had generated, the more easily one can see "the fatuity and pitiful scene one cannot bear to see." The logical inevitability of such a phenomenon lies in the fact that the stronger a society's desire for "invincibility" and "elimination of evils of all descriptions," the more urgent its attempt to activate its people's religious energy and to release it in the forms of mass fanaticism and the blind worship of "the red sun," the consequence of which is the further removal of their pattern of thinking and behavior from the rational principle of civilized society.

4. Since the spread of the "mass movement" was mainly based on a kind of obscurantist philosophy, it severely harmed the mentality of the people, as shown in the following two depictions:

When the boxers arose, foreign goods were condemned; those who used them ran the risk of being executed. Owning something foreign, such as cigarettes, spectacles, umbrellas and socks, was punishable by death. There were once six students who were brutally killed simply because one of them was found by the boxers to have carried with him an imported pencil and a sheet of foreign paper.... Such was their

---

14.Huang Zengyuan, "Some Historical Facts about the Boxer Movement" 义和团事件, in vol. 1 of *Series of Historical Documents of the Boxer Movement* 义和团运动史料丛编 (Zhonghua shuju, 1964), 137.

15. "Chronicle of Jianwei County" 健为县志, in *Historical Materials of the Boxer Movement,* 1065.

detestation of foreign goods! Now [since the taking of Peking by the Eight-Nation Alliance – writer] everything has changed: when someone has an imported hat, or a boot, or a suit, even if they are worn-out ones, he never hesitates to show them off in public. And it is also a fashion to write on either walls or stencil plates in foreign languages; where someone writes in Chinese, he would use both round hand and cursive hand to create a likeness of foreign words, as a way to show his connection with foreign culture. Having done all this, he would then raise his head and throw out his chest, feeling very proud of himself.[16]

When the allies entered the capital, they saw in the streets and lanes thousands of banners bearing welcome messages prepared by passive civilians... After the city had been divided by eleven foreign countries and their armies were stationed within the city and in the suburbs, our passive citizens started to decorate each of their embassies, police headquarters and bureaus of civil affairs with magnificent plaques and couplets eulogizing them in the most adulatory and seemingly sincere terms. Even when we look at them now, we still feel anger and shame, our tears gushing for God-knows what reasons.[17]

Having experienced the duet of political and national myths and an eventual disillusionment with them, people began to tire of things deemed sacred and responded negatively to them. This is also how we felt most strongly after the Cultural Revolution came to an end.

Four, the unscrupulous hunting of and merciless crackdown on heresies in the name of gods. In a socio-cultural system that was dominated by primitive gods, people took as their primary mission the job of eradicating all devils that posed a threat to the authority of divinities. In other words, the "binary mode" of primitive religion was not only manifested in the essential opposition between the divinities and the devils (which recalls the popular distinction between "the two different lines," i.e. socialist and capitalist, during the Cultural Revolution), but also in the fact that the degree of the people's passion for getting rid of devils was proportionate to the degree of their belief in the greatness of divinities.[18] Both the Boxer Movement and the Cultural Revolution gave full expression of this basic tenet of primitive religion.

Evidence of the Boxer Movement's inheritance of such a tenet is that, just as it inflated without bounds the divinity of their gods and of their avatars (e.g.

16. Zuo Yuan Du Jie, "Miscellaneous Records of the Boxer Event" 拳事杂记, in Jian Bozhan et al eds., vol. 1 of *The Boxer Movement* 义和团, 137.

17. Di Pinzi, "Memories of 1900" 庚子纪事, in *An Anthology of Literature about the Turbulences in 1900* 庚子事变文学集, ed. Ah Ying (Zhonghua shuju, 1959), 1001.

18. See my article "The Fad of Constructing Gods in the 20th Century and Its Disillusionment: The Case of Cassiere's Analysis of Fascism and Beyond" 二十世纪造神狂潮的迷惘与幻灭 — 从卡西尔等人对法西斯主义的剖析谈起, in vol. 5 of *The East* 东方 (1995).

the launching of "mass movement" in defense of these gods and those who claimed to be possessed by them), it also magnified without limit the enormity of the devils and their agents.

[....]

The White Lotus Society was a major local religion in the Ming and Qing dynasties. It was wide-spread throughout the country and had many branches and schools, but eventually the rulers of society had come to regard it as no more than a heterodox religious sect. As a religious organization founded by common people, the boxers were originally derived from the White Lotus Society.[19] However, after the Boxer Movement gained the support of the rulers and became the dominant social force, there was a process of constructing and consolidating their religious divinity and political authority, which was necessarily achieved through surveillance and punishment, with great hostility, of the rest of the society, i.e. members other than the boxers, through relentless attacks on and slaughter of the so-called "wicked devils," who were actually their brothers and sisters from the same roots.

[....]

The boxers not only hunted and prosecuted dissidents, they, too, fought relentlessly among themselves:

> The boxers were also afflicted with faction and mutual mistrust. Internal dissension often arose. On July 18th, Zhang Chengzhi, chief of the Qianzi faction, led dozens of his followers to the frontiers of Shandong to arrest ermaozi (i.e. Chinese converted to Christianity – translator's note). When they passed by Haojiawa, they were ambushed by the Kanzi faction led by Pan Rongzuo. Luo Enjun shot an arrow at Zhang Chengzhi, and then decapitated him and hanged his head in the Baolin Temple.[20]

Now that the Boxer Movement was based on a culture dominated by a primitive divinity, the maintenance of the purity of this divinity, and particularly the maintenance of one's own exclusive ownership of this divinity, factions and mutual persecutions were absolutely indispensable. This situation was similar to that of the later Cultural Revolution. Regardless of the wish of the leader of the Revolution to "unite the majority of people" and to "establish a big union of revolutionaries," what actually took place within the socio-cultural system, as it was, was nothing less than increasingly uncontainable armed fights among different factions, which virtually led to a "total civil war" in the name of "defending Maoism at the cost of life."

---

19. "The boxers were in fact a branch of the White Lotus Society," wrote Lao Naixuan in his article "The Religious Origin of the Boxers" 义和团拳教门源流考, in Jian Bozhan et al. eds., vol. 4 of *The Boxer Movement*, 438.
20. "Anti-Imperialist Movement in Ningjin County," 975.

In summary, the reason why the Boxer Movement's external mode of "mass movement" as well as the corresponding internal operating mechanism made a drastic return in the Cultural Revolution is because of their common inheritance of obscurantist cultural genes in both modes of beliefs and behavior patterns. A hundred years after the Boxer Movement, when China faces a new century, especially with the trend of world democratization and globalization, it is now time that we seriously investigate and understand the hereditary relationship between these two disastrous historical events.

(translated by Lin Qinxin)

Part II

Translations

♦ Shanghai History Books

Editors' Note

After three years' experimental use in some Shanghai high schools, the new history textbook, co-edited by Shanghai historians Su Zhiliang and Zhou Chunsheng (professors of history at the Shanghai Normal University), began to be more widely adopted in Shanghai high schools in 2006. What makes the textbook new is that it lays more emphasis on civilizational developments than on heroes, wars, revolutions, and dynastic changes. This shift of emphasis hadn't attracted much public attention until the publication in *The New York Times* of an article by Joseph Kahn, "Where's Mao? Chinese Revise History Book" (*New York Times*, September 1, 2006), which provoked a heated debate among Chinese historians on what should be taught in history classes at high school. Some considered the new textbook a mark of significant progress, while others argued that it "deviated from the Marxist materialist historical view" and "committed serious political, methodological and theoretical errors." In the end, this short-lived history textbook was replaced with a hastily compiled one in September, 2007.

The New History Books in Shanghai: It's a Change, Not a Coup d'Etat*

Su Zhiliang

Gates 1, Mao Zedong 120

Journalist: The article in the *New York Times* [by Joseph Kahn, titled "Where's Mao? Chinese Revise History Books"[1]] on the Shanghai history textbooks has prompted a number of articles by commentators both in China and abroad. How do you view these reports?

Su Zhiliang: The *New York Times* article on September 1 does not fully report the Shanghai history textbooks. The report said one-sided or incorrect things like "in approving the new textbook, the government played the main role ... Marxism has been deleted and socialism reduced ... the banning of books and burying of scholars by the Emperor Qin has been deleted." I think that this type of reporting is not very responsible.

Following the erroneous report, opinions in internet blogs became more and more vehement.

Articles even appeared with headlines intended to shock, like: "Gates to Replace Mao Zedong in China's New History Textbooks"; "A Coup d'Etat Starts Quietly with the Shanghai History Textbooks" and "Shanghai Textbooks are the

---

* This article was first published in *Southern Sunday Post* 南方周末, September 28, 2006.
1. See Joseph Kahn, "Where's Mao? Chinese Revise History Books," *New York Times*, September 1, 2006.

Starting Point of an 'Orange Revolution'." No one with any brain would believe this type of language.

Now the more important point is that almost all of these critics were people who had never seen our textbooks. It is an imaginary problem based on reports with distorted facts, and this is very dangerous. And these translated and republished news stories and reports were spread on the Internet without taking the least responsibility for checking facts, creating a whole series of problems. The strangest was the Phoenix website, whose report on the Shanghai history textbooks used a cover photo of *History* published by the People's Education Press rather than the *History* published in Shanghai.

This type of report could be reprinted, translated and reported as a follow-up by so many domestic newspapers, and then further transmitted by websites, but how was it that not a single one checked the book itself, questioned or verified the facts?

Journalist: How does the new textbook evaluate Mao Zedong?

Su Zhiliang: Mao Zedong is an extremely important historical person. But each textbook and the function of education in different periods are different, and it is impossible that every textbook should discuss a major question in the same way. If they did, then there really would be a problem. I have also paid attention to the new history textbooks from all over the country. It is impossible that every volume in the set of history textbooks should talk about Mao Zedong. Some teachers have gathered statistics showing that Mao Zedong is mentioned at least 120 times in the Shanghai history textbook, especially in the first-year textbook of middle school and the third-year textbook of high school.

The following are relevant extracts:

> The Jinggangshang Revolutionary Base created by Mao Zedong ignited the flames of the 'Workers and Peasants Armed Uprising', which, in turn, illuminated a way for the Chinese Communist Party to use the countryside to surround the cities and use armed force to fight for national political power. (76)

> The Zunyi Meeting in fact established the correct leadership of the new party leadership with Mao Zedong at its core, saving the Chinese Communist Party and Red Army and thus saving the Chinese revolution, and it is a critical life-and-death turning point in the history of the Communist Party. (79)

> The establishment of the People's Republic of China caused one quarter of the then population of the world to escape from their destiny of oppression and enslavement; from this moment the Chinese people stood up. This was a victory for Mao Zedong Thought which combined Marxism with the concrete practice of the Chinese revolution. (118)

There are many other instances where the textbooks discuss Mao Zedong as an individual, but these extracts give the three key points necessary for an evaluation of the great historical contribution of Mao Zedong to the Chinese revolution.

The new textbooks also comment relatively objectively on the mistakes of Mao Zedong in the Great Leap Forward and Cultural Revolution.

> In 1958, when China's economic development appeared to have good prospects, the main central government leaders, from a subjective desire to stimulate the rapid achievement of a prosperous and strong nation and ignoring the laws of economic development, decided in agricultural production to "take grain as the key link," setting high targets that had no basis in reality, opening a mass production great leap forward movement. .....the Great Leap Forward in industrial production was to "take iron as the key link," and the whole nation stopped everything for iron and steel production. (126-127)

At that time Mao Zedong was one of the main leaders of the Party, and of course must bear responsibility for the errors of the Great Leap Forward. That the textbooks do not just point out the errors of Mao Zedong as an individual is in accord with the fact that the Party's collective central leadership system was still working at that time.

There is the following assessment of the Cultural Revolution:

> Mao Zedong mistakenly believed that much of the power in the Party, government and army had already been seized by the bourgeoisie, and that it was necessary to launch a proletarian cultural revolution from the bottom upwards. The trend of the personality cult and the arbitrariness current in the Party meant that the Chinese Communist Party Central Committee could not correct its mistakes in time. Ambitious persons such as Lin Biao and Jiang Qing made use of the Cultural Revolution with ulterior motives, leading to ten long years of disorder throughout the nation. (128)

The textbooks discuss in particular the historical fact of Mao Zedong's promotion of Deng Xiaoping in the year before his death.

We discuss Mao Zedong against the background of the Chinese Revolution, affirming his contribution as a pioneer of the Chinese Revolution in the years before Liberation, as well as his achievements in the construction of Chinese socialism after Liberation. Then, with regard to Mao Zedong during the years between the Great Leap Forward and the Cultural Revolution, we analyze and evaluate his achievements and mistakes. We have written in accordance with the Chinese Communist Party Central Committee's "Resolution on Certain Issues in the History of the Party Since the Founding of the People's Republic of China" (关于建国以来党的若干历史问题的决议).

And one more point in passing: in order to emphasize Mao Zedong's importance, a deliberate choice was made to print Mao Zedong's calligraphy of Lin Zexu's poetry on the cover of the second volume of the lower middle school level textbook. Why choose such a cover? Because, through the calligraphy of Mao Zedong, the two great historical people are related so that students can understand the self-reliant national spirit of the Chinese people from their study of China's modern history.

Less written on peasant uprisings

Journalist: Is it true, as some media have said, that "Mao Zedong has been replaced by Bill Gates"?

Su Zhiliang: In our textbooks Bill Gates is referred to once, and Mao Zedong over 120 times, so is it possible he could replace Mao Zedong? I would like to say a couple of words on Gates. He is without doubt a person who has made enormous contribution to modern human culture. That Gates appears in the textbooks should not be surprising. As a matter of fact, in the high school textbook, Gates is mentioned not in the main body of the lesson but in passing when discussing the US anti-trust lawsuit against Microsoft. To say that in China's history textbooks "Bill Gates has replaced Mao Zedong" can only be the view of an American journalist.

Journalist: Some people have complained that the textbooks do not include the Long March, the Nanjing Massacre and the War of Resistance Against Japan. Is this true?

Su Zhiliang: Of course it is not true. We give substantial space to recounting the Long March. How is it possible to say that there is none? As a scholar, I have devoted my greatest efforts to research on the War of Resistance Against Japan. I accompanied surviving "comfort women" to launch lawsuits in Japan, and have been all over the world to expose this. Do you think it is possible that textbooks edited by someone like me who has studied the War of Resistance Against Japan for a long time and who has rushed about without rest to expose Japan's war crimes would not include it? Would the government permit the distribution of such textbooks?

This subject is mainly discussed in the second volume of the first-year textbook of middle school. The part on the Long March by the Red Army includes Mao Zedong's poem "The Long March". The part on the War of Resistance Against Japan not only narrates the general historical facts, such as the cooperation of the Kuomintang and Chinese Communist Party in the War, but also the crimes of Japanese imperialism such as the Nanjing Massacre, germ warfare and the "comfort women", as well as the Five Heroes of Lang Ya Mountain.

For instance, on the War of Resistance against Japan, we write about the cooperation between Kuomintang and Chinese Communist Party, frontline battles, fighting behind enemy lines, the crimes of Japanese militarism... We have full coverage of the Nanjing Massacre. Through pictures and words, we describe other atrocities perpetrated by the Japanese army.

As for "comfort women", this is the first time this has been recorded in Chinese textbooks. Similarly, it is the first time a textbook has mentioned that during the early period of China's reform and opening up, Japan provided economic aid to China. This demonstrates the truthful mindset of the Chinese people.

There are also people who say that the Cultural Revolution is not mentioned, but this also is not true. There is not much written on the Cultural Revolution, and this is because you cannot have large amounts written on this subject. We used a spread, but I think that we have written clearly, for instance on why turmoil took place, including what kind of person Lin Biao was, and there are also pictures. It includes the language of the Cultural Revolution. It explains the "Little Red Book," "the four olds," "the model Beijing operas," etc. Through the main text, quotations and pictures, we have explained clearly. I hope through that lesson the Chinese people can reflect upon the experience of that age of disorder, draw lessons, and follow a better path in the future.

Journalist: There are also people who say that subjects such as the peasant wars and the banning of books and burying of scholars by the Emperor Qin are not in the textbooks.

Su Zhiliang: In fact the subjects such as the peasant wars and the banning of the books and burying of scholars by the Emperor Qin were removed from the first-year textbook of high school after the first phase of revision. We put these subjects in the middle school *Chinese History*, so that in middle school these basic history lessons are already completed.

There are also people who say that we only discuss autocracy in the section on the Emperor Qin, and there is nothing anywhere else on this. But this view also has problems. We take the Qin dynasty as the starting point of the centralization of power, and the analysis of autocracy is covered in the Ming and Qing dynasties, because in the Ming and Qing dynasties autocracy reached its height.

As for peasant uprisings, in Chinese history there were innumerable large and small peasant uprisings, and it is impossible to deal with them all in a middle school history textbook. We have discussed the peasant uprising at the end of the Qin dynasty, the Taiping uprising, and the Boxers. In the 21st century, is it normal only to write large amounts about peasant uprisings? In the current standard national history textbook, the description of peasant uprisings and peasant wars has also been cut greatly. In fact everyone is in agreement, because we have experienced reform and opening up and, in the past 20 years, there has also been a ceaseless development in our view of history.

What makes the "new" *History* new?

Journalist: What is "new" in the new textbooks?

Su Zhiliang: We hope that the new textbook edition can reflect mankind's struggle for survival and development, embody the process of development of human civilization and delineate clearly the history of human civilization from ancient to modern times.

The last subject in the first-year *History* of high school is "Current and Future Human Civilization," and the lessons are organized around two themes: "man and nature" and "man and society." Students, together with teachers, can analyze the present and freely imagine the future. Another example: there is a chapter on the impact of viruses and contagious diseases on human civilization. Our chosen examples originally were the influenza pandemic in the US and the Black Death in Europe. But as China was hit by SARS in 2003, we use the virus as an example.

In the modern history section we have raised the problem of drugs such as opium. In modern history, our people have suffered greatly from opium and, after 1985, drugs began to spread in China, and we analyze their danger to human life and society. Students very often see news about this on the Internet, in newspapers or on television, so they especially like to participate in discussions in class.

Journalist: What is the overall structure of the new history textbook?

Su Zhiliang: The basic design of the Shanghai middle school and high school history course is as follows:

History textbooks in the past recycled the material taught in middle and high school. Using the example of the textbook from the first phase of revision in Shanghai, in middle school, Chinese history and world history is studied, and in high school, Chinese and foreign histories are studied, and the content is basically the same. It is like first learning 1+1, then learning 1+2, then learning 1+1 and 1+2 together. This does not conform with the pedagogical rule that there should be no significant overlapping in teaching material and because of this most high school students are not interested in history classes.

On the basis of the requirement in the newly-published state standard for history to avoid overlapping, our middle school history textbooks mainly relate Chinese history and world history in the form of comprehensive history, including the history of the wars where the great powers invaded China and the Chinese revolution, and, in the high school stage the textbooks relate the development of human civilization divided into special subjects. In the third year of high school there is an overall revision of the historical knowledge of middle school and the first year of high school so that students can understand the historical process of the suffering and revival that the Chinese people have experienced in the past 100 years from the development of human civilization and the modernization of the major developed countries.

Journalist: Why is it designed on the basis of the history of civilization?

Su Zhiliang: The Marxist historical materialist viewpoint has set the theoretical foundation for our framework of the history of civilization. We believe that, in fact, human civilization includes material civilization, social civilization, political civilization and spiritual civilization. On the basis of this division, we explain the basic subject of the history of human civilization.

In the 1980s and 1990s, the cause of socialism suffered serious setbacks. How can we understand the position of socialism in the history of human civilization? The textbook for the first year of high school does not evade this, rather it points out that socialism is the highest social ideal of mankind and has strong vitality and a brilliant future. Because of this, the style of presentation of the textbook for the first year of high school is different from previous textbooks, but it has absorbed the outstanding successes of the development of historical studies in the 20th century and uses the rich content of the history of human civilization to more deeply embody the historical materialist view of Marxism and the scientific socialist viewpoint.

Journalist: I noticed that you have written about food, clothing, shelter and transport in the textbooks. Why is it necessary to write again on these subjects?

Su Zhiliang: Food, clothing, shelter and transport are the basic materials of life. To ignore the history of mankind's material life would not be the Marxist view of the history of civilization. I would also like to emphasize the basic view of Marxism, because there are certain "Marxists" who were surprised that the Shanghai history textbook included these subjects and ignored the activities of some emperors, monarchs, generals and ministers, and accused us of forsaking Marxism. I think that the question of whether or not food, clothing, shelter and transport are written about, or how they are written about, can be resolved as a technical problem. The real problem lies with the biased view that insists on emphasizing the activities of certain historical figures and suppresses the actual life of millions of people outside the field of history. I find it difficult to understand how this type of bias can occur in the name of "Marxism."

Sometimes changes in the details of food or clothing may produce a profound impact on the history of a people, a nation or even mankind.

For example, one chapter discusses coupons. During class in an experimental middle school, a teacher asked students to go home and collect coupons, and to bring them to class for an exchange. Apart from banknotes, the students had no concept of coupons, but when they went home and asked the old people and their parents, they heard many stories. Finally, during classroom discussion, the students brought out many old ration coupons, rice coupons, vegetable coupons, television coupons and bicycle coupons. Some students even brought salt coupons: buying salt required coupons. What does this show? It shows the lack of material life in the time of the planned economy.

Journalist: According to reports, Zhou Chunsheng, one of the chief editors of the high school first-year textbook, said that the textbook used the views of the French Annales School of historical thought as a reference.

Su Zhiliang: In the process of writing the textbooks we referred to many outstanding Chinese and foreign historical ideas and achievements. The Annales School is a school that was deeply influenced by the Marxist materialist historical viewpoint, and of course we draw from it. But drawing from it is not the same as being directed by it. The American journalist quoted out of context, so that it appeared that drawing from the Annales School meant abandoning the Marxist viewpoint. This is a kind of metaphysical attitude.

Journalist: There are also reports that the Shanghai textbooks will probably spread throughout the country.

Su Zhiliang: Impossible. This is purely guesswork by a foreign journalist without any basis. Because national textbooks have been selected, the writing, research and publishing started long ago and they are already in use. The limit of our authority is use for Shanghai city only. Furthermore, it is only a trial book, which will be constantly revised on the basis of opinion from all sides.

(translated by Duncan Freeman)

Zhu Xueqin Reviews New History Books:
A Cannibalistic View of History Produced Wolves*

Zhu Xueqin

Shanghai in late September: the weather is unusually good, but 33-year-old Han Yunsong's state of mind is a bit confused. He is the Head of the Research Division at Fudan University No. 2 Middle School responsible for all the history teaching in the four classes of the middle school. His confused state of mind began from this term, when the history textbooks used by all the middle and high school students in Shanghai were changed, and these changes have for a whole month been a hot point in internet debates and media reporting.

The debates began with a report published in the *New York Times* on September 1. The report was headlined "Where's Mao? Chinese Revise History Books." It said that the new history textbooks "focus on ... economic growth, innovation, foreign trade, political stability, respect for diverse cultures and social harmony. ... The French and Russian Revolutions, once seen as turning points in world history, now get far less attention. ... In the senior high school text, [Mao Zedong] is mentioned fleetingly as part of a lesson on the custom of lowering flags to half-staff at state funerals."

The article's contents were reported widely in the media in China and abroad and the debate started. It should be pointed out that the different views currently in the media have as their focus the introduction to the table of contents of the new Shanghai textbooks spread on the Internet and reported in the media. Very

---

* This article was first published in *Nandou Weekly* 南都周刊, October 24, 2006.

few of the writers have really had the chance to read the eight Shanghai history textbooks. In fact, the full trial of the set of textbooks, which will start in Shanghai this autumn, is just a normal step taken in accordance with the second phase of Shanghai's curriculum revision plan which started in 1998, and a plan that was already formulated long ago. So the writers have repeatedly emphasized to the media that these textbooks are only on trial, of that opinions from all sides will be taken into account, including those of middle school teachers, and then the books will be revised.

Although the clamour of the debate over the values of the new Shanghai textbooks and the analysis of the facts has begun to slowly quieten down, at the Fudan No. 2 Middle School, discussing the subject with a journalist, the lower middle school teacher Han Yunsong still appears worried. The history classes he gives to students are about to cover a highly sensitive area, the Qin empire and the peasant uprising at the end of Qin.

This journalist interviewed Zhu Xueqin of the history department at Shanghai University on the subject of the new Shanghai history textbooks. As a historian, Zhu Xueqin has his own view.

Revision of history textbooks is unavoidable

Journalist: What did you feel after seeing the new textbooks?

Zhu: They are quite good! I have been a middle school history teacher. There is no comparison between this book and the national textbook I taught 30 years ago, it is a huge advance.

Journalist: Where is this progress shown?

Zhu: First, it is the structure. [The new history books] use the history of civilization to replace the history of class struggle, use changes in the life of society to replace the changes of dynastic systems, use civilization to replace violence, use the changes in the lives of millions of ordinary people to replace the history of a few emperors, kings, generals and ministers. This is a very big advance.

Second, the method of writing the textbook has broken the top-downwards teaching methods of inculcation, dogma and mechanical memorization of the past. It alternates many small teaching modules that will stimulate interest in the classroom. For instance, beside the teaching materials on the voyages of Zheng He 郑和 there is a small box that says that there are different explanations of the motive behind Zheng He's voyages: there are some people who say that they were undertaken to search for Emperor Jianwen. What do you think? Have you heard that he had any other motivation, etc?

If this textbook is used, you can imagine the atmosphere of interaction between teachers and students, the participation of students as opposed to top-down inculcation and the dogmatic memorization method. So I think that it is a big breakthrough in teaching methods.

Journalist: Do you feel that these textbooks have provided a whole new way of thinking?

Zhu: Yes, it is a civilized and open line of thought that engages with the world. If you look at the textbook for the first term of lower middle school, there is Chinese history and world history mixed together and organized around a few themes: the first theme is early human civilization, theme two is human life, theme three is human civilization. Comparing with how we used to teach world history — the five stages of development of society, teaching them one stage after another — it is much more attractive, approachable and convincing.

Abandoning the five stages of societal development is one reason. A second reason is that [the new history books] have diluted and thinned out the previous historical view of class struggle and violent revolution, and they now give prominence to civilization, culture, science and life. They even tell students what the law is. Where was the earliest law produced? Why is there a court system? What is the origin of jury trials? Finally, they pose questions to students, allow students to discuss. It is this kind of questioning that is meaningful. They provoke thoughts on rights and obligations. Children who grow up reading these history books are, I believe, those who will be drinking human milk rather than wolves' milk.

Now, there have been all kinds of responses to the books: misunderstandings, attacks and opposition. I think they should be handled differently.

One view extracts some new perspectives and contrasting examples from the books and deems them to have political implications. It says, for example, they intentionally downplay Mao Zedong and the Chinese Revolution. As I see it, this view does not stand up. Of course, there is some abridgement of the Chinese Revolution and Mao Zedong, the space given [compared to other content] is indeed much smaller than in the past.

Regarding the achievements of Mao Zedong, even today historians have failed to reach a consensus. Given this situation, the writers of the textbooks have handled the subject by means of summarizing and abridging. This is both unfortunate and rational. Not only are these textbooks edited in accordance with an open-ended system of thought, in the classroom every history teacher is completely free to have their own detailed interpretation.

To say that these textbooks on the history of civilization are an "ideological debate" or "the orange revolution is starting from Shanghai" demonstrates that people are really making too much out of it. I would like to say that using this type of language to confront a small advance in textbooks in itself shows that their way of thinking is still bound in the fetters they inherited from the history textbooks of ten or twenty years ago. This way of thinking is the product, or perhaps the victim, of the old violent and revolutionary historical studies that took class struggle as the key. That there are many people on the Internet who use this type of language to maliciously attack this set of textbooks does not mean that these textbooks are not needed; it actually shows the need for such revisions is urgent. We cannot do without reform. Society has been advancing for thirty years, but there are still many people who are stuck in the system of thinking of thirty years ago, and now they are still using this type of language from the Cultural Revolution. This shows that the revision of our textbooks has come too late, not too early!

A cannibalistic view of history produced wolves

Journalist: There are those that say that part of China's history, the part described by historians as the "history of violence", has been excluded from this set of textbooks. They have made history harmonious, softhearted and full of loving stability and unity. Yet Lu Xun has said that, in reality, written between the lines, Chinese history is "people eating people." …

Zhu: First, I do not agree with Lu Xun's view of Chinese history. Lu Xun's view of history is part of the old peasant uprising view of history. If our children are filled with the kind of man-eat-man stories and Lu Xun's simplification of Chinese history, they will drink poison to quench their thirst, and perform the same kind of extremely tragic actions as those of Ma Jiajue. Since our great literary writer tells us that the several thousand years of China is a history of man eating man, I can now take a knife and stab students in my own dormitory to death. Isn't that terrible!

Journalist: Then, is this really a problem of historical outlook, or a problem of our society?

Zhu: Both elements exist, but the historical outlook certainly is a problem. No matter who writes this history, even if it is Lu Xun, I feel it is a great distortion, a deliberate twisting and a great simplification of history. Secondly, inside the social reality of today there are certainly many injustices. Faced with so many injustices, what do you do? Having told the story of Chen Sheng and Wu Guang, do you tell students to go and act like Chen Sheng and Wu Guang, or tell them that we left that period two thousand years ago and that we can try and use civilized and legal methods to struggle for the dignity of people and for justice for ordinary people?

Think what the previous history textbooks taught students. If you come up against unfairness, if you come up against injustice, the fairest, the most just means of resistance, is violence. It is because of this that the Red Guards used such violent methods to attack their elders and teachers during the Cultural Revolution. Apart from the specific political education of the Cultural Revolution period, the history that the children were taught, including the one-sided teachings of Lu Xun, prepared for that day. That is education by drinking wolves' milk, not education by drinking human milk, and it produced wolves, not humans.

If the lesson we draw from history is always that wherever there is oppression there must be resistance, then that lesson is too one-sided. Many other lessons can be drawn. They tell students that apart from oppression and resistance, the resister becoming a new oppressor, and the new oppressor inciting a second generation of resisters in a cycle, there are other means of resolving problems, and these are the law and law courts.

One of the novelties in the new textbooks we have today is that they give a great deal of space to introducing the law. What is continental law? What is Anglo-American law? Of course they do not forget to tell students that in China we have our own ancient law, that there is a Chinese system of law, and they suggest books where students can read further.

The freedom that law brings, the protection of oneself by the law: this is something that more advanced countries have achieved, so why don't we learn from them?

Many points of view are needed to counter colonial history

Journalist: A lecturer at Hong Kong University maintains that this set of textbooks has the edge over the previous one because it emphasizes the spirit of innovation which is essential for globalization. He thinks that an overemphasis of the difficult history of colonized people would make it hard to develop the upper class talent needed by modern society. What do you think?

Zhu: On the history of colonialism and anti-colonialism, I feel that we should discuss both what foreign rule means to people and the meaning of colonial activities on a global scale, or what colonialism contributes to civilization from an objective point of view. If the meaning is restricted to the hatred created by the past history of colonizer and colonized, then the Bund in Shanghai wouldn't exist any more. We can say this: a history of colonizer and colonized is the history of rule and resistance, and at the same time is the history of the export and expansion of civilization. I believe many factors have together created the history of our coastal regions.

Our middle school students carry some psychological problems after they graduate. One of the causes, apart from studying and exams, is the conflict between their textbooks and ordinary life, the ordinary life of every day and every hour. A student who believes our textbooks implicitly will discover every morning on the journey from home to school many things that are different from the textbooks, and he will see even more things that are different after school. Doesn't this trap students in a split personality? This is not to say these new textbooks are completely perfect, but already they are closer to the experiences of a child in a normal life.

Journalist: It seems that many countries have a lot of patriotic education for students in history textbooks.

Zhu: Every country encourages the patriotism of students, but there is no country that has done it as China did in the past. As I see it, American teaching materials are not uniform, and I think that only in this way can a diverse and plural way of thinking be created. Secondly, where Americans discuss patriotism they are not as inflexible and forceful in inculcation as we are. For example, when discussing the colonial and anti-colonial relationship with England and the heroes of the earliest resistance to English colonialists in North America, they do not simplistically cut off the past in one stroke. They begin with how the North-American revolutionary leaders who fought against British colonialism were members of assemblies established by England in each state before the Revolution, and how it is precisely because the revolutionaries had absorbed the lessons of England's parliamentary democracy that they resisted the dictatorship of the English, and that made their resistance more successful, acute and effective.

Of course we don't want to imitate the way Americans write. But I think that previous history textbooks did not have this approach; it has just begun here. I think that today's history textbooks have both historical knowledge and a historical outlook. When transmitting historical knowledge to students, they are livelier and more open, and respect the students more. In the past history was seen in terms of violence, class struggle, revolution and dynastic systems. How is it seen now? The historical view of civilization, culture, society, the daily life of ordinary people and the changes in clothing, food, shelter and transport. Which gives more prominence to ordinary people? Which gives more prominence to the so-called humanistic historical viewpoint? Obviously it is the latter, and not the former.

Journalist: Is this new historical outlook the main trend in historical studies across China?

Zhu: You could put it this way: you cannot say it is the main trend, you can only say that it is becoming more and more the common view of historians.

The unified history exam is a regression

Journalist: As a lecturer in history, how do you feel when facing students who have come from studying conventional middle school history textbooks?

Zhu: When undergraduate and postgraduate students attend class in the first term it is a period for changing their system of thinking. The first thing I say to them is that the historical knowledge they have received, apart from the dates of major events which are quite useful, can be forgotten for the moment. Rather than saying that those things help them to understand history, it is better to say that they prevent them from doing so. So I think that for the postgraduate students and undergraduates whom I tutor, the first term is the most difficult because it is a process requiring them to constantly struggle against the obsolete, mistaken historical viewpoint absorbed from the middle school textbooks. Without this, there is no way they can begin to think independently, and still less be able to write a postgraduate thesis.

Most of my postgraduates finally catch up and are able to help me defeat the obsolete Chinese history textbooks. Not only do I give them historical knowledge but, more important, a sense of life. I want to inspire memories of their own lives. From the age of six, when you start to remember, to the age of eighteen there is already twelve years of history. I will ask them to think about how they spent those twelve years. If in the future a historian were to write about those years, and to do so using the approach of middle school history textbooks, would they recognize that as the history they experienced? So real life can help me defeat this obsolete, decayed and erroneous historical attitude and knowledge.

Journalist: When discussing the problems of history textbooks, middle school history teachers also often raise other difficulties, for example the problem of the upper middle school exam.

Zhu: The upper middle school exam problem has been hanging over their heads for several decades, and now it is over our heads. The Ministry of Education has stipulated that, starting this year, doctoral students in the arts subjects of psychology, education and history must pass unified exams. That is to say, a student in a history department who takes exams for postgraduate studies will not be taking an exam paper set by the teachers of different subjects, but will be taking a national unified exam paper. This is a complete step backwards. How can this be used to differentiate between students who have the ability to carry out research? I refuse this type of student, I reject this type of exam. And so this year I said to the head of our postgraduate department that I would not recruit postgraduate students. To accept students who have memorized books as my own postgraduate students is a humiliation for oneself. So I can tell colleagues in middle schools that we now share your pain, however, we have the right to refuse and they have no right to refuse. Beginning from this term I have already formally told the dean of student admissions that if this system is not changed back I will not recruit students. I refuse this responsibility.

Journalist: A final question. Why did this major revision and change in middle school textbooks first begin in Shanghai?

Zhu: I am really not clear about this. You will certainly have to ask some of the writers. Which department did they go through, which route did they follow to get the instruction to change. I can only say that this reform will arrive in China sooner or later. In China's modern history, the development of civilization has advanced in stages. It is always the east and coastal regions that have advanced civilization first, and then they influence the central regions, which influence the Western regions. If the relevant department wants to do an experiment, it picks the eastern regions first — for example a place like Shanghai — to implement the new teaching materials. This is completely understandable.

(translated by Duncan Freeman)

Part II

Translations

♦ China Maritime Rights

On the Development Strategy for China's Sea Power*

Ye Zicheng and Mu Xinhai

China today is developing rapidly, but its development is unbalanced. From the point of view of geopolitics, this imbalance is above all the unbalanced development of China's land and sea power. China is obviously a land power, but its progress in sea power is relatively limited. But can China become a great sea power through its own development, or become a great power on both land and sea? How should China develop its own sea power? This is a major theoretical and practical problem for China. The authors present some of their own thoughts based on discussions by Chinese scholars.

[....]

China cannot be a Western-style great sea power — China requires new thinking on sea power

The concept of sea power is often borrowed from the West by Chinese scholars which makes it necessary to give a full explanation of how should it be understood. In China, people often argue that sea power is the power to control the oceans, and that it means the development of a strong navy that can control the major

* This article was first published in *Studies of International Politics* 国际政治研究, no. 3 (2005): 5–17.

sea routes. They cite, for instance, the American naval strategist A.T. Mahan. In his famous work, *The Influence of Sea Power Upon History* published in 1890, Mahan expounds his "theory of sea power," arguing that it is the main expression and basic cause of a nation's power and prosperity. Whoever can control the oceans will become a world power.[1] Scholars have pointed out that Mahan believed that the final goal of sea power is mastery of the seas, and that the most powerful naval force was an essential tool to achieve that goal. A nation's prosperity depends on trade, trade depends on sea communications, and sea communications depend on the strength of the navy. Although the capacity to use the oceans to accumulate wealth is a part of sea power, the power to master the seas, that is, the capacity to seize and retain the power to master the seas, is the basic goal and function of sea power. As Mahan argues, since the way to seize and retain the power to master the seas is mainly gained through naval warfare, there is only one measure for the construction of naval armed force, which is fighting for victory; otherwise, the capacity to control the oceans is ineffective. In general, traditional research on the theory of sea power often starts from the military significance of the power to master the seas, which is to say the military scope of sea power is intrinsic to sea power scholarship.[2] This traditional theory of sea power has had a deep influence on the thinking of contemporary Chinese scholars researching to develop China's sea power. For example, some scholars say that only if China has a strong, modernized blue water navy with aircraft carriers at its core can it maximize the combined power of its land and navy forces. A major world power must have an independent global strategy, and the reactions or wishes of other nations cannot and should not be taken as the main basis for the formulation of China's foreign policy.[3]

In the history of the West, sea power was probably as Mahan described, a power won through battle and expressed through great naval strength. But circumstances change and the present cannot be compared to the past. Although Mahan's "sea power" still has some explanatory significance, the times are different. China today faces a different environment. If we still use the kind of traditional thinking on sea power which has as its aim the construction of a powerful navy to control the main sea routes, then the construction of China's sea power will probably end in the same disaster as the Northern Fleet; it will be a dead end. Therefore, it is necessary to go beyond Mahan's concept of sea power, and establish a new approach that is appropriate to the development of China's

---

1.   Sun Fenghua and Liu Yangjie, " 'The Broken Ocean Belt' in the 21st Century" 21世纪的 '的海洋破带' *Human Geography* 人文地理17, no 6 (December 2002).

2.   Liu Xinhua and Qin Yi, "Modern Sea Power and National Maritime Strategy" 现代海权与 国家海洋战略, *Social Sciences* 社会科学, no. 3 (2004).

3.   Yang Yong, "Using the Advantages of Both Land and Sea is the Necessary Choice of Large Land-Sea States" 发挥海陆兼务优势是大型海陆复合国家的必然选择, *Heilongjiang Social Sciences* 黑龙江社会科学, no 3 (2004).

history and culture, and China's maritime space.

If so-called control of the oceans is the mark of sea power, then it follows that that "control" over the main sea routes is maintained by the navy. However, first of all, China never has had and never will have this ambition; second, China probably has never had and never will have this kind of power. China's power and prosperity has never been realized by gaining mastery of the seas, and that is unlikely to change in the future. To put it another way, in the future China will certainly be a world power, but it does not have to gain power through the mastery of the seas. China and the Western countries make different choices which create different routes to world power. The nations discussed in Mahan's book which realized national power and wealth by controlling the oceans through great naval strength are normally typical maritime states. And if these nations cannot control the oceans, which has great significance for their development, then they cannot survive, develop and become great powers. China is different. China has never controlled the oceans, but it has been one of the most powerful nations in the world in 1,800 out of the past 2,000 years. As a Western scholar has noted: "Of all the civilizations of premodern times, none appeared more advanced, none felt more superior, than that of China."[4]

At the same time, it should also be understood that though naval strength occupies an important place in Mahan's idea of sea power, he also points out that it depends in large part on the political system, national character and maritime trade. As Liu Xinhua says: "For a long time people's understanding of sea power has been confused; the belief is that, in military terms, sea power is the power to dominate the seas. ... Sea power's basic meaning is freedom of action in the maritime space. ... In Mahan's view, the meaning of sea power in fact includes two main parts, one is military strength on the seas, the second is non-military strength on the seas. ... Although military sea power is the core of all types of sea power, it is certainly not the final goal of every nation in developing sea power. Comprehensive sea power is the freedom of action of a nation at a specific time in a specific sea area in the political, economic and military spheres, and its actual meaning is much wider than military sea power."[5] And for China these will probably be much more important factors in the development of sea power.

If it is argued that China must now concentrate on the development of sea power, then China's sea power must be defined. Defining China's sea power as

---

4.   Paul M. Kennedy, *Rise and Fall of the Great Powers* 大国的兴衰, trans. Liang Yuhua et al (Beijing: Shijiezhishi chubanshe, 1990), 17.

5.   Liu Xinhua, "Discussion of the Strategy for Development of China's Sea Power" 试论中国发展海权的战略, *Fudan Journal* 复旦学报, no. 6 (2001). It is interesting that Li in "Modern Sea Power and National Maritime Strategy" cited above appears to emphasize more that creation of sea power is the basic aim and function of a sea power.

achieving control of the sea areas and routes that have major significance for China through great military strength on the sea does not conform to China's history, and it does not accord with China's basic goal today of peaceful development without seeking hegemony. It is also behind the times, and a way of thinking that is obsolete. Thus, China must redefine a sea power that has the characteristics of the new era and is in accord with China's present national circumstances.

There are some scholars in China who have begun to reconsider this Western concept of sea power. They believe that it is necessary to differentiate sea rights, strength on the seas and sea power. Sea rights are sovereign interests created through the law. Strength on the seas is a neutral term. Sea power is a form of force which, when used in accordance with the UN and international law, is legal but otherwise is hegemonic. China's sea power should be a form of sea rights based on Chinese sovereignty, and not strength on the seas, and even less maritime hegemony. China's sea power is a limited sea power, its characteristic being that it does not exceed the scope of China's sea rights defined by sovereignty and the international law of the sea, and its naval development does not go beyond the scope of self-defence. Development of underwater weaponry should be considered to be the priority in the construction of the Chinese navy, and never seeking hegemony is the basic principle of the expansion of China's sea power.[6] These are vital considerations. Of course, there are probably some areas in this that require further consideration. For example, whether sea power refers to sea rights, sea interests, maritime strength, maritime power, or whether it is a form of maritime hegemony. But when using the term sea power, we must first ask which aspect of sea power is being referred to. ...

Scholars argue that before developing China's sea power, it is necessary to clear up some errors in China's idea of sea power: (1) The misconception that sea power decides history. In fact it is not sea power that decides history, but history that decides sea power. Victorious sea power depends upon a maritime power's scientific and technological transformation and overall national strength. (2) The mistaken view that globalization requires the globalization of self-defence. It is easy to fall into the trap of seeking absolute security and absolute autonomy. (3) The misconception that the development of maritime force leads to an alliance of sea power with hegemonic power. The view that sea power is the path to win equal status not only disregards history, but also confuses cause and effect.[7]

We think that sea power should be defined from a neutral standpoint as a state's capability and influence in maritime space. This type of capability and

6. Zhang Wenmu, "China's Sea Power" 论中国海权, *Journal of Ocean University of China* 中国海洋大学学报, no. 6 (2004).
7. Xu Qiyu, "Errors and Rethinking of Sea Power" 海权的误区与反思, *Strategy and Management* 战略与管理, no 5 (2003).

influence can be non-military maritime force (for example, the capacity that a state possesses to use, develop and research the maritime space) and the influence that it creates. It may also be military maritime force and the influence that it creates. This military force could be used as a state's means of protection of its own legal national interests in maritime space, or the means to infringe on, damage or destroy another sovereign state's interests on land or in maritime space or the means of attaining world hegemony. Maritime power can be great or small as can its influence. Different maritime forces have different levels of influence, and mastery of the seas is only one kind of influence albeit an important one. This definition of sea power is a not a simple concept but a comprehensive one. The main characteristic of this definition is that it liberates the concept of sea power from the confines of military and strategic studies. It should primarily be a term used in political studies and not a military term. The discussion of sea power does not necessarily imply discussing the development of the navy and aircraft carriers, or how to control main sea routes, or how to achieve maritime hegemony. Of course, there are contradictions and conflicts in the use, development and study of maritime space but there is also cooperation, thus it can be seen that the development of sea power is not just about how to fight and control. The development of sea power has an important but not a necessary connection to the navy and hegemony. Sea power can be the subject of study by military specialists, and can also be the subject of research by many other branches of study.

Furthermore, China's sea power can be defined as its capability and capacity to explore, utilize and exercise a certain degree of control over the oceans, or as its capability to protect its maritime interests and project its influence. This definition indicates that: (1) China's interests in the maritime sphere are increasingly important in the structure of its national interests. The development and protection of these interests in the maritime sphere include the protection of the normal conduct of China's lawful and legitimate maritime trade and transport. Since opening up to the outside world, China's overseas trade has developed greatly; it is already the third largest trading entity in the world and a great amount of trade is carried out through maritime transport. The resources of the Chinese mainland and the needs of China's economic development have produced a major contradiction. China needs to increasingly use and develop resources from the maritime space and overseas. In a world where China is opening to the outside, more and more Chinese citizens are going abroad to reside and engage in investment or other activities. China's overseas interests are greatly expanding but its maritime territorial rights and interests are infringed by some countries. The process of resolution of the Taiwan problem is becoming longer, and the reunification of the two sides of the Taiwan Strait has become complex.

(2) To protect, defend and broaden these interests, China needs to develop an appropriate maritime force. This appropriate maritime force refers both to

maritime military strength and to maritime economic strength: this refers to the use of military strength when needed and to the peaceful use of maritime strength. The development of an appropriate maritime strength also refers to the development of a sea power that neither has control or mastery of the oceans nor exclusive control of the main sea transport routes as its goal, a power that does not have the use of force to fight for ocean resources or the use of maritime military strength to force other nations to accept China's will as its aim. But it does have the protection of China's lawful and reasonable national interests in the maritime space as its goal. This means that the use and development of China's maritime strength is not offensive but defensive and for self-protection. Its aim is the completion of China's national reunification and the protection of the national territory and national interests and not damaging of other nations' interests. It is regional and not global in nature, and it has economic development and not domination by force as its main goal.

Only if China's sea power is defined in this way is it possible that "in the relationship between the development of sea power and China's peaceful rise, the development of China's sea power will not become a structural factor leading to conflict and the obstruction of China's peaceful rise."[8]

Apart from this, it is necessary to note that considering problems only from the point of view of sea and land power leaves many gaps. This is because the development of science and technology today has already gone beyond the concepts of land and sea power. Many things that previously could only be done by developing maritime strength can today be achieved by other options, or can only be done by relying on alternative means. For instance, in the past, in order to obtain mastery of the oceans it was necessary to develop aircraft carriers to gain the advantage of having a maritime offensive force. Aircraft carriers have great power to destroy an enemy's naval vessels or its strategic goals on land, and they are a key to mastery of the seas. Today, aircraft carriers remain very important in obtaining mastery of the seas, but their impact is not as decisive as in the past. The development of long-range bombers, large long-range transporters, land-based, medium-range missiles and mid-air refuelling aircraft has already partially bypassed sea power. It could also be said that without mastery of the air there is no mastery of the seas, that without power in space there is no mastery of the air and without the power of information technology and networks there is no power in space. Therefore, considering the development of sea power only in conjunction with the development of aircraft carriers or naval strength is an outmoded way of thinking. Instead, it is necessary to do some reverse thinking. Since it is possible to control the land through mastery of the seas and control the airspace above the seas through aircraft carriers, why is it not possible to master the seas through development of land power and mastery of the air, space power and the power of information technology?

Heading towards development of sea power with Chinese characteristics

In order to develop China's sea power there must first be a grand strategy. In the future, the development of sea power must be included in the nation's grand strategy. It is certain that 1: The development of China's sea power cannot be separated from the whole of China's national development; it is an important part of China's development. 2. The development of China's sea power cannot be separated from the impact on the whole international and neighboring environment. 3. The development of China's sea power cannot be separated from world political, economic, technical and cultural developments. Some scholars have already proposed that when formulating the grand strategy for the development of China's sea power consideration must be given to the following: a) developing powers should make a cool and objective appraisal of their own capabilities and conditions, and the position of sea power in the whole of the nation's strategy should be decided by this; b) the decision to adopt sea power as China's preferred choice must be made on the basis of whether the development of sea power will be the new point of growth in key areas of international competition; c) relations with the current world hegemonic powers must be considered. China must not become the main challenger to the current hegemonic powers just because it pursues sea power; d) the development of China's sea power must make a full appraisal of security factors. Methods that are too simple and direct may create security difficulties.[9] These views are worth considering.

Then, how should China's sea power be developed? We propose the following considerations.

(1) The position of the development of sea power in China's overall development. Undoubtedly, the development of sea power is increasingly important to China. But the development of sea power is only a part of China's overall development. If it is said that China's development includes the development of land and maritime power, then the development of land power will always be more important and more basic. The development of maritime space cannot override that of the land and become China's most important problem. We believe that China will always be a land power since such power is decided by its position and function in China's overall structure.

---

9. Xu Qiyu, "Errors and Rethinking of Sea Power," *Strategy and Management,* no. 5 (2003).

Therefore, we must correctly consider the position and function of the development of sea power in China's overall development. Zhang Wenmu argues that "a strong navy is the guarantee of the accumulation of domestic wealth and democratic development,"[10] but this raises at least two problems.

1. The relationship between the development of China's sea power and construction of institutions. What exactly is the relationship between the development of China's sea power and the construction of China's political and economic system? The above viewpoint considers that there is a certain internal logic to the development of China's sea power and its democratic development but this view needs to be discussed further. With reference to Western history, it appears that there is no necessary connection between the two; situations in different countries vary. England, for example, was a strong sea power before becoming a democratic nation. Democracy developed first in England, but its democratic development went through a long process, which is normally considered to have started after the English Revolution of 1640. But before this, from 1588, when it defeated the Spanish Armada, it was already a sea power with great maritime strength. The development of the English democratic system is related to its industrial revolution, and its relationship with the development of sea power is weak. In the case of Japan, after it defeated the Northern Fleet of China's Qing dynasty in 1895 and the Russian navy in 1905, it became a newly rising sea power. But Japan's democratic development came after World War II. Before this Japan was always an anti-democratic militarist state. Japan's switch to democracy was not prompted by the development of its sea power but was caused by America which broke its navy and defeated the country. The US implemented a democratic system by force through military occupation, so it can be seen that the democratization of Japan after World War II had no connection with its sea power. The Soviet Union was a great sea power that had been on a par with the US, but the Soviet Union was not considered to be a Western-style democratic state. Even today Russia is not generally considered a Western-style democratic state by Western nations. America's own democratic system took shape after its establishment as an independent state, but it only became a relatively strong sea power a hundred years later and a real sea power after World War II. There is little direct relationship between America's democratic system and its sea power. Therefore, the construction of a nation's democratic system is mainly allied with the development of its politics, economy and culture, and has little relationship with the level of development of sea power. Thus, it is impossible to directly link the construction of a Chinese democratic system and the development of China's sea power. From the lessons of China's most famous navigator, Zheng He, sailing the Western Seas, to the defeat of the Northern Fleet, it should be emphasized

---

10. Zhang Wenmu, "Economic Globalisation and China's Sea Power" 经济全球化与中国海权, *Strategy and Management,* no. 1 (2003).

that the construction of China's institutions has key significance for the development of China's sea power, and not the opposite.

2. The relationship between the development of China's sea power and China's economic development and accumulation of wealth. While there are those that argue that if China had no navy it would not be able to guarantee the development of wealth, the examples given above show that there is no direct relationship between the development of a navy and a nation's economic wealth. Examples like Spain and Portugal at a certain level show that sea power can encourage economic wealth, but these examples are not of significance. Before America developed its navy it had already become the most economically developed nation in the contemporary world. Russia had a strong navy, but it has never become wealthy. China's history demonstrates this point even more clearly.

Even though China borders the sea it has never been a maritime nation and even less a sea power. Although the sea has played a certain role in China's historical development, it has never been an important role, much less a decisive one. China's history is mainly the history of a land power, and China's culture was mainly created and developed from the cultures of the Yellow River, Yangtze River and other large rivers. Although Chinese people have had experience of making sea voyages, and even achieved great successes, they are basically not a maritime people. Thus, today there should be an overall assessment of the position of sea power in the whole of China's history, institutions, culture and life. It is certain that China must develop and improve its maritime strength, and must develop and strengthen its sea power but, no matter what, it is unlikely that its sea power will reach or exceed as a proportion of China's overall strength the level reached by its power based on the mainland and large rivers.

For the past few thousand years, China has existed and developed as a land power. Since its reform and opening-up policy, China's economic development has achieved great success, but this has had little direct relationship with the development of China's navy. From now on China will be a land power that will achieve a quite major development of its sea power and it will emerge as such in international society, but it is unlikely that China's sea power will develop to the same level and degree as its land power. It cannot become as important a sea power as it is a land power, and even less is it possible that it will become a so-called major sea power. The importance of China's land space will always be greater than that of its maritime space. The important space at the heart of China's politics, economy and culture is the land and not the sea, and the great majority of the people of China will live on the land and not in sea areas (even if the population of the coastal regions is greater, these should still be seen as the fringe areas of the mainland, and not as a part of the ocean). The resources for China's existence and development (land, water, oil, minerals) are mainly on the mainland and not at sea. The maritime economy and industry have not been, and probably never will be, a major component of China's economy and industry.

To a great degree, the development of China's sea power is prompted by the need to protect its land power, and is a necessary constituent of the development in depth of China's land power. If it goes beyond the needs of the development of China's land power and takes the mastery of the world's main maritime communication routes as its fundamental direction, this will violate the established national policy of not becoming a superpower dominating the whole world.

Obviously, in a situation where the development of sea power is relatively backward, we can at a future date raise the development of sea power to an important position. Under the circumstances, we can prioritize, strengthen and accelerate the development of sea power; we can speed up the development of the Chinese navy so that it is in balance with the cardinal principle of developing land power. But, in the long term, the development of land power will always take priority over sea power. China needs to change from a land state bordering the ocean to a land state that has a maritime economy that occupies an important position, or a land state that has a few characteristics of a maritime state. But China cannot change into a sea power or maritime state like the UK or Japan, and cannot change into a superpower like the US that makes its global strategic goal the control of the world's main sea routes.

(2) In light of the lessons of Zheng He's voyages to the Western Seas and the 1894 Sino-Japanese War, China must use the construction of institutions as the basic starting point for the development of sea power. This type of institutional construction includes the establishment and perfection of a sound legal system and raising consciousness of doing things on the basis of the law and institutions. As China's famous ancient thinker Han Fei Zi said, in times of struggle for power, nations are not always strong, and are not always weak; when those who respect the law are strong, the nation is strong, when those who respect the law are weak, the nation is weak. The law must be the foundation. Those who understand the law are strong, those who don't respect the law are weak. The construction of institutions includes building the political policy-making system, the consultation system, the military command structure, the logistics system, the system of rewards and punishments and the anti-corruption system. The importance of those institutions related to the development of sea power must be emphasized. For example, civilian resources can be mobilized to participate in the development of islands and, more particularly, regulations should be formulated on how to manage those uninhabited islands that are far from the mainland or large islands so as to strengthen the symbols of national sovereignty.

(3) The development of sea power must be based on China's economic development. Investment in national defence such as the development of the navy must be increased appropriately and proportionately based on economic development. There are two views on building sea power. One is to use a large amount of resources, even if they are limited, on the development of military strength on the ocean. This type of thinking can rapidly increase a nation's military strength on the oceans in the short term, but lacks long-term sustainability and

staying power for development. Prior to modern times, many countries used this method. In fact the construction of the Northern Fleet by the Qing dynasty took this route. When China's national strength was relatively weak, the Qing dynasty Northern Fleet was for a time the most powerful navy in Asia. But its defeat in the 1894 Sino-Japanese War not only exposed the rottenness of the Qing dynasty institutions, it also revealed that the backward economy of the Qing dynasty could not sustain investment in naval construction in the long term. The current situation of the Russian navy is similar. Russia once had a navy to match the US navy, the most powerful in the world, and it still has strength. However, because Russia's economy has retreated it cannot support the enormous military expense of constructing new naval vessels or even carrying out normal maintenance and training for the existing vessels. Because of this Russia's fighting strength has been affected and it must make big cuts in equipment. The second approach is the American style of naval development. The major development of the American navy began at the end of the 19th century, and only reached a significant scale in the early 20th century. At that time, the US economy already occupied the number one position in the world, far exceeding the UK and other European economies.[11] For example, in 1914 America's national income was US$37 billion, exceeding the total of US$35 billion for the five powers: the UK (US$11 billion), France (US$6 billion), Germany (US$12 billion), Japan (US$2 billion) and Italy (US$4 billion). The strength of the US economy provided strong support for the rapid development of the American navy. In 1904 alone America constructed 14 battleships and 13 armoured cruisers. By 1914, the American navy was already the third strongest in the world, behind the UK and Germany. China probably should draw lessons from the American model of naval development. "In the relationship between developing sea power and overall national power, it should not calculate how to reduce the already low investment in naval defence, but to seek ways to raise the contribution of the maritime economy to the overall national strength, thus providing impetus to the development of sea power."[12]

(4) China should prioritize development of the maritime economy and development of the capacity to use and explore maritime resources and change from being a nation that borders the sea to being a nation whose maritime economy occupies a significant proportion of the national economy. This is an important part of China's overall strategy of peaceful and sustainable development.

China will not become a Western-style sea power, but it is possible for it to become a nation with a strong maritime economy, a nation in which non-military maritime strength occupies a significant proportion of its sea power making it a

---

11. Paul M. Kennedy, *Rise and Fall of the Great Powers*, trans. Liang Yuhua et al, 280, 284.
12. Liu Zhongmin, Zhao Chengguo, "Some Considerations on the Development Strategy for China's Sea Power."

major maritime nation. China has the natural geographic conditions to be a maritime nation. It has a coastline of over 18,000 km, more than 10,000 large and small islands, and it has more than three million square kilometers of sea territory. But just as many people who are born by the sea cannot swim, and many people who live abroad cannot speak the local language, these beneficial conditions do not mean that China will naturally become a maritime nation. A coastal state is a concept of natural geography, which means that sea territory, islands, the continental shelf and the exclusive economic zone are a major part of the sovereign nation and its territorial integrity, and sea territory is a major constituent of the total national territory. A sea power is a geopolitical concept and a maritime nation is a geo-economic and geopolitical concept. The political concept refers to a state for which maritime security is a major element of national security; the economic concept refers to a state where maritime sectors occupy a major proportion of the national economy. Maritime sectors include sea transport, offshore oil and gas industries, deep-sea mining, coastal and deep sea resource extraction, sea salt production, marine food production, coastal tourism, marine life and marine medical products, desalination of sea water, ocean ship building and port construction, etc.[13]

The proportion of China's maritime sectors in the overall national economy has been steadily increasing, but is still relatively low. In 1978, China's maritime sectors were only valued at about RMB6 billion. From the 1980s, China's maritime sectors grew annually at an average rate of over 20%, which is three times the rate for China's GDP. According to Chen Lianzeng, the deputy head of the China State Oceanic Administration: "China currently has already become a major nation in the global maritime sector and sea salt production, and is the third largest nation for maritime transport. The overall size of the maritime economy has increased from RMB22.7 billion in the early 1980s to RMB1.28 trillion in 2004, with 20 million people employed in maritime-related sectors. China has entered a period of large-scale, high-intensity development and use of the oceans."[14] But the maritime sector still only accounts for a very small part of the national economy, although its development potential is huge. In 2001 the output of China's maritime sectors reached RMB723.3 billion, or 3.4% of GDP; in 2003 it broke through RMB1 trillion, with a value added of RMB445 billion, and reached 3.8% of GDP; in 2004 it reached RMB1.2841 trillion, with a value added of RMB526.8 billion, and accounted for 3.9%.[15]

---

13. Han Zenglin et al, "The Development and Prospects of Maritime Economic Geography" 关于海洋经济地理学的发展与展望, *Human Geography* 16, no 5 (October 2001).

14. Wu Weizheng, "Clarifying Maritime Resources is Absolutely Necessary" 摸清海洋家底势 在必行, *People's Daily* 人民日报, May 17, 2005.

15. See articles "The Maritime Economy, A New Growth Sector" 海洋经济，新的增长点, "The Healthy Expansion of China's Maritime Economic Development" 我国海洋经济开发稳健展开, *People's Daily*, July 11, 2005.

(5) China needs appropriate development of a certain level of naval strength to protect and control "the four seas and one strait." No nation can attain complete control of the world's oceans and maritime routes, and America is no exception. China can only give priority to selecting, as the key targets for protection and control, the specific sea areas and maritime routes that are most important for its maritime transport, foreign trade and national security. They are mainly China's coastal waters, i.e. the Bohai Sea, Yellow Sea, East China Sea, South China Sea and the Taiwan Strait, hence the four seas and one strait. China cannot have sufficient maritime force to control other main sea areas and maritime routes, even though they may be important to it. Even in the four seas and one strait, China can only achieve a certain level of protection and control (only the Bohai Sea can be completely controlled), and cannot achieve complete exclusive or independent control. In this respect, the importance of the Taiwan problem must be emphasized. The Taiwan problem is a key at the heart of the construction of China's sea power, no matter whether it is maritime economic strength or maritime military strength.

If the above goals are to be reached, it will be necessary to give priority to the development of a strong navy in the near future. Although overall the development of land power must be given priority, this does not exclude giving prominence to naval development in the present period. This is because the development of China's navy bears no comparison to the overall development of land power and is far behind what is required to protect and support the development of land power.

(6) China should develop cooperative relations with major coastal states and sea strait route states, within which it is necessary to prioritize the development of relations with the coastal states related to the "six seas" and "six routes" using diplomatic, political, economic and cultural strength to supplement the lack of maritime force.

The "six seas" are the Andaman Sea, Arabian Sea, Persian Gulf, Gulf of Aden, Red Sea and Mediterranean Sea, and the six major sea routes are the Straits of Malacca, the Panama Canal, the Korea Strait, Strait of Hormuz, the Suez Canal and the Strait of Gibraltar. China does not have sufficient naval strength to effect even minimal control over these sea areas and routes, and can only rely on developing friendly cooperative relations with the countries that neighbor these sea areas and routes. Prominent among these countries are North Korea and South Korea, Thailand, Indonesia, Singapore, Malaysia, Burma, India, Sri Lanka, Pakistan, Iran, Oman, Saudi Arabia, Kuwait, Egypt, Ethiopia, Italy, Yemen, Algeria, Spain, France, South Africa, Panama, Venezuela, Brazil and Argentina. China's maritime transport and also economic and security factors such as overseas transfers, supply, repairs and security protection can only rely on the help and cooperation of these countries. At the same time, the use of strategic cooperation to improve China's geopolitical situation can be considered in order to avoid some sea areas and routes that may be potentially troublesome to the development of

China's sea space. For example, if Thailand intended to open the Kra Isthmus, then the Chinese government could consider this from the strategic point of view of developing the maritime space. Although it may be not very economic, it would have great strategic value, and the friendly relations between Thailand and China can provide a strategic guarantee of the secure long-term use of the isthmus by China.

(7) There is a need to strengthen awareness of the ocean, which means raising "the whole people's consciousness of the ocean," so that they "understand the ocean, study the ocean, explore the ocean, protect the ocean and defend China's sea rights and interests, promote the development of the cause of the ocean, and serve the construction of the national economy."[16] Although in the long term China's consciousness of the land will occupy first place, it must raise the status of the ocean in the people's consciousness.

Consciousness of the ocean is first of all consciousness of the importance of the ocean in the life of mankind. The leaders of China have said many times that "the ocean must be understood at the strategic level and the whole nation's consciousness of the ocean must be strengthened," and also that China should "open up the blue national territory," and "take care of and use the ocean well and promote the maritime economy."

Consciousness of the ocean is consciousness of resources and of sustainable development. The ocean is rich in animal, energy and mineral resources. These resources are an important material basis for mankind's sustainable development and a valuable source of wealth. In a situation where China's continental natural resources are increasingly in short supply, the development and use of ocean resources is important.

Consciousness of the ocean is consciousness of the protection of the ocean environment. The ocean is an asset which is the common inheritance of all humanity, and its development and protection is the common historical mission of all mankind. The ocean is an important part of the earth's environment and its adjustment mechanism. The environmental pollution and over-fishing of ocean life in China's oceans are very serious. Economic fish species in the Bohai Sea are already close to extinction, there are almost no fish to catch in the Yellow Sea, overall fish catches in the East China Sea are declining and over-development on the mainland has also caused serious pollution of China's sea areas. For example, 95% of the sea waters of the once-rich Pearl River estuary are now seriously polluted, and in dozens of miles of coastal waters have practically no fish to catch. The four main causes of this phenomenon are land reclamation from the sea, dredging of sand, pollution from the land and artificial aquaculture.[17] Therefore, it is urgently necessary to adopt measures to protect China's sea territory.

---

16. Han Zenglin et al, "The Development and Prospects of Maritime Economic Geography."
17. "Four Major Problems Threatening the Sea Waters of the Pearl River Mouth" 四大难题威胁珠江口海域生态, *People's Daily*, June 17, 2005.

Consciousness of the ocean is consciousness of national security. China's modern crisis started from a maritime crisis when the Western powers breached China's closed doors from the sea, creating a life and death situation for the Chinese people. Today, the greatest threat to China's national security also comes from the sea. Following the deepening development of China's reform and opening up to the world, the national interests in China's maritime space are increasingly important, becoming an important constituent of China's national interests and national security. Guaranteeing the unification of Taiwan with the mainland, protecting sovereignty over the Diaoyutai ("Pinnacle Islands") and islands of the South China Sea and ensuring that China's exclusive economic zone and its legal rights and interests on the continental shelf are not infringed upon are important parts of China's national security.

(8) It is necessary to study, use and encourage the cooperation of the UN, international organizations and the major sea powers to protect China's maritime interests. Today there are many nations that have global interests. If every nation established a global navy then there would be more naval vessels than commercial ships in the main sea areas. Even if China had a strong navy it is unlikely that it could protect the security of its own commercial ships at any time in any place. Therefore, China must learn to use the existing international institutions to protect its own legal rights and interests, and cannot completely rely on so-called methods of self-reliance to resolve problems.

In summary, the development of China's sea power must start from the overall situation of China's peaceful development and modernization, take into account both the land and the sea, and strike a balance between economic development and military development. While it is unlikely that China can develop into a major sea power, the goal should be to develop from being a land power with relatively weak sea power to being a big land power with strong sea power.

(translated by Duncan Freeman)

On China's Sea Power*

Zhang Wenmu

Sea power first presented itself as a problem for the Chinese during the Opium War. It has still not been theoretically resolved although it urgently requires a theoretical answer. This article examines the idea of sea power by going from the general to the specific, and seeks to provide a theoretical system of sea power that fits the sense of the Chinese language and the practice of China's modernization in the new century. It also uses these concepts and theories to solve the current problems concerning the realization of China's sea power.

[....]

The characteristics of China's sea power

China's sea power was born at the same time as its sovereignty, but its recognition of sea power and efforts to defend and strengthen it only began in recent times. Currently, China's sea power has only the strength to protect legal sea rights and falls far short of what could be its goal. For example, the unification of Taiwan and the other islands that are within the limits of China's sovereignty is a major element in the realization of its sea power. However, this only amounts to the

*   This article was first published in *World Economics and International Politics* 世界经济与
政治 no. 10 (2003): 8–14.

protection of China's sovereignty and its related sea rights and maritime interests in these areas. Such use of sea power is not an attempt to gain hegemonic sea power. From this it can be seen that China is within its rights to defend national sovereignty, but the military intervention of the US in the Taiwan region is a hegemonic naval action designed to show its sea power. If we do not make a distinction in the translation of sea power - haiquan (海权) — between power and rights, it will lead to neighbouring regions and countries having a significant misunderstanding of the realization of China's modernization and its related sea power.[1]

China's sea power is the lawful protection of its sea rights within Chinese sovereignty. It is not power over the oceans, let alone maritime hegemony. "But in today's world, it is impossible to obtain justice only with the law and without power,"[2] thus, if China wishes its sea rights in legal theory to be China's in reality, it must have greater sea power. Therefore, China's sea power is the unification of the end and the means. The concept of China's sea power should include both "sea rights" drawn from China's national sovereignty and the "sea power" to realize and protect these rights although that does not include the "sea power" that is commonly seized by Western hegemonic states.

The "sea rights" element of Chinese sea power includes the realization of both China's "sea rights" and "maritime interests." The former includes international sea law, the provisions of the UN Convention on the Law of the Sea and the sea rights recognized by international law that are enjoyed by sovereign states. These rights evolve slowly with changes in international sea law, and are well defined. The latter includes economic, political and cultural interests created by the sea rights. These rights change with economic, political and cultural changes in various states at different periods, and are the elements of sea power that can vary considerably. Different states enjoy the same sea rights under international sea law, but sovereign states that have the same sea rights have

1. John J. Mearsheimer, professor at Chicago University and director of the Program on International Security Policy is a well-known representative of the "China threat" point of view. In his new book *The Tragedy of Great Power Politics*, he draws the conclusion: "Obviously, in the early 21st century, probably the most dangerous prospect faced by the US is that China will become the potential hegemonic power in northeast Asia. Obviously, the prospect that China will become the potential hegemonic power mainly depends on whether its economy can maintain its rapid growth. If this happens, China will not only become the main inventor of leading technology, but also will be the richest of the world's large powers. It will almost certainly use its economic strength to establish a powerful military machine, and will develop rational strategic principles. It will certainly seek regional hegemony, just like the US did in the Western Hemisphere in the 19th century." *The Tragedy of Great Power Politics* (New York: W.W. Morton & Company, Inc 2001), 401.

2. Alfred Thayer Mahan, *The Influence of Sea Power upon History* 海权论, trans. Xiao Weizhong (Beijing: Zhongguo yanshi chubanshe, 1997), 418.

different maritime interests because they exist in different stages of economic, political and cultural development. Hence, excluding maritime hegemonic factors, generally speaking the maritime interests of traditional powers and rising powers are larger than those of small powers and declining nations. In addition, there are "maritime interests" that are neutral and even wider than sea rights. They may be legal interests that derive from sea rights or illegal interests prompted by a desire for hegemonic power. Because China's current capacity to realize its sea power has not "overflowed" the limits of its sovereignty, it bears no relation to hegemony. China's maritime interests can be described as seeking and realizing its legal sea rights.

China is a large country with a growing economy and it is in transition to modernization. It is one of the five permanent members of the UN Security Council and exercises a major influence in international affairs. In 2000, China's GDP reached RMB8.9 trillion, exceeding US$1 trillion for the first time. In 1999, China's GDP was ranked seventh in the world.[3] As the economy grows rapidly, China's demand for energy from the rest of the world was also rising quickly. China's oil imports increased between 1994 and 2000 from 2.9 million tons to 70 million tons. The oil import dependency greatly increased, from 1.9% in 1994, to 30% in 2000. At this rate, by 2010 over 40% of China's oil requirements will be imports, and by 2020 the proportion will be well over 60%. The main source of China's oil imports is currently the Middle East. Over half of oil imports (56.2%) come from the Middle East, followed by North Africa.[4] As China enters the international market it has become a country with broad links to the world. Its maritime interests have expanded throughout the world, and will continue to widen following the growth of the Chinese economy. At the same time, and in common with other countries, the internal demand that China realize its sea power amid external pressures is also increasing.

However, China's sea power must be unique. What are the features of this uniqueness?

First, the process of national reunification and the realization of national sea power is the same. China is currently a nation that has not completed full unification, and the regions where unification has not been achieved are mostly concentrated in China's eastern sea areas. These areas are both Chinese territory and also the maritime strategic fulcrum for the realization of China's sea power. For example, Taiwan and its neighbouring Chinese islands are the forward base for China's entry to the Pacific and also are the forward defence for East China's

---

3. State Statistical Bureau, "International Comparison of Economic and Social Development Levels." [Available online] Available from http://www.stats.gov.cn/tjfx/ztfx/jwxlfxbg/200205300095.htm.

4. Quoted in Liu Xinhua, Qin Yi, "China's Oil Security and it Strategic Choices" 中国的石油安全及其战略选择, in *Contemporary International Relations* 现代国际关系, no. 12 (2002): 37.

golden economic zone: the Spratly Islands are also the forward base for protection of China's right of free passage in the Straits of Malacca. The realization of China's sovereignty over Taiwan and the Spratly Islands will be both the achievement of the just cause of China's reunification and also a key step to show whether or not China's sea power can be actualized. The twin aims of actualizing sea power and unification give China's sea power both its special character and its advantage. That special character will determine the legitimacy and justice of the realization of China's sea power for a long time to come and will also exclude the possibility that its realization will turn into maritime hegemony. Thus we can say that the belief that China realizing its sea power interest and developing a navy is a "China threat" and the view that China should not develop its navy are both unfounded and illogical.

Secondly, specific geopolitical conditions determine that China's sea power will be limited. These conditions are similar to those of France, and unlike those of the UK and the US. China is both a land and a sea state, but the UK and the US are both protected by the sea. This maritime security aspect required that the UK and the US gave priority to the realization of sea power and expansion of maritime interests to the point where they finally became world maritime hegemonic states. Geographically, China has the ocean on only one side, and land on three sides. Because of pressure on security at its land borders, China has historically developed a strong land army rather than a navy. Its geopolitical character and the features of China's sea power described above also determine that China's sea power — even if it had the same financial resources as the UK and US — would not need to be used to pursue global maritime power. From the end of the 20th century, China's eastern regions have faced a security threat, especially from the growing pressure caused by the separation from Chinese sovereignty of Taiwan and part of the Spratly Islands. To date, China's policies to deal with these crises have been very inadequate. It is only under these special historical circumstances that we stress the need for the protection of sea power, and call for the development of China's naval strength. But this does not mean that China should attempt to emulate the unlimited sea power and hegemony of the UK and the US, and especially the Soviet Union. China's sea power should be limited and characterized by the fact that it does not go beyond the limits of sovereignty and the sea rights provided for by international sea law and that its naval development does not go beyond the limits of self defence.

Thirdly, the development of China's naval power involves the marriage of the limited nature of the long-term strategy described above with the unlimited nature of short-term tactics. The Chinese people's awareness of maritime strategic interests began with the defeats of the Opium War and the Sino-Japanese War of 1894-5; their awareness of sea power from the point of view of economic globalization began during the transformation of China from a planned to a market economy. In the ancient world, because of the lack of technology to power long-distance voyages, the coastal seas to the east became the natural protective screen for China's eastern borders. Then came the naval defeats of the Opium War, the Sino-Japanese War of 1894–5 and earlier stages of the Anti-Japanese War, but they only caused Chinese people to consider the meaning of sea power from the point of view of border defence. In the 20 years from the start of reform and opening up in the 1980s to the beginning of the 21st century, the Chinese economy has entered profoundly into the process of economic globalization, which has produced an ever-deepening dependency on international markets and resources. In view of this, China cannot avoid the need to develop a naval power that can protect its global overseas interests, and which will grow with the widening of these overseas interests. The process of this growth is without limit, but its nature does not go beyond the limits of self-defence.

In the process of the ever-growing interdependence between China and the world, China's eastern coastal region has become the golden zone with the most rapid growth of output in the Chinese economy. At the same time, the conflicts between China and the Western hegemonic powers, especially the maritime conflicts, are increasing. In order to block China's power, especially the extension of China's naval power to the Pacific Ocean, the US is encouraging the alliance of Japan, Taiwan, the Philippines and Australia, promoting Japan's military capacity and instigating the strengthening of Taiwanese separatism. In the struggle with Taiwan separatism, and also through giving close attention to the increasingly serious naval security situation to its east, China has realized that the slow development of a navy cannot protect its most basic maritime interests. This realization further induces "Taiwan independence elements" to constantly take risks, challenging the central government policy on Taiwan. Even more seriously, the negative effects of Taiwan independence may influence the political situation in the whole of East Asia from Japan to the Association of Southeast Asian Nations. This naturally has an influence on China's eastern regions and, in particular, results in an invisible centrifugal effect on the south-eastern coastal provinces. The result is that the deterioration of the Taiwan problem will affect the whole of China's modernization. The key power to contain "Taiwan independence" is the strength of China's maritime strategy, which is the rapid rise of the Chinese navy. The Chinese navy is the key to China's maritime strategy. In light of this, it is necessary to concentrate all resources on rapidly developing China's navy, transforming global military weakness into regional strength, and thus resolving the problems of sea power in China's maritime areas.

In essence the Taiwan problem is a problem of the Chinese navy, and the essence of the problem of the Chinese navy is the problem of the peaceful reunification of the motherland. The completion of the peaceful return of Taiwan together with its modern culture is impossible without a major expansion of the navy.

World military transformation and China's strategy for swift naval development

The navy is the core of China's maritime strategic strength, and is the military arm that provides the necessary prop for China's sea power. In the same way, sea rights must necessarily rely on sea power, although it is not the whole of the state's maritime strategic strength. Strategic strength, whether on land or at sea, is military strength that has the capacity for total warfare against an enemy. Thus, China's maritime strategic strength should not only concern the navy, but should also be an overall expression of the strength of national defence in the wake of the transformation and development of world military technology. Before World War I, navies were mostly an adjunct to land forces. Land forces in this period were the core military arm of a state's strategic strength. In the period before World War II, naval warfare had already become a decisive factor in victory or defeat in war. A state's strategic strength was increasingly expressed through the navy. The aircraft carrier was the most powerful warship that emerged in World War II. This was not because of its size but because, for the first time, it clearly broke through the limits of the different military arms; it transformed warships into three-dimensional fighting platforms uniting land, sea and air fighting capability. Today, the aircraft carrier's fighting capability is not just the simple fighting capability of naval vessels, it is a unification of the military arms of land, sea, air and electronic communications in a single entity. The giant fighting platform of the aircraft carrier exercises a new type of flexible strategic strength at sea. The aircraft carrier's fighting capability and its fighting systems are no longer naval, it is the strategic strength of the state.

From the second half of the 20th century, following the rapid development of satellites, space early warning systems and the pinpoint accuracy missile technology that followed, the technological factor in the maritime strategic strength of the state and the level of its organic synthesis greatly increased. It has grown from the small three-dimensional warfare of the World War II period, which used a combination of the firepower of aircraft, submarines and aircraft carriers, to large, three-dimensional fighting with satellite surveillance technology in outer space, inner space early warning technology, deep-sea[5] submarines, sonar technology and accompanying land and sea pinpoint missile strikes. Warfare at sea is far from being conducted using only the naval arm; today it is the overall expression of the national technological foundation and the fighting capacity

---

5. According to the standards of depth measures of ocean silt set out by *China Science Encyclopaedia: Atmospheric Sciences, Oceanography, Hydrology* 中国大百科全书：大气科学、海洋科学、水文科学 (Beijing: Zhongguo dabaike quanshu chubanshe, 1987), 302, 623, 11 and 664, we designate the concept of "deep sea" a depth of 200 meters or more.

formed from it.[6] With each passing day, following the appearance of outer space satellite telecommunication technology and the advance of deep-sea technology, the large three-dimensional warfare model is replacing the small three-dimensional warfare model that focuses on the aircraft carrier. If there were no combination of outer space telecommunications technology and deep sea submarines, aircraft carriers, no matter what their technological capacity, could, at most, "only act as floating coffins"[7] rather than form an effective fighting force. Currently, an American aircraft carrier, apart from the protection of satellite positioning, satellite early warning and other surface ships, also has massive protection from submarines. In comparison, China's naval fighting strength is still far from reaching this level. China has not yet developed an aircraft carrier and, even though it has made certain advances in outer space satellite technology and deep-sea submarines and acoustic technology, it has been left behind in the last 20 years. It follows that the danger to China's maritime security is great, and the task of naval development will be more urgent in the future. Therefore, the proper use of China's limited defence resources and science in the construction of the navy should be considered from the standpoint of both the theory and realization of China's sea power.

[....]

The construction of China's navy started early, but development has been slow. This is a characteristic of the history of the Chinese navy, and is also to its advantage. In the same way that China did not have the military strength to participate in the strategic nuclear competition for "mutually assured destruction" between the US and USSR and is saved from the burden of reducing strategic nuclear weapons, the relative backwardness of the Chinese navy meant that it was able to have the advantage of the late developer in developing new fields. The current problem for China is that the model of warfare which relies on outer space satellite telecommunications technology — pushed forward and led by the US — not only has increased the military technology gap between the US and China, but has also had a serious impact on China's national security, especially on the security of China's sovereignty in sea areas. As a result, China must urgently take steps to make proper use of its limited defence resources and science to develop the navy, and make efforts to close the technology gap between the US and China within the shortest possible time. How can we achieve this goal? Do we have to follow the path set by the Americans starting from outer space and instigate a broad race in space with the US? On the basis of historical experience, if we use the advantage of the late developer and give precedence to the use of

---

6.   In view of this, my concept of "navy" has departed from the traditional meaning of "service arm." It means "national maritime strategic strength."

7.   Thomas S. Burns, *The Secret War for the Ocean Depths* 大洋深处的秘密战争, trans. Wang Xinmin and Xin Hua (Bejing: Haiyang chubanshe, 1985), 84.

limited defence resources for deep-sea development, it will probably create an effective deterrent force within a comparatively short period of time, and will drive forward the development of China's navy. This is because: (1) The outer space technological revolution which began in the 1980s has reached maturity, but the development of deep-sea technology is just unfolding. (2) Deep-sea weapons are more flexible and more easily concealed than aerospace weapons, and are more beneficial to achieving the national strategic offensive and defensive task. (3) Compared to land-launched ballistic missiles, deep-water, nuclear-powered strategic weapons can better guarantee that the nation's second strike capability can exist for longer. (4) The development of deep-water arms, including submarines, is the basis for the development of surface warships including aircraft carriers. The final capacity of the nation's navy to wage war lies not in the fighting strength of surface warships but in the fighting strength of underwater vessels, which is to say, following a large-scale nuclear attack only deep-water warfare capability enables strategic retaliation and second strikes. (5) China is a developing nation, and its defence tasks are by nature strategic. Giving priority to the use of limited resources in deep-sea development is not only beneficial to the aim of blocking the strength of "Taiwan independence" and realizing national reunification, it will also guarantee the final effectiveness of the national strategic defence policy.

In early August 2003, during a visit to Heilongjiang and Jilin provinces, Premier Wen Jiabao emphasized the strategic significance of reviving the economy of the northeast.[8] The northeast is the centre of the national defence equipment industry, and Liaoning is the major base of R&D and production for China's military equipment.[9] If the naval defence industry in the northeast can follow the space industry in the west and grow in the new century so that east and west work in concert, it will provide a strong guarantee for China's large three-dimensional national defence systems, in particular, the swift development model for the naval defence system.

The principles of expanding China's sea power

The navy is the main means of expanding national sea power. Noting the lessons of the crushing defeats of some nations in the past, some people claim that China has no need to develop its navy. There are also people who emphasize the

---

8. "Wen Jiabao Visits Heilongjiang and Jilin and Says Revival of the Northeast has Strategic Significance" 温家宝考察黑龙江吉林 称振兴东北具有战略意义, http://news.sina.com.cn/c/2003-08-05/1235508708s.shtml.
9. "Bo Xilai: Six Values and Five Relations for Reviving Liaoning" 薄熙来:振兴运辽宁的六个价值和五个关系, http://www.cas.ac.cn/html/Dir/2003/07/10/7051.htm.

importance of developing China's navy from the point of view of the struggle for hegemony between the great powers. However, in our view, these views are not correct. In reality, the widening of China's sea power has its own specific principles which it cannot depart from and which must be used in service of the meaning and scope of China's sea rights.

But what are the meaning and scope of China's sea rights?

In the short-to-medium term, China faces the serious task of unifying the motherland and regaining sovereignty over its island territories. This is not only the great historical mission that the Chinese government must bear, but it is also the main element in China's defence of its sea rights. Therefore, regarding the problem of reunification of Taiwan and the neighboring islands under Chinese sovereignty, no matter how it is calculated, the significance of China expanding the navy could not be greater. The future military actions of the Chinese navy to reunify the nation will be similar to those by Bismarck to unify Germany and Lincoln to unify the US. No matter whether peaceful or non-peaceful methods are used, the thing is to achieve the goal which has great significance. With regard to the goal of reunification, China's sea rights within the scope of its sovereignty are without limit. At the same time, China's sea rights and the power to realize them, like the expansion of the Chinese navy, have limits in regard to protecting overseas political and economic interests. This is because in these fields there are many problems that must be resolved through multilateral negotiation within the framework of the international law of the sea. The goal of the Chinese navy is only to provide a guarantee for the lawful implementation of the outcome of these multilateral negotiations. Seen from this point of view, the construction of the Chinese navy is limited to deterrence for self defence. The goal of developing the Chinese navy will always be in service to the needs of China's independent, equal standing in the world. "China will never be a hegemonist,"[10] is not just a slogan, it is also the mature lesson for strengthening the nation drawn by China's politicians from the history of the rise and fall of the great powers of the world. We did not need to look far for a lesson. It was precisely the unlimited military expansion of Germany, Italy, Japan and the USSR that led to their national decline, and it was precisely the inability of such nations as Yugoslavia and Iraq

---

10. China News Net 23 June: State Council Premier Wen Jiabao was recently jointly interviewed by journalists of the Press Trust of India and *The Hindu*. Wen Jiabao pointed out that the Chinese people have suffered invasion and humiliation, and especially appreciate peace and tranquillity. China is not yet developed now, and it will not seek hegemony even when it is developed. China will never seek hegemony. China's development will benefit the collective development of the region, and will not be a threat to any nation. See http://cn.news.yahoo.com/030623/72/1o3fc.html.

to keep up with advances in world military technology that led to them being broken up or defeated. In light of these historical experiences, choosing either the unlimited expansion of China's navy or basically abandoning the modernization of the navy would be disastrous for the future of China. We should adopt a dialectical attitude toward the problem of China's sea rights and the development of the navy. In the process of consideration through debate, we achieve greater advances that are beneficial to the rise of China.

The historic events occurring today provide an opportunity for the rise of China. Bush's foreign policy has departed from the realistic policy of a continental balance of power promoted by such presidents as Franklin Roosevelt, Richard Nixon and George H.W. Bush and has returned to the problematic idealistic foreign policy which was pursued from Truman to Johnson after World War II, a policy that supported unilateral interventionism in the Asian regions and attempted to resolve regional conflicts by removing the ruling ideological systems in these regions. The result, inevitably, was that the US showed the courage of Hamlet seeking to reverse the course of events but achieved the results of Don Quixote tilting at windmills. Before the war in Afghanistan, the balance of power between the Taliban authorities, Iran and the Commonwealth of Independent States (CIS) in central Asia was favorable to the US but, after the overthrow of the Taliban, relations between the Karzai government, Iran and the CIS states in central Asia improved. Following the US war in Iraq, the longstanding opposition between Iraq and Iran suddenly turned to harmony and resulted in US allies Kuwait and Saudi Arabia being put in an awkward position. It is certain that if US foreign policy is not promptly readjusted back to that of Nixon, the result of the US attempting to change Islam by force will be that Islamic resistance to the US in the Middle East will continue to rise, the unity of Muslim nations will continue to strengthen and anti-America terrorist activities will increase further. This will cause the threadbare Bush foreign policy to be even more exposed, and destroy the balance of power established by previous American administrations that was advantageous to the US and also the strategic benefits derived from this. Before 9/11, Bush pointed his spear at China, and China had to avoid his strength; after 9/11, the military strength of the US was directed at Afghanistan, and China had to be circumspect; now the US is trapped in Iraq, its morale is suffering, and its domestic economy is in a long-term slowdown. The US has gone from having a strong fighting spirit to losing its fighting spirit. During this period, if China, while establishing good relations with the US, can also make military preparations in case of need, especially preparations for naval modernization, the first 20 years of the 21st century will be judged a strategic opportunity for China, and its rise will be unstoppable.

(translated by Duncan Freeman)

On China's Foreign Policy Strategy*

Yu Xilai and Wu Zichen

First, we should make the parameters of foreign policy strategy clear. Put simply, it is both the assessment of the general global situation and the definition of overall diplomatic goals, and also what people commonly speak of as "situations and tasks." As for specific tasks according to region, area and time, and strategies, methods and measures for completion of such tasks, these are minor matters of small-scale strategy, campaigns and tactics.

I. A basic assessment of the global situation

1. *The importance of situational assessment.* When leaders make reports, they often discuss China's situation by starting from the global situation, and discuss the local situation by starting from China's situation. If they always say "everything is fine," "everything is getting better," this is unquestionably a way of toeing the party line but this type of analysis of the situation going from the macrocosmic to the microcosmic follows the natural logic of human thought. For a nation, a ruling party or a citizen, the international situation is a major factor and, as such, it must be given priority.

* This article was first published in *Tribune of Social Sciences* 社会科学论坛, no. 8 (2003): 7–16.

When Mao Zedong criticized Zhou Enlai for the last time in his life, going as far as saying, "[he is] not discussing important matters, [he is] reporting small matters every day and, if this does not change, it must be corrected," he was taking into account the assessment of the world situation. In July 1973, Zhou Enlai endorsed an article in issue 153 of *New Situation* titled "Initial Views on the Nixon-Brezhnev Meeting". It analysed and reviewed the world situation after the signing of the US-USSR agreement on the prevention of nuclear war and said that the US-USSR meeting was "fraudulent," and that "the atmosphere of US-USSR world domination is even stronger." Mao Zedong criticized this report, saying: "Recently the Ministry of Foreign Affairs has had some problems, which does not make one satisfied. I often speak of major turbulence, division and restructuring, and the Ministry of Foreign Affairs comes up with something about a big fraud and massive domination. When there is revisionism in the future, do not say that I haven't warned you." Zhou Enlai took political responsibility for this criticism, and undertook self-criticism in the Politburo.[1] There was a reason why Mao Zedong was angry. If the global situation was really under the combined domination of the US and USSR, there was no future for his new foreign policy strategy of uniting with the US to oppose the USSR.

To tackle the problems of war and peace, it was essential to break the bonds of the "two whatevers"[2] and make a realistic assessment of the external conditions that China faced. Indeed, that was the premise and foundation of the line of reform and opening-up policy with "economic construction as its core" which was formulated by the 3rd Plenary Session of the 11th Chinese Communist Party Central Committee. As early as 1962, Wang Jiaxiang, then Director of the CCP Foreign Liaison Department, was already urging leaders to take a realistic world view in his letters to leaders and drafts of document outlines. "Do not say that the basic contradiction between the socialist camp and the imperialist camp must lead to world war, do not say that only after the destruction of American imperialism can the Third World War be avoided. ... Do not overemphasize the threat of world war and dilute the possibility of preventing world war," he said, adding: "Such views as 'under the existing conditions of imperialism, there cannot be peaceful coexistence', 'imperialism must be overthrown, and only then can there be peace', 'imperialism and colonialism must be thoroughly exterminated, and only then can peaceful

---

1. See CCP Central Document Research Office edited: vol. 2 of *Zhou Enlai Chronicle (1949–1976)* 周恩来年谱 (一九四九——一九七六) (Central Committee Archive Press, 1997), 603–5.

2. "Two whatevers" 两个凡是 was coined by Hua Guofeng right after the end of the Cultural Revolution and the arrest of the Gang of Four in a CCP Central Committee meeting held on October 26, 1976. It refers to the statement "whatever decisions are made by Chairman Mao will be resolutely upheld, whatever instructions given by Chairman Mao will be unswervingly followed." [Translator's note]

coexistence and world peace be realized' are mistaken."[3] Mao Zedong, however, did not accept the views of Wang Jiaxiang, and, on the contrary, made him into one of the advocates of the 'three surrenders and one extinguish' revisionist line. Instead he proposed the development of a strategy where "we must base ourselves on war, start out from preparation to fight a war and give priority to the strengthening of national defence."

When Deng Xiaoping re-emerged for the second time, he said: "We can probably strive for some more time to avoid fighting a war," and "we can strive to delay the outbreak of war."[4] Hu Yaobang finally formally declared in the political report to the 12th CCP Congress: "It is possible for world peace to be safeguarded." If the leadership of the CCP had persisted in Mao Zedong's line of preparing to "fight a world war," and "fight a major war, fight early and fight a nuclear war," it would be difficult to imagine the success of economic development over twenty years of the opening-up policy and reform.

2. *Subjective and objective factors in situational assessment.* When people carry out an assessment of a situation, it is very difficult to avoid the influence of subjective factors, but they should still make every effort to stick to the objective facts and take seeking truth from facts as the basic starting point. The changing assessment of the situation in the Korean War is a very good illustration. When the Chinese People's Volunteers were victorious in their first and second campaigns, Peng Dehuai telegraphed Mao Zedong, suggesting that the army adjust its positions and, for the moment, that it should not cross the 38th parallel. The same day Kim Il-sung issued an announcement with the slogans, "March to victory in the war for liberation of the motherland" and "Send the American armed invaders and the Syngman Rhee traitorous clique to their graves", Mao Zedong took the side of Kim Il-sung. In a telegraph to Peng Dehuai he said: "Our army must cross the 38th parallel. If we arrive to the north of the 38th parallel and stop, this will be a major political disadvantage."

On January 13, 1951, after the Chinese army gained victory in the third campaign by occupying Seoul, the Political and Security Committee of the UN General Assembly passed the report on the basic principles for resolving the Korean problem suggested by the Three-man Commission on the Korean Problem. This report suggested: immediate implementation of a ceasefire; holding a political conference to restore peace; withdrawal of foreign military forces in stages and organization of elections for the Korean people and making preparations for a unified Korea. Following a ceasefire, a meeting with the participation of the UK, US, USSR and Communist China would be arranged to

---

3. See Xu Zehao, *Biography of Wang Jiaxiang* 王稼祥传 (Beijing: Dangdai Zhongguo chubanshe, 1996), 560–1.

4. Vol. 2 of *Selected Works of Deng Xiaoping* 邓小平文选 (Beijing: Renmin chubanshe, 1994), 77.

resolve problems in the Far East, among which would be the problems of the status of Taiwan and the representation of China in the UN. But on the basis of his assessment of the situation, Mao Zedong believed that that it was possible to obtain complete victory, and therefore rejected the ceasefire proposal. After the defeat of the fifth campaign, Mao Zedong, Stalin and Kim Il-sung conferred repeatedly and made a new assessment of the war situation: the Korean War was a partial clash of the two camps in the world, and not the final decisive battle; America's strategic centre was Europe, and its military strength in the Far East was auxiliary; the goal of the UN forces in the Korean peninsula was to return to the original situation, and was not to occupy the north; the Chinese People's Volunteers did not have the strength to annihilate at one time an organic unit made up of a complete battalion or more of the US army. Following this relatively realistic assessment of the situation, those in favor of a ceasefire and peace negotiations gained strength and finally achieved a halt in the fighting. At the time, American generals also had different views about the war situation. MacArthur preferred to risk spreading the flames of war to the northeast of China, and was determined to allow the army to fight to the banks of the Yalu River. Because of this, President Truman removed him from the post of Commander in Chief of the UN forces and the US forces in the Far East. If Mao Zedong had not learned from experience and changed the assessment of the situation in time, and persisted in trying to drive the UN forces into the sea, it could well have resulted in the resurgence of the views advocated by MacArthur which might then have become the strategic policy of the American government.

An optimistic assessment of a situation can be helpful in raising morale. Because of Lin Biao's pessimistic mood manifest in his letter to Mao Zedong, Mao introduced, in his reply, the famous line "a single spark can light a prairie fire" to describe the situation of the Chinese Workers and Peasants' Red Army in 1930. Another important analysis of a situation by Mao Zedong, and one of the most successful in his life, was made in 1947. Many experienced people believe that the most brilliant article in the fourth volume of the *Selected Works of Mao Zedong* is "The Present Situation and Our Tasks." When the enemy was strong and China was weak, Mao Zedong bravely predicted that war between the US and the USSR and the Third World War would not break out and that Chiang Kai-shek would certainly be defeated. The civil war between the KMT and CCP had already reached a turning point, he said. This turning point mainly referred to a change in the aims of the war. Prior to this, the CCP had always said that the civil war was a war of self-defence, but the emphasis changed with the slogan, "Overthrow Chiang Kai-shek, liberate the whole of China." Mao Zedong's analysis of the situation had the effect of killing three birds with one stone: one was to boost the ambition of his own side, the second was to win over the strength of the middle ground and the third was to break the enemy's will to fight. The leaders of the KMT and CCP were about the same age, they had grown up in a similar political environment and ideological atmosphere, and many of them were originally classmates (Deng Xiaoping and Jiang Jingguo, Hu Zongnan and Chen Geng) or colleagues (Mao Zedong and Chiang Kai-shek at the KMT Party Central, Zhou Enlai and He Yingqin and Chen Cheng at the Huangpu Military Academy) and some military and political leaders of the KMT were former CCP members or underground CCP members (for example Shao Lizi, Liu Fei and Guo Ruhuai). Because of this, it was easy for subjective factors to influence the assessment of the situation, with mixed results.

3. *Simple review of assessment of the global situation.* As a person with inside knowledge, Li Shenzhi has published an article in which he reviews the whole process of the theory of the "three worlds," from its being an impromptu judgment to its final self-dissolution.[5] The writer points out that the assessment of the world situation by the CCP leadership can be simply summarized by the four numbers "2,3,4,1."[6]

In the early Mao Zedong period, the world was viewed as being divided into the two big camps, the socialist and capitalist states. In the 1950s, the famous assessment was that the "east wind will overcome the west wind." In the 1960s, the classic formulation was: "The overall trend is that imperialism is heading toward total collapse, and socialism is heading toward victory throughout the world." Because Mao Zedong had insisted at the Moscow meeting that the socialist camp must "take the Soviet Union as the core," when relations between China and the USSR worsened, the two camps formulation disappeared from the scene. In retrospect, this type of assessment and the foreign policy based on it was obviously doomed to a short life. In less that half a century, the camp with the Soviet Union as its leader was split and then disappeared, and so what can be said of its "overcoming" and "victory" now?

On February 22, 1974, at a meeting with Zambia's President Kaunda, Mao said, "I see the US and USSR as the First World. The Second World is the group in the middle: Europe, Japan, Australia and Canada. We are the Third World. ... The US and USSR have many nuclear weapons, and are relatively rich. The Second World ... does not have so many nuclear weapons, and is not so rich, but is richer than the Third World." He added: "The population of the Third World is very large. ...The whole of Asia except for Japan is in the Third World.

---

5. See Li Shenzhi, "Discussion of the Foreign Policy of the People's Republic of China" 谈谈 中国人民共和国的外交, *Strategy and Management* 战略与管理, no. 4 (2002).

6. See Yu Xilai, Wu Zichen, "The New World Order and the Historic Choices of the Newly Arising Powers" 世界新秩序与新兴大国的历史决择, *Strategy and Management*, no. 2 (1998); Wu Zichen, "The Evolution of China's Foreign Policy Ideology: from 'Peaceful Coexistence' to 'Peaceful Development'" 中国外交思想的演变：从'和平共处'到'和平发展' *Strategy and Management*, no. 2 (2002).

The whole of Africa is in the Third World, Latin America is part of the Third World."[7] After Deng Xiaoping re-emerged for the first time, he represented the Chinese government at the Sixth Special Session of the UN and gave a speech where he developed these ideas further. Against this background, the "three worlds" analysis of the situation continued to be used in the early part of the Deng Xiaoping era. Later, following the views of foreign affairs experts such as Li Yimang, who was then the Executive Deputy Director of the CCP Central Committee International Department, the Political Report at the 12th CCP Party Congress did not use the "three worlds" formulation any more.[8] The abandonment of the theory of the "three worlds" was the result of the disjuncture of theory and reality. According to Mao Zedong's analysis of the three worlds, China should unite with the Third World, draw over the Second World and oppose the First World. This was like the Warring States period when the weak states to the east united to oppose the strength of Qin. But the foreign policy actually carried out by China at the time was "linking," i.e., uniting with the US, the major power in the First World, and most of the countries in the Second World and Third World to stand on a "single line" to oppose the Soviet Union and its bloc.

In the period of the gradual dissolution of the "three worlds" policy, Deng Xiaoping put forward the four-character formulation "east, west, south, north." He said during a discussion with Japanese officials: "The real major current world problems, the strategic problems with a global nature, are firstly the problem of peace and the other is the economic or development problem. The problem of peace is an east-west problem, [that of] development is a north-south problem. In short, the four characters east, west, south, north."[9] The statement that the problem of peace and development is the subject of the era is still used today despite the fact that some avant-garde scholars have cast doubt upon it recently. The theory of "four characters: east, west, south, north" was never fully developed, and was dropped later. The reason is very simple: after the split and change of the Soviet Union, one character – the east – is missing from the "east, west, south, north" theory. After 9/11, the situation was even clearer — the new global war and peace problem was also a north-south problem, and not an east-west problem.

During the latter part of the Deng Xiaoping era, there was an elementary understanding of the "one world" concept. He said many times: "I can clearly and definitely say China is a force to protect world peace and stability, and is not

---

7.   Mao Zedong, "On the Problem of Defining the Three Worlds" 关于三个世界划分问题, in vol. 8 of *Collected Works of Mao Zedong* 毛泽东文集 (Beijing: Renmin chubanshe, 1999), 441–2.

8.   See He Fang, "Remembering the Conduct of Li Yimang and Some of His Views" 记李一氓同志的为人和他的几个重要观点, *Hundred Year Tide* 百年潮, no. 5 (2001).

9.   Vol. 3 of *Selected Works of Deng Xiaoping* 邓小平文选 (Beijing: Renmin chubanshe, 1993), 105, 104, 282.

a destructive force. ...There are two things that must be done in the world, one is to establish an international political order, the other is to establish a new international economic order."[10] The "one world" concept became the official discourse at the APEC conference in November 1993 in Seattle. Jiang Zemin said that the leaders of the last century should carry "a peaceful, stable and developing world" through to the 21st century. In the Sino-French Joint Communiqué signed by Jiang Zemin and Jacques Chirac on May 16, 1997, the two sides declared that they would strive for "a more prosperous, more stable, more secure and more balanced world." The political report at the CCP 15th Congress pointed out for the first time that globalization "is an irresistible historical trend." It added: "Facing the trend of economic and technological globalization, we must have an even more active posture of going out into the world, completing a structure of opening to the outside world in all directions, at many levels and in broad spheres, developing an outwardly oriented economy, increasing international competitiveness, encouraging the optimization of the economic structure and raising the quality of the national economy."

The "one world" analytical framework has already been stirring and is about to come on stage, but even more fashionable and exciting are the formulations of global "multi-polarization" and the north-south "division into two poles." The basis of the former is geopolitics — the belief that the US, Europe, Japan, Russia, China and probably India already constitute rising, mutually competitive and interacting global power "poles." But critics point out that the existing global structure does not consist of "multi-polar" independent equality, but is one of a "single superpower"; apart from China, the other "powers" are either old allies (the EU, Japan) of the US, the only superpower, or are its new quasi-allies (Russia, India). The basis of the latter is Marxist or quasi-Marxist political economy, which believes that the result of globalization can only be "division into two poles," with the developed countries of the north becoming richer and richer and the developing countries of the south becoming poorer and poorer.

In "one world", it is an incontrovertible reality that two extremes exist. On the one hand there are the developed countries represented by the OECD, and on the other there are the poorest countries where the average national income is less than US$1 per capita per day. From the political point of view, there are the liberal democratic states, and then there are the totalitarian dictatorships, and the economic classification and the political classification are basically identical. A few Middle Eastern oil-producing nations are the only exceptions. But it should not be forgotten that between the two there are some transitional states – newly industrializing nations and transitional democratizing states. Tony Blair's foreign affairs adviser Robert Cooper recently wrote an article which pointed out: "This leaves us with two types of states: first there are now states – often former colonies

---

10. Ibid.

— where in some sense the state has almost ceased to exist, a 'premodern' zone where the state has failed and a Hobbesian war of all against all is underway (countries such as Somalia and, until recently, Afghanistan). Second, there are the post imperial, postmodern states who no longer think of security primarily in terms of conquest. And thirdly, of course there remain the traditional 'modern' states who behave as states always have, following Machiavellian principles and raison d'état (one thinks of countries such as India, Pakistan and China)."[11] It is the fate of the third group of "modern states" that will decide the appearance of the "one world." If their economic and political transformation fails, then people will face a world "in the form of a gourd," where the forces of dissolution will overcome the trend towards integration. If their transition is successful, then people will face a "distributed" world. With the study of the domestic class situation and political stability, the "distributed" global system can be a stable system.

In Chinese society, the general opinion is that the transition of their country to modernity will be successful. The situation in India is the same. On August 16, 2002, India's Deputy Premier Lal Advani said at the opening ceremony for an exhibition in New Delhi that India should make sure that nobody calls India a developing country. Just as the 20th century belonged to the West, India was now striving to make sure that the 21st century belonged to India and in the next 20 years India would be able to prove this.[12] If the aspirations of the roughly two billion people in China and India could be realized, "a more prosperous, more stable, more secure and more balanced world" would undoubtedly appear in the mid 21st century.

4. "*Very good*" or "*very bad*." Previously, the official media and scholars with an official affiliation had the habit of shouting "very good" — in the domestic situation everything was good and, naturally, everything should be "good" in the international situation. But in recent years a few people have suggested that the urgent task we face now is to oppose "peaceful evolution." At present, public opinion emphasizes the class-struggle nature of peaceful evolution, and this is undoubtedly correct. But peaceful evolution also has another and more important characteristic. At a time when the international market place is increasingly restricted, resources are increasingly scarce and the world is still divided using states and nationalities, peaceful evolution also means Western nations using a strategy of containment and disintegration against socialist countries in order to maintain their control of the international market and resources. In the new era, the global situation is evolving, and the form of the expression of class struggle is changing from a domestic to an international clash of interests between different states and ethnic groups. If prominence is given to this aspect when

---

11. "Background Materials: What is 'Neo-liberal Imperialism'?" 背景资料：什么是 "新自由帝国主义"？, *Guangming Daily* 光明日报, April 26, 2002.
12. "Indian Vice-Premier: No Longer Call India a Developing Country 21st Century Belongs to India" 印度副总理：勿称印度为展中国家21世纪属于印度, *People.com*, August 17, 2002.

opposing peaceful evolution, it will be more effective, and, as important, it will awaken the people's self-respect and sense of self-protection.[13] Because of this, some opinion-makers and scholars are beginning to change direction, and shouts of "very bad" are becoming fashionable, and becoming louder. We should use the insight of history and comparison to see whether the global situation is "very good" or "very bad."

China's international environment is not as favorable as in the early period of reform and opening up. It is possible to estimate the position of China in the world from international reaction to the bombing of the Belgrade embassy and the aircraft collision incident. From the point of view of big power relations, in the early period of reform and opening up, China and the US, the EU and Japan were quasi-allies on "one line" and on the other side were the Soviet Union and India in a disadvantageous position. After 1989, the "one line" was broken by disturbances and violent change, and China and the US changed from strategic partners to competitors. But China still had strategic choices which could have been substitutes: one was the alliance of Russia, India and China suggested by some Russian politicians, the second was the "B2B" (the Baghdad-Beijing axis including Iraq, Iran, Pakistan and China) suggested by some Western scholars. But after 9/11, these strategic choices became impossible. Russia became a member of the G8 and G20, and gained the status of a quasi-ally of the US, with much closer relations than those between China and the US. India, in the same way as Russia, greatly improved its political and military relations with the US. The relations between the US and NATO allies and Japan also underwent a qualitative change, from regional defence cooperation to global military intervention. Because President Bush had already clearly announced that Iraq was an "evil state" and Saddam was overthrown, and also because the US had occupied Afghanistan and directly threatened Pakistan, the B2B axis had been cut off at the waist.

The situation on China's borders also altered following the changes in relations between major powers. After 9/11, the US and its allies and quasi-allies formed a strategic encirclement of China. The international capabilities of ASEAN are increasing, and Singapore, which is a leading spirit of ASEAN although by extraction mainly Chinese, anchors its foreign policy tightly to the US, voluntarily providing it with an aircraft carrier base.

Although the international situation is not very beneficial to China, it is far from being "very bad." In the first half of the 20th century, particularly the early years, China's international situation was at its worst. At that time the Eight-Nation Alliance occupied Beijing, and forced the Chinese government to sign the Boxer Protocol that humiliated and betrayed the nation. The period when the international situation was best was the few years before and after victory in the

---

13. See "China's Actual Response and Strategic Choices Following the Huge Change in the Soviet Union" 苏联巨变之后中国的现实应对与战略选择, *China's Spring* 中国之春, no 1 (1992).

War of Resistance against Japan. Because of China's correct stance in Word War II and its positive contribution, the former unequal treaties were completely abrogated, and China was a permanent member of the UN Security Council. At the Dumbarton Oaks Conference, President Roosevelt said that China would be "one of the four major powers responsible for the preservation of peace." Roosevelt's idea for the order of East Asia after the war was to "use China to replace Japan." US Secretary of State Cordell Hull put it very clearly: "Japan has lost the status to be a great power in the Far East for a long time to come, and the only real great power in the Far East is China…. Therefore, if we wish to guarantee the stability of the Far East, any arrangement must be done with China at its core."[14]

If the agreement signed by Mao Zedong and Patrick Hurley, ambassador to China,[15] on November 10, 1944 had been accepted by Chiang Kai-shek, and a united government established before the end of World War II, China would not only have recovered the North East and Taiwan but would probably not have had to abandon sovereignty over Mongolia and would have recovered Hong Kong and Macau earlier. In October 1945, the US government officially telegraphed China's Nationalist government to invite China to send a military force of 50,000 men to assist the American occupation of Japan. The Nationalist government designated the 67th division to go to Japan to act as the Chinese occupational force. In early June 1946, the Ministry of National Defence of the Nationalist government issued an order for the advance party to go to Japan. In mid-June the advance party, through the Chinese military delegation in Japan led by Zhu Shiming, arrived in Japan. Unfortunately, two weeks later the large-scale civil war started in China and the 67th division was not able to reach Japan. In mid-August, it was destroyed by the New Fourth Army led by Su Yu in the battle in central Jiangsu.[16] After this, the positions of China and Japan in East Asia changed again, and the Far East order "with China as its core" referred to by Hull has never appeared.

In the half a century since the founding of the People's Republic of China, the worst international situation was during the early part of the Cultural Revolution. To the east, the US and its allies Japan, Korea and Taiwan looked on fiercely. To the south, the Vietnam War had broken out and China had sent several hundred thousand auxiliary fighters and also undertaken military expenditure of tens of billions of RMB. To the west, China had just fought a small-scale war with India. The greatest threat was to the north, where there were continuous

---

14. Drawn from Zhao Zhihui, "The Cairo Conference and the Turning Point in America's Policy Toward China" 也谈开罗会议与美国对华政策的转折—兼与时殷弘和陶文钊同志商榷, *World History* 世界历史, no 2 (2000).

15. CCP Central Document Research Office, ed., *Biography of Mao Zedong (1893–1949)* 毛泽东传1893–1949(Central Document Publishing House, 1996), 688–93.

16. See Liu Zuokui, "China's Occupation Force Did Not Go to Japan" 中国占领军没去日本, *Global Times* 环球时报, August 19, 2002.

border clashes between China and the Soviet Union in the North East and Xinjiang, and the Soviet military threatened to carry out a "surgical strike" on China's nuclear bases. The period when the international situation was the best was the first few months of 1989 — the Chinese and US militaries were considering cooperation and, with the handshake of Deng Xiaoping and Gorbachev as a symbol, Sino-Soviet relations were completely normalized. Unfortunately, this golden period for foreign relations in China's contemporary history passed quickly and, two weeks after the handshake between Deng and Gorbachev, there was a major turn in the situation.

Careful comparison demonstrates that neither the "very good" nor "very bad" view can be sustained. The international situation China currently faces could be better, but it could also be worse. What is more important than whether the existing situation is good or bad is the direction of its evolution. If China's economy develops and national power strengthens, then the international situation will naturally evolve in a good direction and thus, at present, it will only be necessary to follow the established principles and it is completely unnecessary to spend too much thought and effort on foreign affairs. However, the development of the international situation is not only decided by how China perceives and approaches the world, but even more by how the world perceives and approaches China. The world referred to here is mainly the developed nations led by America and China's neighboring countries. Up until now, the US has not seen China as its most pressing and threatening strategic opponent. America's most threatening enemy is Islamic fundamentalist terrorist groups and "axis of evil" nations that are currently developing weapons of mass destruction, and the most pressing task is global anti-terrorism and "anti-axis of evil" action. Meanwhile, the US believes that China still does not have sufficient strength to threaten its security and execute its global strategy in the same way as the former Soviet Union. However, without long-term planning, there will be problems ahead. Should the US take ten to twenty years to win the "fourth world war" against terrorism and the "axis of evil" nations, how will it then approach China? When the time comes, will China's national strength be sufficient to contend with the US and its allies? In international scholarly circles there is currently a popular democratic peace theory. Its main points are: firstly, there are never (or very rarely) clashes between democratic nations; secondly, if there are clashes between them, they are unlikely to use force or the threat of force, because this is contrary to democratic principles and reason; thirdly, it is more easy for clashes to take place between dictatorships, or between dictatorships and democratic nations, and more likely for force to be used to resolve the disputes. To put it another way, non-democratic nations are more warlike than democratic nations.[17] In a situation where the democratic

---

17. See Zheng Anguang, "The Theory of Democratic Peace and its Influence on America's Post-Cold War Foreign Policy Strategy" 民主和平论及其对冷战后美国外交战略的影响, *American Studies* 美国研究, no 2 (1999).

peace theory has become the dominant discourse of the world, how will neighboring nations perceive and approach the increase in China's national strength? Will they compete to throw themselves into the heart of China or, out of fear of the "China threat," will they draw even closer to the US and Japan? People who advocate the "very bad" viewpoint often exaggerate and add a few contradictory ideas, but they have sharply observed that, if there is no major adjustment of foreign policy strategy, China's room to maneuver on the world stage will become more and more restricted.

II. Foreign policy goals – the choices ahead

On the basis of a more thorough understanding and more sober judgment of the global situation, China must make a fundamental choice over its foreign policy goals. Is it a revolutionary, overthrowing the existing world order, or is it a participant and reformer, on the one hand accepting the existing order and rules, on the other actively seeking improvement and perfection? In other words, should the world be changed so that it fits one's own existence and development, or should one start by changing one's self, and enter "one world"?

Mao Zedong was undoubtedly a great world revolutionary. According to Li Shenzhi; "Mao Zedong's greatest wish was to be a person like Stalin, as Hu Qiaomu, Mao's political secretary for twenty years, reveals in his *Recollections of Mao Zedong*. Stalin's highest title was 'leader of progressive mankind,' and it looks like that was the goal Mao pursued. In the 1960s, during the great criticism of Soviet revisionism, [he] attempted to replace it and become the 'pole' to oppose the US in the world, and even to 'kick open the UN and make revolution,' to use the Games for the New Emerging Forces to replace the Olympics.... During the Cultural Revolution Mao Zedong openly used the slogan 'liberate the whole of mankind.' In his view, allowing China to become somewhat rich and powerful was nothing; it was just vulgar bourgeois shortsightedness. In fact, China's Red Guards also shouted the 'liberate the whole of mankind' slogan, which can truly be called a lofty sentiment. At that time Mao Zedong's revolutionary slogans influenced many people from the rich countries of Western Europe and North America to the poor countries of Asia, Africa and Latin America, and all over the world there appeared communist parties that added 'Marx, Lenin, Mao' or even 'Lin [Biao],' to their names. Pol Pot in the east and Che Guevara in the west were influenced by Mao, and even today a faint influence remains. For Mao Zedong personally this is a great honor and comfort.

"Deng Xiaoping was a pragmatist, his goal was to make China's foreign policy omni-directional [to benefit] the advance of his pragmatic policy of reform and opening. ...Because Mao's theory was entirely made up in his head, and Deng's view was in conformity with reality, it was easy to advance, and did not receive any strong opposition. Only in recent years have some extreme nationalists appeared who think that the US is too arrogant in the world, and is too aggressively rude toward China, so that it can be seen that its basic imperialist nature has not changed. They advocate saying 'no' to the US, question Deng Xiaoping's two themes of 'peace and development,' and criticize the Chinese government as being too soft. This is a trend that is worth paying attention to."[18] After twenty years of China's reform and opening up, the choice of either a revolutionary or pragmatic foreign policy strategy has again become a problem. Let us investigate these two different strategic choices from the point of view of necessity and feasibility.

1. *Utopia and the world of the jungle.* Henry Kissinger proposed two models for research on international politics: the first is the stable system, the second is the revolutionary system. He thought that stability was not achieved by "the pursuit of peace, but is produced by commonly accepted legality." "Legality", he argued, "means the system of international order accepted by all the major nations." The characteristics of the stable international system are that national actors all have a common view of means and goals in foreign policy, and this view determines the foundation of each country's internal political structure. If one of the major states in the order is not satisfied, and intends to change the situation, then the order becomes revolutionary. When there is a large separation from the internal political structure and the concept of legality based on it, politicians lose a common language. Although they can still engage in meetings, their debate is no longer related to how to resolve differences within the accepted structure, but whether this structure itself is still effective.[19] According to Kissinger's models, both Mao Zedong and Hitler sought a revolutionary new world order, but the former was a proletarian internationalist and the latter was a nationalist and racist, which made them completely different in mind and spirit.

Using Marxism's theory of social evolutionism as his basis, Mao Zedong devoted himself to the great cause of "liberating the whole of mankind," and hoped to replace today's capitalist world with a communist utopia. Hitler, on the basis of the social Darwinist theory of *Lebensraum* (space to live), devoted himself to the "racial destiny" of the establishment of a new order in Europe dominated by the German Reich, the annihilation of the Jewish people and the purification of the Aryan people. What is sad is that in recent years in the name of "national interest" and "ethnic interest," the ideas of "profit before everything" and "profit over principles" have suddenly entered China's temple of political correctness in the new century. World revolutionaries like Mao Zedong are dying off with each passing day. […].

---

18. See Li Shenzhi, "Discussion of the Foreign Policy of the People's Republic of China" 谈谈中国人民共和国的外交.

19. Drawn from James Dougherty et al, *Contending Theories of International Relations* 争论中的国际关系理论 (Beijing: Shijiezhishi chubanshe, 1987), 123–129.

Internationalists aspire to universal wellbeing. When they discover the fact that other people are better off than they are, they will start to make themselves richer without forcing others to become like them. Racists believe in the law of the jungle and the theory of Lebensraum: If you live well, it is the reason why I live badly, and as I want to live well, I cannot let you live well. They believe that the earth's resources are limited, and that the social Darwinists in the dominant Western culture will not let developing nations really develop; that the superpower "has not given up its ambition to destroy us," and if the existing world order is not changed China will never be able to realize the goal of ethnic revival.

The logic of Nazism has no place in contemporary Germany. History has given a deep lesson to the German people: Germany started two world wars with the aim of establishing a new world order, with the result that it ended in failure. Today, by accepting the existing order it has obtained the economic and social development that it previously did not have. Similarly, the disciples of Hitler's theories in China cannot gain support from the facts of history. It is already more than a century since social Darwinism was proposed in the West, and if it really dominates public and government opinion, why did Western countries abandon colonialist policies and also allow non-Western societies to increase their population four or five times in the same period? Furthermore, while the population is booming, the average per capita GNP of the world has also increased greatly. Should opening new Lebensraum for mankind rely on raising productive powers and international cooperation or rely on world war and racial extinction?

If a people, including a former great power, want to achieve economic revival, it is not necessary to make changing the world order a precondition. The US did not volunteer to participate in the two world wars. It did not voluntarily challenge the contemporary world order led by the UK. The losers of World War II, Germany and Japan, achieved economic revival under the post-war Yalta system, and are now steadily becoming political powers. Russia, led by Putin, having lost the status of a superpower, has passed the low point of decline, and the goal of national revival is now attainable. India is also thinking about how to make the 21st century the Indian century, but we have not heard that they consider the world order, in which they have no permanent seat on the UN Security Council, an obstacle to their own development that must be broken.

In fact, the law of the jungle is a type of fiction, which could be said to be a form of anti-utopia. In the *Leviathan*, Hobbes imagined the "war of every man against every man" in a so-called "condition of mere nature" in order to prove the lawful origin of the state's possession of the power of coercion. He said: "During the time men live without a common power to keep them all in awe, they are in that condition which is called war. …The only way to erect such a common power, as may be able to defend them from the invasion of foreigners, and the injuries of one another, and thereby to secure them in such sort as that by their own industry and by the fruits of the earth they may nourish themselves and live contentedly, is to confer all their power and strength upon one man, or upon one assembly of men, that may reduce all their wills, by plurality of voices, unto one will[.]"[20] Beginning with Locke, political thinkers used the "state of nature" concept to expound the theory of the social contract to replace the "condition of mere nature." Anthropologists have demonstrated that "the war of every man against every man" is not the nature of mankind and is not the agent of evolution. There is greater equality between males, who are able to cooperate more than other primates, and this is the socio-biological reason that mankind advances towards culture and civilization. From clan to tribe, from chieftains to empires, from the nation state to a unified world, every advance of civilization signified an increase in security, the broadening of cooperation, raising of prosperity, and the poor masses of society gained the most. The aim of reviving the brute force of the law of the jungle (or "martial spirit") to challenge the "world hegemony," is not a "clash of civilizations" but is the challenge of brute force against civilization. No matter whether it is the brute force of Nazism, or the brute force of Islamic fundamentalism like bin Laden, or the brute force of "contemporary Chinese nationalism" that has been recklessly promulgated on the Internet (saying, for instance, that China has nuclear weapons and a large population, and so can withstand the results of starting a nuclear war), such force can only slow down the advance of civilization, and cannot bring national revival.

2. *Hide one's capacities and bide one's time; and take some action.* The above analysis shows that a world revolution is not a necessary condition for China's revival. The following analyses whether it is feasible for China to promote a revolutionary foreign affairs strategy.

On this question Deng Xiaoping's attitude was very clear. When he announced his retirement,[...] the Berlin Wall fell and a series of events occurred, particularly the revolution in Romania and the execution of Ceaușescu, which were truly extraordinary changes which left us stunned and panic-stricken. Fortunately Deng Xiaoping proposed the "sixteen-character strategy": observe calmly, take steady steps, take cool measures, hide one's capacities and bide one's time. He also later added the two phrases "never claim leadership" and "take some action" and further said: "Don't think of carrying the flag, even if you want to carry it you won't be able to." This enabled China to calmly deal with and pass through this sudden conflict. Given the fact that "hide one's capacities and bide one's time" is a saying which has a very clear tactical meaning, and that Deng Xiaoping later said "take some action", it was unavoidable that it would lead to some people questioning whether China would proudly raise the flag of world revolution after a lengthy period of "undergoing hardships to prepare for a comeback," when, for instance after 2050, its national strength had been increased.

The existing world order was born during World War II with the UK and US signing of the Atlantic Charter. It continued to grow with the Cairo Conference

---

20. Thomas Hobbes, *The Leviathan* 利维坦 (Taibei: Shangye yinshuguan, 1985), 94, 131.

between the US, UK and China, the Tehran Conference between the US, UK and USSR, the four-power Dumbarton Oaks Conference and the Yalta and Potsdam Conferences between the US, UK and USSR, and became established after the war. The United Nations and its subsidiary organizations, the International Monetary Fund and World Bank, the General Agreement on Tariffs and Trade (GATT) were the main global organizations supporting this order. Without doubt the US had a decisive role in the process of creation of the new world order after World War II, and its wartime allies, the UK, the USSR and China also exercised a certain leadership role. After the Cold War, there was a partial change in the world order based on the so-called Yalta system. GATT became the World Trade Organization (WTO). Apart from the permanent members of the Security Council, the G8 was added to the structures for consultation by the major powers, the role of regional organizations was strengthened (in Europe, the European Community changed to become the European Union (EU), in Africa the Organization of African Unity became the African Union, APEC was established, etc). NATO was expanded to the east, and possibly became the embryo of a global military organization. Because of the disintegration of the Soviet Union and the "big family of socialism," the US became the world's only superpower. In the adjustment of the world order after the Cold War, the role of Russia and China declined, and the enemies of World War II, Germany and Japan, by contrast gained a certain degree of influence. If China is to remould the world order in 50 years according to its own will, it will at least need to have the overall national strength, influence, allies and followers that the US had at the end of World War II or the end of the Cold War. Can China be confident of having these attributes when the time comes?

When World War II ended, the GDP of the US accounted for one third of world GDP, and its industrial output capacity and foreign investment accounted for two thirds and three fourths of the world totals respectively. Apart from this, for a time, the US had a monopoly on nuclear weapons, and was the only nation with the capacity to fight wars on two oceans. When the Cold War ended, the proportion of US GDP in the world total had fallen to one fifth, but the global leadership for innovation, science and technology, scholarship, culture and the new economy had shifted from Europe to the US. Furthermore, the US was still the only nation in the world that had a major global power projection capability, and also had a decisive advantage in cyber warfare and space warfare. If everything goes well, by 2050 the overall size of the economy of greater China (the mainland, Taiwan, Hong Kong and Macau) will be comparable with the regions of greater East Asia excluding China (Japan, Korea, Australia and the countries of Southeast Asia), greater India (the nations of south Asia), greater Europe (the EU and AFTA [Asian Free Trade Area]), North America (the US, Canada and Mexico) and other nations in the world (the nations of Western Asia, South America and Africa), but it can only account for about one sixth of world GDP, which is far from the proportion reached by the US. In 2050, there will probably still be a quite big gap between China's military power and that of the US, so they may be able to treat each other as equals, but China will still not have the dominance that the US has had.

A nation's economic and military power does not automatically confer international influence and a capacity for foreign affairs. In the 1880s, Germany's industrial production capacity was the biggest in the world and, for a long period after, it was the second largest (after the US) but, in the world order led by the UK, it did not have a decisive role and felt aggrieved for a long time as a result. Japan has been the second economic power in the world for 20 or 30 years, but today it is not a "normal state" with the "right to make war," and it is far from being a major political power. In 2050, even if China is the number one economic power in the world, will it have a large group of allies and followers?

Soft power is as important, or even more important, than hard power. In the 20th century, the US underwent Wilsonianism, the Roosevelt's "four freedoms" and the human rights foreign policy of Carter, and always held the ideological high ground. In the 21st century, what ideology can China rely on to vie for dominance? If it has no creativity and breakthroughs in theory, it will not be the world leader in the 21st century. [....]

Deng Xiaoping's "take some action" encouraged active participation in, and gradual reform of the existing world order, and discouraged potential revolutionaries. Within the framework of "one world," China certainly has the chance to rise from being a participant to being one of the leading groups and, in peaceful conditions, even to receive the mandate of world leadership, and become the main formulator of the international rules for the next century.[21]

3. *The necessity of integrating with the world.* The history of the 20th century shows that if any country does not integrate with the world and fully use the world markets and the international division of labor, its economic development will suffer from serious impediments. Comparisons between West Germany and East Germany, Austria and Czechoslovakia, North Korea and South Korea, the newly industrializing countries of Southeast Asia and South America, and China and India in the 1980s all illustrate the point. Today, China's economic development is at a key stage. In order to realize industrialization and urbanization, allowing 800 million peasants to enter the cities, the following three goals must be achieved: 1. China must become the "workshop of the world"; 2. imports of food, energy and all strategic resources must be guaranteed; 3. a number of pivotal projects for development and reform of the national territory must be carried out.

In order to make China the workshop of the world, the most critical factor is not China's manufacturing capacity, capital or labor resources, it is the openness of the world market to China. When there are disputes between China and the

---

21. See Wu Zichen, "The Evolution of China's Foreign Policy Ideology: from 'Peaceful Coexistence' to 'Peaceful Development.'"

US, America's most powerful weapon is not nuclear weapons or aircraft carriers, but its market. Today, according to US statistics, China's net exports (surplus) to the US are about US$100 million, which is roughly equivalent to one tenth of China's GDP. This surplus is not only increasing daily, but is also increasing faster and faster. This fact is the fundamental reason why Deng Xiaoping emphasized that "Sino-American relations must in the end be improved."

In 1992, environmental analyst Lester Brown said that if the whole of China's state machine concentrated entirely on increasing the output of grain, not only would China delay the process of marketization and urbanization, it would also carry the burden of several billion yuan of financial deficits and bad bank debts. Such a scenario will not happen in the future. In order to give play to the comparative advantage of its economy, and not add to investments in scarce raw materials that are ineffective or have low efficiency, China from now on must reduce its rate of self-reliance for grain to 70% or less, and increase its import dependence for energy, timber and mining products to 70% or more. If it does so, China's foreign policy psychology will be close to the current situation in Japan and Korea. It will no longer be delighted by "great upheaval, great divisions, and great reorganization," but will make guaranteeing the peace and stability of the oil and gas fields of the Middle East and Central Asia and the countries through which the international transport routes and pipelines pass the main task of foreign policy.

The Three Gorges Dam and its generation of electricity, the transfer of water from South to North, sending electricity from west to east, the transport of gas from west to east, the Hangzhou Bay bridge and several dozen nuclear power plants are the major projects that are required for the development and transformation of the nation. But the premise for the construction of these projects is avoiding war, especially nuclear war. Otherwise, these projects themselves will become a pile of rubbish and even an extremely powerful time bomb. In a situation where there are many people who say "war is inevitable" or "it is better to fight earlier rather than later," it would not be appropriate to undertake these projects. Even urbanization itself is also in doubt. If China's population increasingly concentrates in large cities, China, like the US, will not be able to survive a nuclear war.

Therefore, China's foreign affairs strategists must make a decision: first unify Taiwan and then integrate with the world or first integrate with the world and then unify Taiwan, or both together, each promoting the other. Fight first and construct later or construct first and fight later, or actively participate in the unification of the global economy and struggle for long-term global peace.

4. *Changing one's own possibilities.* Shi Yinhong and others have pointed out that the precondition for changing the world is for China to change itself. He said: "Changing itself is the main source of China's strength, and changing itself is also the main means for China to influence the world. ...A complete strategy is to actively take the initiative, and not be passively reactive. ...Apart from

deciding in which direction to change according to the world's basic trends, the key problem is to have clear national goals and unwavering political determination."[22] China has in fact been pursuing the basic national policy of changing itself and integrating with the world for over 100 years. Sometimes it has been relatively active, and at other times relatively passive, sometimes it has taken the correct route, and sometime it has taken the wrong direction.

Liang Qichao sought the basis of "self-renewal" in the poetry of the Yuan dynasty:

> *The Book of Poems* says: 'The Zhou dynasty is old, but its mandate is renewed.' In governing an ancient nation, new means must be used. The *Book of Changes* says: 'When all means are exhausted change is necessary, when changes are made a solution is found, when a solution is found it is possible to continue.' Minister Yi said: 'Use the new, get rid of the old, then the defect will no longer exist. If one is not able to innovate, he is not a sage; if one is not able to follow the times, he is not a sage. The ancient sages were never ashamed to learn.' ... To put it simply, the means are the tools of everyone, and change is the logic of everyone. The world is one, and many nations are disappearing, the days are passing, the main trends are pressing and they cannot be blocked. Change also changes, even if there is no change it also changes. Changing and the changed, by changing those who hold power can protect the nation, can protect the race, can protect the religion; not to change and be changed, so that power falls to anyone to bind it and gallop with it. Woe. These are things I cannot give voice to.[23]

Since Liang Qichao said these words, China has already had five big movements of "changing oneself." The first was to reform the government by adopting a new policy, the second was the establishment of the republic, the third was the establishment of the Nationalist government, the fourth was the establishment of the People's Republic and the fifth was reform and the opening-up policy (to use Deng Xiaoping's words, this was the second "revolution").

In the process of self-renewal, China's idealists have followed three teachers. The first was "to take Japan as teacher," but the Japanese themselves mainly took Germany as teacher. The second was "to take Russia as teacher," but the Russians mainly took France as teacher. Since history has shown that the Japanese and Russians took the wrong turn on the road to modernization, China must oppose two erroneous tendencies in order to smoothly change itself and integrate with

---

22. Shi Yinhong et al, "Consideration of China's International Attitude, Foreign Policy Philosophy and Basic Strategy in the Early 21st Century" 21世纪前期中国国际态度、外交哲学和根本战略思考, *Strategy and Management*, no 1 (2001).

23. Liang Qichao, *On Change* 变法通议, in *Collected Works of Yinbing Room* 饮冰室合集 (Shanghai: Zhonghua shuju, 1989), 1–2, 6–8.

the world. One is cultural essentialism, which believes that China's essential nature cannot be changed, and the freedom, democracy, constitutional government and rule of law originating in the West cannot find a home in China. The second is cultural nihilism, which believes that everything in China is backward, and that there must be complete change, complete Westernization, etc. According to the popular fragmented and divided social engineering and "gradual mending" outlook, from now on when changing itself China should do more addition and multiplication, and do less subtraction and division. If something is lacking, remedy it; if something is broken, replace it. Change the radical attitude of "without destroying the old we cannot build the new" and "first destroy and then build" to a stable plan of building the new first and then destroying the old and first build and then destroy.

Since we plan to take twenty years to achieve a breakthrough in reform of the market economy and integration with the unified world economy using the WTO as the standard, we can also take twenty years to achieve a breakthrough in reform leading to democratized politics, the signing and ratification of the UN Human Rights Convention, participation in the G8 and OECD and the establishment of an Asian collective security guarantee system as the standard for integrating with the global unified political system.

(translated by Duncan Freeman)

Contributors

Jonathan Arac is Andrew W. Mellon Professor of English at the University of Pittsburgh and a member of the *boundary 2* editorial collective. His books include *Commissioned Spirits* (1979), *Critical Genealogies* (1987), *"Huckleberry Finn" as Idol and Target* (1997), and *The Emergence of American Literary Narrative* (2005). His recent work has addressed questions of world literature. The essay in this volume opens a new inquiry: how the internationalization of English in the United States has affected American fiction.

John M. Carroll is an associate professor of history at the University of Hong Kong. His research interests are in modern Chinese history, Hong Kong history, and imperialism and colonialism. Author of *A Concise History of Hong Kong* (Lanham, Maryland, 2007; Hong Kong: University of Hong Kong, 2007) and *Edge of Empires: Chinese Elites and British Colonials in Hong Kong* (Cambridge, Massachusetts: Harvard University Press, 2005; Hong Kong: Hong Kong University Press, 2007), Carroll is currently working on a history of foreign communities in late-imperial and republican China and on a study of the 1967 riots in Hong Kong.

R. A. Judy, Professor of Critical and Cultural Studies at the University of Pittsburgh, has received prestigious honors from the Ford and Mellon Foundations, and been a Fulbright Fellow at the Institut Bourguiba des Langues Vivantes, Université de Tunis I. A member of the *boundary 2* Editorial Collective, he was editor of two groundbreaking special issues: *Sociology Hesitant: W. E. B. Du*

Bois's Dynamic Thinking, which was awarded second place by the Council of Editors of Learned Journals in the category of Best Special Issue of 2001; and *Ralph Ellison: The Next Fifty Years,* co-edited with Jonathan Arac.

Douglas Kerr is Professor in the School of English at the University of Hong Kong. His publications include *Wilfred Owen's Voices* (1993) *George Orwell* (2003), and *A Century of Travels in China: Critical Essays on Travel Writing from the 1840s to the 1940s* (2007), co-edited with Julia Kuehn. *Eastern Figures: Orient and Empire in British Writing,* (HKU Press, 2008), deals with the history of representations of Eastern people and places from the time of Kipling to the postcolonial period. He is a founding co-editor of *Critical Zone.*

Kwai-Cheung Lo is currently teaching at the Humanities Programme of Hong Kong Baptist University. Author of *Chinese Face/Off: The Transnational Popular Culture of Hong Kong,* he has recently finished a book manuscript tentatively entitled *Excess and Masculinity in Asian Cultural Productions.*

Q. S. Tong is Associate Professor and Head of the School of English at the University of Hong Kong. He has been at work on issues and problems of critical significance in cross-cultural studies, with special attention to the historical interactions between China and Britain on different levels, political, cultural, and intellectual. He is an editorial member of several international journals including *boundary 2: an international journal of literature and culture,* and is a founding co-editor of *Critical Zone.*

Wang Shouren is Professor of English and Dean of the School of Foreign Studies at Nanjing University. He is Vice Chairman of the China English Language Education Association and Vice Chairman of the China Association for the Study of American Literature. His research interests are British and American fiction, literary history and English education in China. His publications include The *Theatre of the Mind (1990), Gender, Race and Culture* (1999; 2004), *New Literary History of the United States* (2002) and numerous papers on English literature and cultural studies. He is a founding co-editor of *Critical Zone.*

Bell Yung was born in Shanghai, grew up in Hong Kong, and holds degrees from UC Berkeley, MIT, and Harvard. He has taught at HKU, CUHK, Cornell, UC Davis, and is currently Professor of Music at the University of Pittsburgh. His publications include *Cantonese Opera: Performance as Creative Process; Celestial Airs of Antiquity: Music of the Seven String Zither of China; Harmony and Counterpoint: Ritual Music in Chinese Context;* and *Understanding Charles Seeger, Pioneer in American Musicology.* His latest book is *The Last of China's Literati: The Music, Poetry and Life of Tsar Teh-yun,* forthcoming from the HKU Press.